You Are Worth It

Discover Self-Love, The Key To Happiness

AMY LYNN

outskirtspress
DENVER, COLORADO

The opinions expressed in this manuscript are solely the opinions of the author and do not represent the opinions or thoughts of the publisher. The author has represented and warranted full ownership and/or legal right to publish all the materials in this book.

You Are Worth It
Discover Self-Love, The Key To Happiness
All Rights Reserved.
Copyright © 2015 Amy Lynn
v3.0

Cover Photo © 2015 thinkstockphotos.com. All rights reserved - used with permission.

This book may not be reproduced, transmitted, or stored in whole or in part by any means, including graphic, electronic, or mechanical without the express written consent of the publisher except in the case of brief quotations embodied in critical articles and reviews.

Outskirts Press, Inc.
http://www.outskirtspress.com

ISBN: 978-1-4787-5263-9

Outskirts Press and the "OP" logo are trademarks belonging to Outskirts Press, Inc.

PRINTED IN THE UNITED STATES OF AMERICA

Om Namah Shivaya
In honor of the strength and divinity within us all.

Contents

Introduction 1

Section One: Health 5
Lesson 1: Drop the Baggage 7
    Roles & Expectations 8
    Routines and Habits 10
    Work and Career 11
    Relationships 12
    Surrendering Attachments 13
    Leave the Comfort Zone 14
Lesson 2: Break the Chains 21
    Healing Emptiness and Pain 21
    When Eating Hurts 23
    Hurt in Relationships 23
    Guilt and Shame 25
    Surrender the Past 26
    Becoming your own parent 27
Lesson 3: Finding Balance 35
    Quit beating yourself up 36
    Unraveling Self-Doubt 37
    Workaholism 38
    Perfectionism 39
    Self-Forgiveness 40
    Pace Yourself 41

Lesson 4: Be Good to Yourself... 49
    Speaking the Language of Love...50
    Daily Affirmations...52
    Reward yourself..53
    Surround yourself with people who care 54
    Spend time doing things you enjoy 55
    Say no when you don't want to..57
    Self-Massage..59
    Aromatherapy 60
    Vacation 61

Lesson 5: Discover your Beauty 68
    Inner Charm 68
    Accept Yourself..70
    Feel your beauty 70
    Focus on your Positive Qualities...71
    Show your beauty..72
    Quit Comparing 73
    Inner Confidence 74
    Smile...75

Lesson 6: Take Care of Yourself 82
    Get Enough Sleep 84
    Get Plenty of Rest 85
    Eat Right and Exercise...86
    Read Encouraging Literature 87
    Satisfy your deepest needs...88
    Surround Yourself with Love 89
    Ask for what you need...91
    Do at least one thing each day that makes you happy 92
    Take care of yourself emotionally...93

Lesson 7: Nourish Your Body... 101
    Eat Right...103
    Fruits and Vegetables...103
    Proper Portions 105
    Avoid Emotional Eating..106
    Eat Colorful Foods..107
    Antioxidants..108

    Protein Linking 108
    Homeopathic Health..109
    Ayurveda 110
    Drink Plenty of Water 111
    Spice up your Life 111

Lesson 8: Stay Fit 120
    Getting Started...121
    Find a form of exercise you enjoy 122
    Tai Bo 123
    Relaxation and Exercise 123
    Yoga and Pilates...124
    Interpretive Dance...124
    Belly Dancing...125
    Power Walking 126
    Hiking...127
    Kayaking/River Rafting 128

Section Two: Wealth:.. 137
Lesson 9: Get to Know Yourself 139
    What makes you Tick? 140
    What are your inner resources? 141
    What are you good at?..143
    What do you need?...143
    What makes you smile? 145
    Know your limits 146
    Feel when you are depleted 148
    Search out your Destiny 148

Lesson 10: Invest in Yourself 155
    Read, read, read..156
    Never stop learning 157
    Build a nest egg 159
    Buy gifts for yourself 160
    Take yourself on a date 161
    Develop your talent 161
    Pursue a career that is rewarding.....................................162
    Find your purpose 164

Lesson 11: Discover your Talent... 171
    Surrender Busyness..172
    Experiment and Learn 173
    Rekindle your Dreams...174
    Discover your Inner Strength 175
    Discover your Natural Poise 176
    Be Patient...177

Lesson 12: Inventory Your Strengths.. 184
    Brainstorm 184
    Inner Strengths versus External Supports..........................185
    Be Optimistic...186
    Strength in Limitations 186
    Preserve your Strength...187
    Mindfulness Meditation 189
    You are your Strength 190
    Strength joins us to Destiny 190

Lesson 13: Nourish your Mind 197
    Challenge Yourself Intellectually.......................................198
    Stay Open Minded and Flexible 200
    Consider Alternatives 201
    Learn from Everyday Experiences......................................202
    Appreciate the Simple Lessons in Life...............................202
    The Power of Positive Thinking 203
    Soften and Brighten your Outlook 205

Lesson 14: Believe in Yourself 211
    Building Self-Confidence..211
    Excavating the Obstacles 212
    Encourage Yourself. Be Your Own Cheerleader.................214
    Have Faith in Your Abilities..214
    Dare to try new things...215
    Live Courageously 216
    Develop a network of support 217
    Believe in your Dreams 218

Section Three: Wellness **225**
Lesson 15: Live with Ease **227**
   Lighten Up 228
   The Law of Least Effort 230
   Retire from the Guilt Committee 232
   Let go of Regret 232
   Only look back if it makes you smile 233
   Release the heavy weight 234
   Feelings Exercise 234
   You can't change the past 235
   You are alright just the way you are 236
   Surrender Perfectionism 237
   Practice Unconditional Love 238
Lesson 16: Be Content **245**
   Quit Postponing Happiness 245
   Accept Yourself 247
   Accept your place in life 248
   Quit looking around 249
   Quit wishing for more or that things were different 250
   Let go of worry 250
   Enjoy the moment 253
   Find Inner Peace 253
   Express your love and show affection 254
   Live in Gratitude 255
   Loving Kindness Meditation 255
Lesson 17: Be Yourself **263**
   Let your guard down 264
   Accept your imperfections 265
   You're enough 267
   Express yourself 268
   Do not worry about what others think 268
   Don't be afraid to do your own thing 269
   Pursue your interests 270
   Enjoy what you love 271
   You're amazing 272

Lesson 18: Be True to Yourself 278
    Don't sell yourself short 278
    Create your own roles...279
    Our Decisions Become Us..280
    Remember your Heritage 281
    Practice traditions that are meaningful to you........................281
    Treasure your life...282
    Appreciate your experience..283
    Honor the Journey 284
    Honor your values..284
    Honor your relationships..285
    Honor the Divinity within you 286
    Find your destiny 287

Lesson 19: Boundaries 294
    Self-Definition 295
    Internal versus external boundaries...................................296
    Boundaries are affirming 297
    A Boundary Matrix 298
    Navigating the journey..299
    Boundaries are the framework of self-truth..........................299
    Boundaries lead the way to self-respect..............................300
    Boundaries give us room for ourselves 301
    Boundaries can help us realize our hopes and dreams 301
    Boundaries help us achieve our destiny.............................302

Lesson 20: Nourish your Spirit 309
    Discover your inner light...310
    Take time to worship...310
    Nirvana 311
    Marvel upon the universe 312
    Enjoy Nature..313
    Have meaningful ceremonies and rituals 314
    Surround yourself with meaningful things.......................316
    Dance and Sing 316
    Spend time with females..317
    Seep into the treasures of the moment............................318

Lesson 21: Old Me, New Me 324
   Remember what you have learned 325
   Does this fit anymore? 325
   The journey is a process of discovery 326
   The Sky is the Limit 327
   A New Outlook 327
   New Behavior 328
   Lead your most incredible life 329

Section Four: Joy 335
Lesson 22: Fall in Love with yourself 337
   Let go of your fear of abandonment 338
   Embrace Intimacy 339
   Pamper yourself 339
   Focus on loving thoughts 340
   A Romantic night alone 341
   Take a long walk on the beach 341
   Balance your love 342

Lesson 23: Enjoy Yourself 349
   Have fun 350
   Vacation 350
   Spend time with people who make you happy 350
   Spend time with the ones you love 351
   Limit your work week 352
   Explore new hobbies 353
   Get lost for a day 354
   Be Creative 355
   Delight in Nature 356
   Giggle and Laugh 356

Lesson 24: Self- Satisfaction 364
   Please yourself 365
   Go after what you want 366
   Pursue your interests 366
   Chase your dreams 367
   If it is uncomfortable, quit it 368

    Small ways to create satisfaction 368
    Check in with your feelings...369
Lesson 25: Nourish your Soul 376
    Live in reverence..377
    Quiet Solitude...377
    Metta Practice 378
    Prayer and Meditation..379
    Read spiritual books 379
    Spend time outdoors 380
    Bask in the gifts..381
    Live in Abundance 381
    Share your gifts with others 382
Lesson 26: Have Faith 389
    Believe in Abundance...390
    Everything happens for a reason 391
    Surrender 391
    Have faith in the universe...393
    Trust in a higher power 394
    Have faith in yourself..395
    Have faith in the journey..396
    Believe in the power of love 396
    Believe in miracles 397
    Have Hope..397
    Rest in the care of the universe 398
Lesson 27: Redefine your Life 405
    Define your journey the way you want to................................405
    Leave the status quo behind 407
    Choose what is important 407
    Chart your course toward the future.......................................408
    Don't limit yourself 409
    Experience all life has to offer 410
    You can make your life beautiful...410
    Discover and experience your destiny 411
    Appreciate each step along the way...412

Introduction

I love to walk along the shore of a sparkling beach. Watching the colorful waves smoothly drift back and forth in perfect rhythm across the golden sand eases my spirit. My mind drifts with each wave as I loosely ponder all the wonderful days that I have experienced in my life. So many treasured memories, like delicate grains of sand, they make up a beautiful place in my heart; a place that is sacred and precious. Do you have a special place?

The rhythms of my life have not always been this peaceful. I have encountered many struggles and challenges, like we all do. But amidst the many trials, I have always returned to the beach to gather my thoughts and spend time with my Creator. There is something marvelous and miraculous about the water. Light dances in magical colors upon the water's empty slate which becomes an ever changing masterpiece showing the love and mercy of the universe. It is peaceful and healing. Where do you go when things bother you?

One of my favorite beaches is in Cozumel, Mexico. It stretches across seven miles of creamy white sand, speckled with Caribbean blues and greens. I like to gaze across the deep blue sea beneath an umbrella of robust white clouds that hang lazy and low against the horizon. The rhythm of the waves is especially powerful here. Nature energizes my mind, body, and spirit like no other force. It helps me become one with the universe, if only for a moment.

On one of my walks in Cozumel, I met a Mayan teacher. He eventually became an invaluable spiritual mentor to me. We quickly became friends as he joined me in my walks on the beach in the early dawn. He seemed to appear out of nowhere. He was helpful and sincere. After we strolled along the beach for several yards talking, he would stop me and draw my attention to the ground. There, he would teach me lessons by drawing pictures in the sand with a long stick from a nearby tree.

The first thing he taught me was how to sail the strong gale winds. I have loved to sail since I was five years old, and sailing the Caribbean is spectacular, but challenging. It is not easy to turn the boat around, especially against the unpredictable gale. He drew pictures of the boat, sail, and wind patterns in the sand where we sat; and on both knees, he showed me three effective turns to be used when maneuvering the boat alone. His strategies later proved very effective. But that was not his only advice that proved beneficial as I moved into my future.

On one particular trip to Cozumel, I was experiencing especially hard challenges. When he found me that first morning on the seashore, he said he could see the stress on my face. I told him I was just under a lot of pressure and things would be alright. But remembering our previous conversations, and seeming to understand my journey as he did, he sat me down on the beach and asked me to watch as he drew a circle in the sand. When he was finished, he told me it represented my life. Then, he started dividing the circle into pie shaped pieces. The first one was very large, and he said this represents the time and energy I spend with my children. Next, and not much smaller, he drew the piece representing my work and career. After that a smaller, but still sizable piece that he labeled my love relationship. Lastly, he showed me my own piece of the circle, which was very narrow.

He went on to tell me that my problem is that the part of my life I devote to myself is very small. I need to make my piece of the pie larger. He saw all the energy I expended on kids, work, career, and relationship; but said he is left to wonder how much energy this leaves for me. He had listened to me hope and dream and told me it is time to learn

INTRODUCTION

to care for myself; embrace my dreams and follow my heart. Time is too precious to waste, and although taking care of others is rewarding, we must take care of ourselves as well. We have only one life to live, one journey- a destiny that belongs incredibly to us. What does your destiny look like?

This divine intervention was exactly what I needed. Although it did not resonate at first, this image carried forward to change my life. Through a series of changes and after some trial and error, I finally learned to care for myself. That is the purpose of this book. I would like to share this miracle with you. I want to help you understand you are priceless, valuable, and worthy of your full attention, affection, and devotion. I spent many years wondering how I could possibly increase the size of my part of the circle. Eventually, it all came down to one common thread, self-love. I finally discovered "I am worth it."

This book is designed to show you that you are worth it too. It is divided into four sections: health, wealth, wellness, and joy; categorizing many thoughts and ideas in the form of lessons that will guide you to self-love. They are based on the many theories and techniques I have learned throughout my Graduate Studies in Clinical Mental Health, empirical research, creative and experiential techniques, the interactions I have had with women through my outreach programs, workshops, and clinical experience; as well as my own personal discoveries, and spiritual inspiration and growth.

You may be feeling challenged and discouraged. Perhaps you are expending the majority of your energy at work, on others; or you feel overwhelmed by responsibilities and obligations. You may be feeling like you are just barely staying afloat, merely surviving. Or, perhaps you struggle with life's challenges or even mental health issues. Well, the tide is changing. It is time to learn to love yourself as much *if not more* than you love and care for others. It is time to treasure the beautiful, wondrous creation you are… to discover self-love. You can find an intimate romance that far exceeds your greatest expectations for joy and happiness. Learning self-love brings deep satisfaction and contentment. The time is here. You are worth it!

Section One
Health

1

Drop the Baggage

I find the new baggage rules in the airline industry quite frustrating. It can be difficult struggling through the airport with my suitcase, especially stowing it above my head; but it is even more disheartening to pay high baggage fees. For those of you who refuse to pay the added cost like me, you will identify with the following analogy.

Picture yourself at the airport between flights. You have 20 minutes to catch your next plane, and the flight attendant announces you must make your way to gate B31, which happens to be clear on the other side of the airport. They finally open the airplane door and you squeeze out of your seat, straining upward to recover your luggage. The line of people in front of you finally begins to move, and you carefully align your suitcase between the narrowly encroached seats that crowd the small isle to the door. After pulling and bumping, you finally make it off the airplane.

Then is the mad dash to the next plane. Your luggage rocks back and forth as you begin to run until you finally stop, turn around, and reset it on its wheels. You decide to walk swiftly rather than run, but your suitcase still does not cooperate. It almost completely rolls over as you hop off the moving sidewalk. Frustrated and sweating you continue to glance at your cell phone to see if you will arrive at the connecting gate on time. Your arms begin to shake. Your wrists are tired. If only you didn't have the baggage, you might make it. You hold on tight and keep on going. If only you didn't have this cumbersome weight behind you. Sound familiar?

Sometimes we live our lives similar to this illustration. We pick up baggage along the journey, and do not realize that we are weighed down until it is too late. Our hearts become weary. Our spirits are worn out. We quit doing the things that once made us happy and begin taking the comfortable, "familiar" route. We fall into routine and life begins to weigh on our shoulders.

My hope is that if you are feeling worn down by too much baggage, things can change for you. We can excavate our lives of anything and everything that is standing in the way of becoming all we want to be. This might involve letting go of a variety of things, however, there are certain pieces of excess baggage that many women have in common. This is where we begin.

Sometimes, we need to let go of certain things before we can even begin the journey of discovering self-love. This lesson will provide examples of some of the more common obstacles that can get in the way of you living your most spectacular, beautiful life. We will discuss the various ways women can compromise their best journey. Hopefully, learning to drop excess baggage will help us begin to discover what we really want in life. It can free us to embrace our hopes and dreams.

Roles & Expectations

The first item we will look at is roles and how they relate to our expectations of who we are. Clinical studies support the fact that roles have a large effect on women, especially on our well-being. The majority of research indicates that roles can have a positive influence on our emotional landscape. For example, theories of adult development suggest that both personality and social roles are sources of adult well-being. Further research supports the impact of social roles on psychological wellness. Studies have also confirmed that the "quality" of our roles is an important component of the path to well-being. (Foster et. al, 2004)

For these reasons, it is important to explore our roles periodically to assure they are what we really want for our lives. Some of our roles are handed to us by others including our families of origin, the educational system, our current families, careers, and community (church, social clubs, political affiliations). Women often get stuck in roles they do not choose. This can challenge the truth and integrity of our inner being. It can cloud our most perfect vision of who we would like to be.

Other studies have illustrated the dilemmas women face in juggling social roles and expectations. Tensions between responsibilities toward themselves and others in conjunction with the fulfillment of social roles have a definite impact on women's positive decision making skills and well-being. (Segraves, 2003) Again, roles are heavily integrated in our psyches.

Maintaining roles that do not resonate with who we are can take satisfaction and value away from our journey. Instead, we can choose roles that are congruent with our innermost selves. We can engage in activities and responsibilities that support our aspirations and values. It is important for us to monitor our roles and the expectations others place on us. As indicated above, our emotional well-being depends on it.

So, where do we begin? Perhaps the best place to start is to take a current inventory of the various roles that make up your life. Consider all the arenas of your life…home, work, leisure, community, and family. List all your roles. Next, place a check mark beside the roles you enjoy and draw a line through the roles you would rather not fulfill anymore. This might represent some of your baggage.

Then, make a new list that contains the roles you would like to carry forward along your future journey. By letting go of roles that no longer fit, you are beginning to reframe your life. This is something we will do in every lesson throughout this book. The goal is to move toward a place that is more satisfying, edifying, and joyful.

Part of moving away from the roles you no longer wish to play might involve the release of the expectations of others. This can be especially difficult, but well worth the effort if some of your roles create conflict or dissatisfaction in your life. Women are nurturing. We are caretakers by nature. Making others happy gives us great pleasure. The problem begins when we forget about our own happiness. Some of us learn to put our own needs on the backburner in the quest to please others. We try to do what is "expected" of us. We do not like to rock the boat.

Releasing the expectations of others paves the way for us to achieve our greatest expectations for ourselves. We can increase the size of our piece of the pie in life by spending time on the things we find most fulfilling. In the final analysis, we are the ones we must satisfy. We can only affect our own happiness anyway. It is an illusion to think we have control over others, or that they should have control of us. We will discuss many illusions in this book in order to paint a more realistic picture of true happiness and inner peace. Each lesson is designed to encourage self-awareness. We will begin to see how truly beautiful we are.

Routines and Habits

Other pieces of baggage to be considered are old habits and worn out routines. Many of us are creatures of habit. Doing the same things over and over brings a sense of comfort and security, even if it is false (another illusion). But doing the same things over and over and expecting different results is also a popular definition of insanity. If you have been feeling burdened, worn out, disillusioned, or despondent; this may be a good time to consider your current routines.

A list may be the best remedy again here. You can take inventory of your daily routines, from morning to bedtime, including weekdays and weekends. Like we did in the last exercise, place a checkmark beside those routines that give you pleasure and make you happy. But unless something on your list is absolutely necessary such as work or fixing dinner for the kids, draw a line through it and do not carry it forward to your new list. This can help you identify your true responsibilities. We all have obligations in life, but at least some of our activities can be classified as needless routine. It is helpful to outline the differences on paper.

DROP THE BAGGAGE

We can also consider old habits. These can be especially detrimental. Some of us don't even realize we are in the habit of acting in certain ways, even though they may be negative or harmful. We are in the comfort zone. (We will talk more about this toward the end of the lesson.) We become used to behaving the way we do. Hopefully, our actions are advancing our most precious journey, but we may be sabotaging our life. It is time to begin considering all of our actions, in order to drop the baggage of old habits that no longer belong. We are on our way to creating a healthier, happier life, a new beginning. Let's leave the negative behind, once and for all.

Work and Career

Now, let's examine our work and careers for a moment. It was mentioned that we have certain obligations such as work, but the kind of work we do is optional. Not all of us enjoy our careers. Some of us are unaware of the fact that work can be enjoyed. Or perhaps you enjoyed your career at one time, but now it is another worn out routine you are carrying like old baggage into the future.

Whatever the case may be, it is liberating to consider the fact that we spend a great deal of time in work and career and by all means, we need to be doing something we enjoy. It is even more rewarding if we can also do something we believe in, work that adds meaning to our lives. Women have the luxury in this country of being able to choose their career path. We have many choices. We are not held back by social norms or even laws that require only certain occupations for women. This is a gift we can all enjoy.

Perhaps an exercise in self-reflection fits well here. Consider your job, visualize your career. Then, on a scale from 1 to 10, rank how satisfied you are, with 1 being least satisfied and 10 being most satisfied. Where do you fall on the scale? Considering how much time you spend at work, approximately 50% of your day, it is especially worth evaluating. Many women get "trapped" in dead end jobs and stagnant careers. This could be due to a number of things including exaggerated feelings of loyalty or a lack of self-confidence. Whatever the cause, it is worth stepping aside for a moment and considering how happy you are. Next, think about what it would take for you to increase your rating one or two points on the satisfaction scale? What would it look like? Ponder these questions… We will return to these considerations throughout this book. For now, just keep in mind you're worth it!

Relationships

Moving on to another important item in our life, we can consider our primary relationship. What I mean by this is your relationship with a significant other -your partner- perhaps your husband, boyfriend, or girlfriend. This can be a difficult area for many women (as we will discuss more in the next lesson). Some women allow relationships to define who they are. We have the tendency to get lost or lose sight of who we are. Even in a good partnership, it is not always easy to determine where your lover ends and you begin.

At some point, it is healthy and healing to take a step back and find your center. Connect with your thoughts, feelings, and desires; and make sure you are heading in a direction that is truly adding happiness and satisfaction to your life. We are meant to share our lives with one another. We are designed to be in relationships. We grow at a higher rate inside a partnership than we grow on our own. Sharing our life with another is not only rewarding, it is maturing. And yet, we can be careful we are not getting hurt. We can make sure we are caring as much *if not more* for ourselves than we are for another. Taking some time to evaluate our love is healing and renewing.

Hopefully, you will discover your love is supporting, nourishing, satisfying, and joyful. But what if you don't? What if you find your love life disheartening, discouraging, frustrating, or worse yet, hurtful? If you identify with the latter description, you may consider dropping the baggage. Some of us are only meant to travel together for a time. Others hold on way beyond the point their time is up. It could be you are done growing together in this particular relationship. Perhaps you have learned all the lessons it holds. If this is the case, you can lovingly surrender. You can confidently embrace your own path. You will be alright. If it is meant to be it will be, whether you are together or apart. You do not have to fear being alone any more.

Consider a simple analogy. You have outgrown your favorite pair of blue jeans. You have either worn them out or you no longer fit into them. They used to be comfortable, even flattering. You have many good memories in those blue jeans, but most recently they have begun to feel tight, uncomfortable, perhaps even confining. What do you do? You have two choices. Keep trying to squeeze into the jeans, continuing in discomfort and maybe even misery, hoping someday they might fit again…or get a new pair, perhaps a size larger or a pair with more room in the legs. You can wear the new jeans more comfortably. You now have the space you need to feel good again.

Surrendering Attachments

The pieces of baggage we have discussed can be viewed as attachments. We have both secure and insecure attachments in life. In order to discover self-love-to really fall in love with yourself- and in order to find an intimate, fulfilling relationship with "you"; we can prepare to surrender insecure attachments. These are the attachments that stand in the way of you living your most satisfying life. They are the persons, places, and things that get in the way of your happiness and destiny. Unfulfilling roles, old routines, bad habits, dissatisfying jobs, hurtful relationships, and the expectations of others can be just some examples. There are also material attachments such as homes, cars, gymnasiums, and money (just to name a few). Insecure attachments contribute to an external locus of control, which shifts the focus away from your inner spirit. Hopefully in reading these lessons, you will find your locus of control shifting inwardly. This is where the healing happens. It is where happiness begins.

This is also part of simplifying your life, which we will discuss in more detail later. Sometimes too much gets in the way. There may come a time for us to pare down our life to continue moving forward. This creates room for the sacred and profound. Light can enter in and changes us. We are no longer busied by external distractions or diverted by needless obligations. Simplification adds beauty, the very depths of peace. Letting go of insecure attachments is a huge part of simplifying the journey. It helps clear the way to a more delightful future.

Leave the Comfort Zone

Have you ever considered leaving the comfort zone and pursuing your dreams? The term comfort zone here refers to the familiar. It is what we are "used to". Remember what the Mayan teacher taught me on the seashore? Part of increasing my part of life was to embrace my dreams. I had been pursuing my destiny at one point, but through the process of some very painful trials, I lost hope. I decided not to dream anymore.

I have since reclaimed my hopes and dreams and can tell you there is no better way to live than inside the deepest desires of your heart. We all deserve our dreams. They may not all come to fruition, but we are guaranteed the journey will be spectacular when we are following our heart. We can drop the baggage of our past, and reach forward to a bright and brilliant future. We can dare to leave the comfort zone and embrace the unknown, the road not yet traveled, the outskirts of our destiny.

It may not be easy, but it is possible. We all have an innate ability to change. We are intelligent, resourceful, gifted women. Many of us only know a fragment of our full potential. When we are no longer weighed down by the things that don't belong, the sky is the limit. We can literally soar. My hope is through this book you will discover more about yourself, your needs, and what makes you happy. We are on the brink of a brilliant, miraculous horizon. We are at the beginning of the journey to self-love.

References:

Foster, Claire, Eeles, Rosalind, Ardern-Jones, Audrey; Moynihan, Clare, Watson, Maggie; Psychology & Health, Vol 19(4), Aug, 2004. P. 439-455

Segraves, Mary Margaret (2003) *Midlife Women's Narratives of Living Alone*

YOU ARE WORTH IT

Reflections

DROP THE BAGGAGE

YOU ARE WORTH IT

DROP THE BAGGAGE

YOU ARE WORTH IT

2

Break the Chains

Before we continue discussing health and well-being, let's evaluate some of the destructive ideas and behaviors that reduce our health and happiness. In this lesson, we are going to explore our inner landscape in order to break any chains that may exist in our inner psyche, deep seeded beliefs that stand in the way of our continued journey toward self-love. This may not be comfortable, so please try to keep an open mind as we reflect upon and review some of the negative patterns that hold women down. Our goal is to reach a place where we are finally willing to release any chains that may hold us back from moving into a life that is more joyful and edifying. Like a gardener, we must first prepare the soil in order to grow healthy, hearty plants. We can cultivate our hearts to be able to receive joy most fully.

Healing Emptiness and Pain

Beginning our search within, many women carry an underlying emptiness and pain. Somewhere beneath the surface we may feel a festering or aching. We do many things to try and cover this feeling. We may try to patch it or numb it with our daily activities, engagements, and encounters; however, it never really goes away. We may try to avoid feeling it, but it is there. It haunts us when we are still for too long. When we are quite, it whispers fear and insecurity.

It might scare us to be alone with these feelings. We may try to divert them at any cost. But trouble begins when we are afraid to embrace our core emotions. We may know deep down we are not comfortable. We sense there are things to be resolved in us. We may have hurtful childhoods and painful memories of days gone by. Perhaps we have lost loved ones along the way. We may have even lost touch with ourselves.

And yet we can begin the process of healing and restoration when we lovingly face our emptiness and pain. We can let go of regret, abandonment, and fear with acceptance and compassion. No matter what hardships we have encountered, no matter the challenge or trauma, we can let go and move forward. We are resilient and capable. We are not victims.

Facing our emptiness and letting go of past pain are two critical components to finding out who we really are and what we want and need in life. It is also the beginning step to learning how to truly care for and love ourselves. We can open the door to revealing negative emotions and behaviors and then deal with them in a way that is kind and compassionate. Some of us have hurt ourselves for too long and in many ways. Not all emotions are good; in fact, some can be detrimental if we allow them too much space in our hearts and minds. The Latin root word for emotion is *emovere*, which means to move away. Sometimes our emotions move us further away from our positive center of energy.

In this lesson, we will discuss some of the destructive patterns women struggle with. These are some of the issues that might lie just below the emptiness, or they could be defense mechanisms we use to try to fill the void. My hope is through exploring these forms of destruction; we can lift the veil of illusion and turn our faces into the light; preparing the path for a better tomorrow. You might be fortunate enough not to identify with any of the items we will discuss. If that is the case, you can count your blessings. But I am guessing that many of you will relate to at least one if not more of the following ways women hurt themselves. You might not realize it, but some of us are masochistic. We may not overtly hurt ourselves, but we can harm ourselves in more subtle ways.

One researcher, who has devoted a great deal of time to the study of masochism, says that masochistic traits develop as an attempt to repair the painful memories of early childhood experience.(Cooper, 2009) He goes on to say diagnostically it is long past to acknowledge the existence of the masochistic personality disorder. But what does this mean for us? How can we translate this into our lives in a way that can help us learn to live more freely?

Let's explore some examples.

When Eating Hurts

Many women use food to abuse themselves. We overeat and under eat, gorge and starve. Many eating disorders exist such as anorexia nervosa and bulimia. There are bingers, restrictors, runaway eaters, and other labels for hurtful forms of eating. Instead of appreciating food and nourishing our bodies, some women hurt themselves with food. We become obsessed. How many calories, how much exercise? Or, we feel remorse after eating a whole box of donuts, several pieces of cake, or a large bag of chips. Perhaps we are eating to fill the emptiness inside or starving to gain control or ease the pain. Whatever our reasons, we can lovingly stop. It is time to quit fighting food.

It is important to nourish our bodies. Lesson seven is dedicated solely to this topic. For now, we can become willing to consider changing our eating habits. We can surrender to nourishing our bodies and quit using food to manipulate our feelings. We can spend time with our core emotions and experience what is really going on with us. We can embrace the emptiness and allow ourselves to seep into the quiet and still. This may be difficult and uncomfortable at first. Patience… baby steps. There is no rush; in fact, healing cannot be rushed. It happens like magic when we are peaceful and ready.

Hurt in Relationships

Another way women hurt themselves is through abusive or hurtful relationships. Some women don't know any other way. You may have encountered one or more abusive partners in the past. You may currently be in a harmful relationship. A good question to explore is what needs the relationship might satisfy in you? Everyone makes choices for a reason. We are instinctually needs driven. You may feel trapped, but staying in a hurtful relationship is a choice. Doing nothing is a conscious decision we make. So what might you be getting out of the deal?

Cooper postulates in the absence of alternatives, the assurance of continuity and familiarity, even with a disappointing object, is safer and more reassuring than confronting the danger of a total break of attachment. In fact, some women view any form of attachment as preferable to abandonment. He says in effect, any sense of continued safety through the maintenance of an attachment to an object of power and control (like an abusive partner) becomes the primary pleasure need, overriding the usual sources of pleasure and safety. (Cooper, 2009)

Although we may be hurt physically, emotionally, or sexually by someone else; our decision to remain in the relationship is a form of self-infliction. It is another covert form of masochism. We may think by kidding ourselves that we are really victims, but isn't it true some of us are choosing pain and sorrow. It is familiar. In fact Wikipedia defines masochism as pleasure in receiving the pain.[1] How might our world change if we dare consider alternatives? Do we even want to? Are we really comfortable or is it time to try something different?

These are not simple questions to ponder or answer. Change can be difficult. It is not always easy to openly gaze upon our true motives and feelings. But as we learn to face our emotions, we grow. Self-awareness leads to better days. Again… baby steps. Spend a little time each day picturing what your life would be like without pain. Visualize your life with people who support, encourage, sustain, and unconditionally love you. How does it feel? Stay with this feeling as long as you can. Perhaps your current partner is causing you pain. Partner or couples counseling might be the answer. Or maybe you envision someone else (or the single life) and decide you are ready to move on. Whatever the case may be, you can begin to move toward hope and healing. These are not light considerations.

Guilt and Shame

Another way we can hurt ourselves is through the process of guilt and shaming. Some women do not think they "deserve" to be happy, deep down. There is a place in us that may be saturated with remorse and regret. It might be a place deep within where we had hoped for the best and experienced the worst. We had good intentions. We may not have consciously realized life would go wrong. Perhaps you have suffered severe trauma in your life? Some of us have seen and experienced nightmares. In fact I have encountered such a horrible tragedy, I literally had to pinch myself in hopes it was just a bad dream. Unfortunately, I felt the pinch.

How about you? Are there certain dark memories in your past that still haunt you? Are there tragedies so great you cannot seem to get beyond them? Do you still carry guilt and remorse for things you did or did not do, just because you were there? Sometimes we take on more responsibility than belongs to us. Or even if you were responsible, can you forgive yourself? God has. The universe has. We are only human.

But despite unconditional love and forgiveness, we may go on sabotaging our lives in fear we do not deserve the best. We continue to live in the illusion that we are not worthy of joy and happiness. We subconsciously live as if we are paying penance. We sentence ourselves to a life of reciprocity. The light of the journey surrounds us, but it cannot penetrate our thick walls. These are more of the chains we carry.

Cooper's article in the Psychiatric Annals labels self-sabotage as a self-defeating personality disorder. He says it is a pervasive pattern of self-defeating behavior, beginning by early adulthood, and present in a variety of contexts. The person may often avoid or undermine pleasurable experiences, be drawn to situations or relationships in which he or she will suffer, and prevent others from helping him or her as indicated by at least 5 of the following:

1. Choosing people or situations that lead to disappointment, failure, or mistreatment, even when better options are clearly available.

2. Rejecting or rendering ineffective the attempts of others to help him or her.
3. Following positive personal events, responding with depression, guilt, or a behavior that brings about pain.
4. Inciting angry or rejecting responses from others and then feeling hurt, defeated, or humiliated.
5. Rejecting opportunities for pleasure and reluctant to acknowledge enjoying himself or herself.
6. Failing to accomplish tasks crucial to his or her personal objectives despite demonstrated ability to do so.
7. Uninterested in or rejecting people who consistently treat him or her well.
8. Engaging in excessive self- sacrifice that is unsolicited by the intended recipients of the sacrifice. (Cooper, 2009)

If you identify with some of these qualities, I want you to know it is time to break the chains. No one deserves to spend their life working out a painful past. It is time to quit hurting yourself and learn to forgive and love yourself unconditionally. Ultimately, we can even *fall in love* with ourselves. It is the goal of this book. My hope is by the end of lesson twenty- seven; you will have discovered an intimate and meaningful love affair with yourself. You can become your best friend. We all deserve the very best. We are worth it!

Surrender the Past

If you are still living in regret, the time has come to deal with it and then move on. Surrender the past. Step beyond the painful memories and embrace and cherish the good ones. We can hold our golden memories in the forefront of our minds. These are the only ones we need to carry forward. We have wasted enough time ruminating, attempting to alter moments past that cannot be changed. Letting go of this self -defeating prophecy creates valuable space in us where we can develop an abundant gratitude for all the many blessings we have experienced in our lives. We do not need to be weighed down or darkened by the things we cannot change any longer.

Becoming your own parent

Bottom line, it's time to grow up. Many of us have spent much time healing and working on our inner child, but we have reached the point where our adult selves are ready to blossom. We can quit manipulating, acting out, crying, screaming, and hiding. We can stand up and brush the dust off. We have a bright future ahead. It will be as bright as *we make it*. We are the artist and a magnificent canvas lies before us. It is time to begin our masterpiece.

One strategy that can help you grow is to consider becoming your own parent. Try loving yourself until you feel lovable. Become the parent to yourself that you always wanted, a supportive encourager, someone who makes you feel satisfied and safe. Periodically ask yourself, "What do I need"? We will talk more about this in section three. You can learn to nurture yourself and treat yourself with kindness and unconditional love. Although this may sound hokey, this concept is truly amazing when practiced. We can give ourselves all the support we want and need. We can begin the journey toward providing ourselves happiness and satisfaction.

Learning to nurture and care for yourself may involve changing your internal dialogue and firing your inner critique (if you have one.) Women have the tendency to judge themselves harshly. Many of us are in the habit of speaking to ourselves in negative messages. We evaluate everything we do and gravitate toward being displeased with our performance. When it comes to our self-concept, we might be "glass half empty".

To become a good parent or friend to ourselves, we can change the way we interact cognitively. We can begin sending ourselves positive messages. We will discuss how to change your internal dialogue in the next lesson. Most importantly, we can quit hurting ourselves with our words. Good friends do not deliberately hurt one another. We can surrender masochism once and for all.

YOU ARE WORTH IT

Many of these ideas will be explored in greater detail in later lessons. For now, try to begin discovering and accepting that you are a valuable, lovable woman. We can soften our minds to the idea that we are beautiful and worthwhile. We can make a firm commitment that we will no longer cause ourselves harm, whether it is through eating, starving, relationships, negative thoughts, or withholding joy from our experience. We do not deserve hurt. We can let go of pain. Our lives will be different, and different can be spectacular.

We are all created to live a miraculous journey. We are born to discover joy, which is the goal of the last section of this book. Let's pause for a moment before we continue. Let's become totally ready to break the chains and surrender the emptiness and pain. We are making room for happiness and abundance. We are on the brink of discovering the beauty of who we are.

Reference:

Cooper, Arnold M.; Psychiatric Annals, Vol 39(10), Oct, 2009. pp. 904-912

YOU ARE WORTH IT

Reflections

BREAK THE CHAINS

YOU ARE WORTH IT

BREAK THE CHAINS

YOU ARE WORTH IT

3

Finding Balance

In this lesson, we will begin to consider the concept of energy, since it is a foundational component of our strength and well-being. The purpose of many of these lessons is to help you learn how to harness your energy in positive, enriching ways. The goal is for you to discover how to tap into the miraculous source of energy in the universe. Ultimately, we can offer our positive energy to the world.

Women have an abundant source of energy within. Our bodies are over 99.9% energy and less than .0001% mass. In the realm of quantum physics, there is no well-defined, tangible barrier between our physical bodies and the universe. When we extend our thoughts, we are extending our minds into the vastness of the universe. We affect our environment, others, and the world.

It is crucial to learn how to balance our energy. Finding balance is something we all strive for. Phrases like "If only I had more time in a day" or "I'm exhausted" might sound all too familiar. We can get caught in the cycles of negative energy if we are not careful. Before we know it, we are overwhelmed. We can reach a more comfortable state of balance by focusing on positive, loving energy.

In the universe, there are two distinct and opposite polarities that stand at each end of the spectrum of emotional energy. These two extremes are love and fear. Our emotions vacillate between the two ends of the spectrum. Think about it for a moment. Let's meditate on this idea. Pause and try to clear your mind of all worry and concern. Surrender all plans, judgment, and agendas for just a while. Open your mind to warmth and light and let your heart fill with pure love. Stay with this feeling for a while. Breathe deeply, fully, lovingly, compassionately…

This meditation is designed to help you shift your focus away from fear and toward love. Taking the time to let love fill your heart and mind can reduce stress, anxiety, and fear. Hopefully, this gives you a taste of the polarities that exist within us, and how love can push fear away. They are like two magnets of opposite attraction. This exercise sets the stage for our discussion.

There are many sources of negative energy in the world. Fear based thoughts are an example. I am not referring to healthy fear, where your body reacts in response to an actual threat, but rather the fear that lingers unnecessarily in our lives. Some women use negative thoughts to beat themselves up. We discussed masochism in the last lesson. Fear can be looked at as an extension of self-harm. We can learn to let go of fear in order to find health and balance.

In this lesson, we will review some of the common types of negative energy like fear, which can throw us off balance. The goal is to help you become willing to surrender the negative energies that can interfere with the balance and harmony of your life.

Quit beating yourself up

We have already touched upon the topic of the inner critic. Some of us are prone to self-criticism. We are our own worst enemy. We have an inner dialogue that is negative and self-defeating. We are unable -or unwilling- to give ourselves credit when we accomplish anything. We minimize our successes and generalize our failures. We are catastrophists. Thankfully, we can work through these issues by restructuring our inner dialogue. We can change the way we speak to ourselves, choosing words and thoughts that are more positive, balanced, and affirming.

In one recent study, it was determined that self-criticism is strongly correlated with a range of psychopathologies such as depression, eating disorders, and anxiety. In contrast, self-assurance is inversely associated with such psychopathologies. (Longe, Maratos, Gilbert, Evans, Volker, Rockliff, and Rippon, 2010) Positive self- regard leads to good health.

Self-blame can be another source of negativity. Research has suggested that internal attribution for negative events (i.e.) self-blame is especially correlated with depression. (Steinhauser, 1997) Some of us illusively exaggerate the amount of control we actually have over situations and others. If something goes wrong it must be our fault, or at least we should be able to "fix it". Many women live their lives as though they have more influence over others than they actually do.

It can be refreshing to learn the only person we can control is ourselves. It places the locus of responsibility where it belongs, on caring for ourselves. It also helps us balance our energy. When we are not expending energy needlessly trying to change things beyond our control, we are free to utilize more energy on tending to our own precious needs.

Unraveling Self-Doubt

Another negative thread that can tangle our thoughts and interfere with our balance is self-doubt. Doubt holds us down. It prevents us from realizing our full potential. It stops us from taking chances, whereby causing us to miss opportunities. When we doubt our talent and abilities, we are reluctant to embrace our journey in its fullest. We sell ourselves short.

Self-doubt stems from a disposition of fear. It results in us not believing in our innate ability to live victoriously. It robs us of all the chances we could have taken, opportunities that could lead to many successes and miracles for us. It is the unfortunate cloud that lurks in the minds of many women who do not yet realize how incredible they are.

The opposite of self-doubt is self-confidence. Self-confidence helps us succeed and grow. We are talented and gifted women- capable, brilliant, and creative. We can develop the confidence we need to believe in ourselves and succeed. An openness and willingness to see ourselves in a new way is all we need to get started. We can begin relating to others in ways that are confident and support our value. It may not feel natural at first, but notice how you feel as you begin to interact in secure, confident ways. Your life will begin to change for the better.

Workaholism

Another way we can be thrown off balance is by overworking. Workaholism is becoming more commonly accepted and even "expected" of women these days. It becomes a problem when we spend more energy on work and career than we do anything else including family, friends, and our own emotional and spiritual well-being. It is a socially acceptable way of hurting ourselves. We may not realize it, but it can make us numb. It deadens our feelings or at least prevents us from fully experiencing our feelings.

It is especially important for women to learn to balance work, family, community, and all the many responsibilities we have with caring for ourselves. It wasn't until the past century that women even began working outside of the home. Now, even though many of us maintain careers that include full work schedules, we are also primarily responsible for home, family, and other social obligations. Although career and profession can be very rewarding, a problem develops when we spend all of our time occupied in obligations. It can result in little time for us. We sacrifice tender moments of self-care to meet over packed agendas. It might not hurt at first (or at least we don't feel it) but eventually, it catches up. We begin to lose our center of positive energy.

Let's reflect for a moment on how much time we are dedicating to work. It is good to consider all of your obligations (not just career) in establishing how much time you are actually working in a week. Many only calculate their work week and do not count time spent on caring for children, housekeeping, cooking, laundry, etc… If you add up the amount of time you spend on all of your jobs, you might easily be putting in 80 hours. Perhaps you are in a position where career is your only real obligation and this does not apply. But for the many women

FINDING BALANCE

who struggle to balance family and career, by all means do the math. You will be amazed.

The solution is balance. Learn to spread your energy in a way that leaves an ample supply for you. You're worth it! Self-care takes time and attention. It's not something you can do just a little of while on the road stuck in the traffic jam. Deep breaths between business meetings are not enough. You can carve out time each day for you and only you. This may involve reducing your hours on the job. It may require you to hire a housekeeper or a nanny. Be creative. Think outside of the box. The most important thing is to create a life that is encouraging and supportive of your emotional and spiritual growth. Happiness is important. You deserve it.

Perfectionism

Another negative energy that can throw us off balance is when our expectations for ourselves are too high. Many are perfectionists. We do not do anything in half measures. Some of us go to extremes. We demonstrate this at work, at home, and in our private lives. We think if we hold everything together tight enough, we will not lose anything. We are so scared of abandonment and failure. These thoughts make us cringe.

It is good to know there is an easier, softer way. Let's try another exercise. Close your eyes and visualize your life at a slower, more comfortable pace. You are not trying so hard. You are rolling with the resistance of the difficult situations you encounter. Nothing is that big of a deal *really*, at least not compared to your level of peace and serenity. You are happy. You are joyful. You are free. Stay with this vision for a while. Your life can be this good if you let it be.

Perfectionism is a cunning enemy. It tricks us into thinking we have more control than we really do. It causes us to deny our humanity. Nobody is perfect. It is our imperfections that make us unique and incredible. They distinguish our characters. They make us beautiful. It is time to embrace all of who we are; the bright and dark sides of our personality, our successes and our mistakes. We are alright just as we are. We are magnificently and wondrously created. We don't have to try so hard. We can relax and enjoy the journey.

Self-Forgiveness

Self-forgiveness helps us lead a more balanced life. This may seem like a foreign concept. Perhaps you have not forgiven yourself for a past that is filled with mistakes and missed opportunities. Maybe you just haven't been living the way you would like. You have taken the wrong paths and made poor decisions. Perhaps self-centered fear darkened your journey. Maybe you were caught in the illusions of narcissism and you wish your life had been more fruitful. You continue to carry the burden of regret and sorrow. You might not think you deserve forgiveness from anyone, let alone yourself.

Let's take the time right now to open our hearts and let the golden light of transcendence grace our mind and soul. Pause and meditate on the grace and mercy of unconditional love in this moment. Bask in the energy and light of self-compassion. Then, consider the following question. What have you done that is so bad it cannot be forgiven? Weigh this in your mind along with the idea you did the best you could at the time with the resources available to you. Reflect on your humanity. Accept your finite nature. Stay with these thoughts and continue meditating. Let self-forgiveness flow in. Do not fight it. Forgiveness is available to everyone. It is our gift.

This is one way to experience self-forgiveness. You can also begin living it out by treating yourself with love and kindness. You can make a living amends to yourself and those around you by doing the best you can today while letting go of the past. Your current actions and behaviors can make up for anything and everything you have encountered up until this point. One day at a time, you can erase the past by making better decisions. You can create a life filled with new experiences, joyful and wonderful.

When you choose to forgive yourself, the weight will be lifted. You will feel refreshed and vibrant. You will have more energy to give yourself, others, and the universe. The journey of personal discovery and

FINDING BALANCE

growth is not for us alone. As much as we can enjoy our lives, there is an even greater purpose at work, which we will continue to discuss throughout this book. The magic of learning to care for yourself is that ultimately, it prepares a miraculous way for you to care for the world. It leads to the beauty of sharing your love.

Love and balance go hand in hand. Love yourself. Learn to love and really appreciate others. We will no longer feel the need to criticize, judge harshly, blame ourselves or others, doubt our abilities, overwork, or hold too high of expectations for ourselves. The battle is over. Love balances everything. It brings healing.

Pace Yourself

Balance involves pacing yourself. Relax. Let's try to put our visualization and meditation into practice. When you feel yourself spinning and exhausted, slow down. Connect with your body. Ease your mind. Remember, you are in control (of you that is.) You have the ability to settle down and let the peace and abundance of the universe flow in and through you. It will not happen overnight, but with patience and perseverance, you will learn how to relax and care for yourself. Trust me if I can learn how, anyone can. Have faith in the process.

We can also learn how to balance work with play. I encourage you to play as hard as you work, if not harder. Play leads to the realm of creativity; the field of pure potentiality where anything is possible. Recreation prepares the mind, body, and spirit to accomplish greatness. It helps us become more effective. Sometimes we work so long that the harder we push ourselves, the further we fall from objectives and solutions. Give yourself a break. Give yourself a lot of breaks. Take some vacation time. Reduce your hours if that is what you need. Ultimately, you will accomplish more. We will discuss the law of least effort in the next section. It basically purports that many times the harder we try the more resistance we encounter. We get much further ahead when we work in a more relaxed manner, trusting that God and the universe will meet our needs. It is remarkable. It really works.

YOU ARE WORTH IT

Hopefully this lesson has helped you begin to tap into your positive energy source. Positive energy is the foundation for inner strength. It leads to balance within ourselves and in our lives. We are slowly shifting the focus away from fear into the realms of love, where hopefully we will find ourselves. It may have been a long time since you have paid much attention to *you*. Perhaps you have ignored your needs or even hurt yourself for many years. Some of us have treated ourselves worse than enemies. We can end the tragedy now. We do not have to extend it any longer. It is time for forgiveness, self-love, and happiness. It is time to embrace a life balanced with self-compassion.

References:

Longe, Olivia; Maratos, Frances A.; Gilbert, Paul; Evans, Gaynor; Volker, Faye; Rockliff, Helen; Rippon, Giva; Neuro Image, Vol 49(2), Jan 15, 2010 pp. 1849-1856

Steinhauser, Darren Craig; Dissertation Abstracts International: Section B, The Sciences and Engineering, Vol 58(4B) Oct, 1997 pp. 2141

YOU ARE WORTH IT

Reflections

FINDING BALANCE

YOU ARE WORTH IT

FINDING BALANCE

YOU ARE WORTH IT

4

Be Good to Yourself

The next concept we will begin considering is how to be good to ourselves. This lesson consists of various ideas to help you learn to treat yourself better than you ever have before. It is exciting to consider what life can be like when you dedicate your heart to treating yourself with dignity and kindness. Be prepared for change. You will never want to go back to the way things were.

First, let's look at what we mean by dignity. *The Writer's Digest Flip Dictionary* defines dignity with words like character, elegance, excellence, grace, honor, majesty, nobleness, poise, prestige, pride, standing, stature, virtue, and worth. When we possess a feeling of dignity, we can feel all these fine qualities. Self-dignity can be the foundation for learning how to think and behave in new and different ways, ways that are enriching and edifying. It is the key to discovering a life that is filled with peace and happiness. It is the core of being good to ourselves.

We have already discussed the concept of relating to others in a way that promotes value and self-worth. Now, let's take this a step further. Consider relating to yourself and the world in a manner that projects dignity, grace, and beauty. We can act "as if". It might not feel natural at first, but we can continue to practice interacting with pride, poise, confidence, and elegance until it feels comfortable. It will not take long. You will be surprised to see how quickly you can reshape your life.

So what are some ways we can begin treating ourselves with dignity and kindness? First, we can quit being so hard on ourselves. We can treat ourselves as if we are precious and worthy, even royalty. This may seem a bit extreme, but in the universe we are royalty. We are royalty in God's eyes. We are beautiful, unique creations. When we perceive ourselves in a higher standard, we are sure to fall along the prism of self-love where we are healthy and satisfied. It will be a big improvement over viewing ourselves critically and negatively.

Speaking the Language of Love

This is a good place to return to the concept of the "inner critic" in an effort to become willing to give up unhealthy, negative patterns of thinking. Two renowned therapists who have done a lot of work in this field, Hal and Sidra Stone (1993), claim that the inner critic is an inner voice that criticizes us and makes constant judgments about our worth. They say that this aspect of our personality develops early in life and absorbs the judgments of people in our environment. The inner critic checks our thoughts, controls our behavior, kills our spontaneity and creativity, and leads to feelings of shame, anxiety, depression, exhaustion, and low self-esteem. (Hal & Stone, 1993)

In their book titled *I Never Knew I had a Choice,* Gerald and Marianne Schneider Corey (2010); list some of the negative consequences of listening and adhering to the voice of your inner critic:

- It constricts your ability to be creative.
- It prevents you from taking risks.
- It makes you particularly vulnerable to fearing mistakes and failure.
- It warns you never to look foolish.
- It takes the fun out of life.
- It makes you susceptible to the judgments of others.

BE GOOD TO YOURSELF

Part of treating ourselves with love and kindness involves changing our inner dialogue for good, permanently firing the inner critic, and adapting a style of language that enhances self-love. Hopefully, lesson three already encouraged you to begin speaking to yourself in better ways. Here, we will consider specific words and phrases we can begin using to substitute the negative with the positive. We are changing the flow of energy within us. We are becoming healthier and happier. We are coming closer to joy and peace.

First, let's consider what you call yourself. You might not realize it, but we all call ourselves something. I used to use negative names for myself. Now, I try to call myself encouraging names like sweetie, honey, or even "OK you" (when I am messing up). The point is I am much kinder to myself than I used to be. Even when I am disappointed in myself, I try to be gentle. I no longer consciously abuse myself with words.

What positive, supportive names can you think of for you? What makes you feel secure, loved, comforted, and encouraged? Perhaps it is a nickname your grandparents used to call you. Maybe it is a soothing, positive name like sweetheart or dear. Whatever you choose, make sure it works for you and most importantly, be prepared to use it to replace the negative. Changing how we label ourselves is the beginning of learning to talk to ourselves in more healthy ways. We are adapting a more loving inner dialogue.

Next, let's look at replacing some of the negative phrases with positive, supportive ones. Here are some suggestions you might try in your future:

If you make a mistake, or wish you would have done something differently, consider saying, "I gave it my best shot. Next time, I will try something new."

If you are having a day when you just feel ugly (some of you can identify) try telling yourself, "You are beautiful and worthy. You are going through a tough time right now, so just try to relax and smile."

If you accomplish something, try rewarding yourself by saying something like, "Good job. You really worked hard and deserve to appreciate and enjoy yourself."

If someone challenges you, try saying to yourself, "Not everyone will agree with me, and I will listen to their opinion and then confidently make my own decision."

These are just some examples of rewriting the language of your heart. Now, take some time to write down some new phrases that will work for you. Begin by writing down situations in particular that are challenging for you. Perhaps you have not been feeling good about yourself or someone is disagreeing with you. You can even get more specific. Divide your situations by the various settings in your life such as work, home, family, or in particular social circles. Write down the events that are causing you grief in each of these categories. Then, next to each situation, write a positive phrase you can say to yourself to replace the negative one which may be attempting to burst forward first.

Practice these new phrases. Practice calling yourself a name that carries dignity and love. We are reframing our minds. Positive energy is beginning to abound. It feels good. It soothes the soul and brightens the heart. Another benefit of this is soon, other people will begin to relate to you differently as well. Our energy surrounds us. We exchange energy with others. They will sense our self-confidence. They can literally feel our value and worth. We will be surrounded by beauty, peace, and ease; and all of our interactions will be made more positive and fruitful. It is like magic. It will change your life.

Daily Affirmations

Practicing daily affirmations is another way to be good to ourselves. It is important to send ourselves positive messages, and self-affirmation is a good way to get in this routine. There are many ways you can incorporate affirmations into your life. There are several wonderful meditation books that provide daily affirmations. You can also spend some time in direct meditation each day reflecting on your strengths, virtues, and self-compassion. If you need help getting started, here is a good exercise to begin.

List at least 5 things you like about yourself. Everyone has at least

BE GOOD TO YOURSELF

five positive qualities. List more if you can. Then, hang this list somewhere where you will see it every day. Some women hang affirmations on their mirror in the bathroom so they can read them each morning. Others hang them on the refrigerator, or a door they pass through regularly. Where ever you choose, make sure you will see your list often.

Many years ago, someone asked me to write down 5 things I liked about myself. I cried after realizing I couldn't think of anything. That was shortly after a tragic time in my life, one that stole my self-worth and self-love. Thankfully, it slowly got better. I went on to eventually come up with 3 things. I decided I was creative, caring, and resourceful; and so that is where I began. That proved to be enough as I eventually reached a place in my life when I could write this book. All we need is a modest place to start.

So where will you start? It might be hard for some, but keep with it. The only way you can start loving yourself is to try. Are you helpful, caring, smart, flexible, or creative? Perhaps you are quick, full of ideas, or patient? Brainstorm. You have good qualities, you just need to discover them and write them down. Then, find a good spot and hang your sign. Remind yourself of your good qualities every day. We forget so easily.

Reward yourself

Another important way we can be good to ourselves is to reward ourselves for a job well done. This was already mentioned in the reframing exercise, but it warrants further discussion. Some of us push ourselves very hard. We jump from one accomplishment to the next without taking the time and energy to pat ourselves on the back for a job well done. It is healthy to pause between activities to relax and rejuvenate. We need this time to prepare for our next endeavor.

Rewarding ourselves is a way to express self-love. We are acknowledging the fact that we are grateful for being the healthy, capable, intelligent creations we are. You might even consider giving yourself tangible rewards for your larger achievements such as a nice bottle of perfume, a fine piece of jewelry, a new sweater, a manicure, a nature hike, or a bouquet of freshly cut flowers. We can treat ourselves for the hard work we accomplish. We can show ourselves that we're worth it.

Learning how to reward yourself is contingent upon accepting your value. You are appreciating yourself for the time and effort that was necessary to accomplish your goal. Many of you may be in positions of authority such as managers, supervisors, executives, teachers, or moms. Just think about it for a minute. You make sure to take the time to show your employees, subordinates, or children that you value their effort, don't you? We already have the natural tendency to praise others. All we need to do is make praise transparent in our own lives. We can treat ourselves as well as we treat others.

Another way to be good to ourselves is to slow down. I mentioned earlier the importance of pausing, relaxing, and enjoying your time between responsibilities and tasks. We may even need to catch our breath, especially when we are really busy. Some of us hold our breath and don't even realize it. We let stress overcome us and before we know it, our breathing is shallow and broken. It becomes more rapid the faster we move. The next time you are rushed, check in with yourself. It might feel almost like your panting. A simple way to change the pace of your life is through regulating your breathing. We can take the time to slow down and deepen our breaths. This can help us slow down and enjoy. It helps us relax.

People who pause to relax between responsibilities are more effective. We replenish our energy supply when we take some time off. It can be for 10 minutes or 2 weeks; the length of time does not matter as much as the quality of time. We can practice skills such as meditation, reflection, prayer, or simply basking in silence. We can call upon these skills when we need them. We can practice them regularly. Our lives will change. We will become more effective, happy, and healthy.

Surround yourself with people who care

Another important way to be good to yourself is to surround yourself with people who care. Hopefully, you already have a circle of friends and loved ones who make you feel good. If so, make sure to give them the attention and affection they deserve. In caring for them, you will be caring for yourself. When we are with our loved ones, we feel the most sacred realms of love. Our hearts overflow with abundance.

There is no substitute to spending time with those who are dear to your heart. These are times to create precious memories. Together, we can experience the grandest miracles of love. Whether you are having a nice dinner together, taking a wilderness hike, or sharing a cup of tea, these are times that fill the soul. They are nurturing and fulfilling moments. We can release our worries and enjoy the presence of someone who is dear to our heart. Our spirits connect. We are renewed.

Perhaps the best example of this is children. I could not be any happier then when I spend time with my kids. We have created many precious memories throughout our journey together, and now that they are both adults, we continue to experience golden moments as we journey on separate paths. My kids have always been the light of my life and so spending time with them illumines my journey.

We can experience these same gifts through friendship and relationships. When we develop close intimate relationships we discover there is someone to lean on, to share our life with. We do not have to face the world alone. We will have someone to turn to when the going gets tough. They might not have the answers to our problems, but it is healing to simply talk. We can give voice to our concerns, and this in itself releases well-being, freedom, and peace. It leads to a healthier perspective. It helps us know we are part of a great universe.

Spend time doing things you enjoy

Another way we can be good to ourselves is to take time to do the things we enjoy. The American culture is so busy. We spend much of our time at work. We take far less vacation time than other countries around the world. Our vacations are often long overdue. We think we "should" work hard before we play. In Italy, they place pleasure before other obligations. They believe in the beauty of doing nothing. In France, several hours are spent each day on mealtime and conversation. These cultures have a zest for life. They realize the importance of enjoyment.

YOU ARE WORTH IT

We can learn from other countries. We can surrender our need to cling to work and structure; and relax and enjoy life. We miss so many beautiful wonders in the rat race from point A to point B. We can grab a bicycle or put on walking shoes and take our time getting around. We can take the whole month of vacation we earn each year and begin traveling more. We can learn firsthand how spectacular life can be. The journey is truly as magnificent as we let it be. We can begin doing the things that make us happy.

You might be wondering at this point what kinds of things even make you happy. Don't worry. You're not alone. Many of us are used to the status quo. We have fallen deep within the comfort zone we talked about earlier, and therefore considering what makes us happy or brings us enjoyment may seem like a foreign proposition. So let's brainstorm. Let's do another exercise in self-reflection.

Think back to when you were a child, before life became so busy. What was important to you? What were your dreams? What did you hope your future would be like some day? What did you want? What did you need? These are all questions that can hopefully get the wheels turning toward remembering your interests.

Now, go to the reflection pages and begin listing the things that were meaningful and important to you. List the things you enjoyed and the events, people, and situations that made you happy. Write them all down so you do not forget your ideas later. You may have liked to draw or paint. Perhaps you enjoyed writing poetry or knitting. Maybe you dreamed of becoming an artist or a singer or perhaps you wanted to be a doctor, nurse, or teacher. Take some time here to remember. This is an important brainstorming exercise. It can become the foundation for a brighter and happier life.

Now that we have contemplated a life filled with enjoyment, it is time to surrender. We can release worry and control… and relax. We are so used to taking care of everything and everybody around. We are comfortable diving into work and schedule day in and day out. One way we can begin enjoying ourselves and doing the things that make us happy is to evaluate our current mode of operation. We can slow down and smell the roses. It is time to seep into the moment at hand, take a deep breath, and enjoy.

The last section of this book is dedicated solely to finding enjoyment in life and many of these topics will be readdressed. The important lesson we can learn for now is it is OK to enjoy ourselves. There is nothing wrong with relaxing, or even playing. It is good to let go. It is replenishing to spend time doing the things that make you happy. It is healing to let the stream of life lead you to your next adventure. The universe *will* care for us. We can surrender and trust.

Say no when you don't want to

For some reason, many women find it hard to say no. Because we are so equipped and resourceful, it is not uncommon to be asked to do many things. We are given several opportunities and so it becomes challenging to prioritize. It feels good when people ask us to take on responsibility. We feel worthy and appreciated. It contributes to our sense of value and accomplishment.

Now, let's look at the flip side of this equation. There are twenty-four hours in a day. This is the only real restriction women face. I have such a strong, unfaltering belief in the strength, power, and ability of each and every woman on this earth; that I think our only true constraint is time. It forces us to prioritize. It is refreshing to learn to make choices that include doing those things that are important to us.

Managing our time well invariably results in the importance of learning to say no. We can pick and choose the opportunities we would like to pursue. We can take ownership of our lives. We can create the path we want to follow, in fact, our actions create our journey. We can keep a healthy perspective of our true responsibilities and conserve our precious energy. In this way, we will not be easily swept away by distractions and diversions. We will discuss this in more detail toward the end of this book, but a large part of healthy living is learning how to listen to your heart's desires. Being able to say no is an important tool when you do not think something fits with how you picture your "ideal life".

For the purpose of this lesson, let's practice saying no with a role playing exercise. We will begin by reviewing some helpful phrases. First, there are many ways to say no. Finding ways to say no respectfully and with kindness usually works best.

Here are some examples: (Someone asks you to take on a task that doesn't fit your agenda.)

"I appreciate your faith in me, but I am currently overcommitted and could not do the project justice."

"That certainly sounds like a great opportunity and I appreciate you considering me for the job, but I am currently committed to a full schedule, so I will have to pass."

Or

"That sounds fascinating. I appreciate that you want to include me, but at this point I will have to pass. I have been spreading myself too thin and need to make sure I effectively accomplish what is currently on my plate."

These are a few examples of saying no in a way that is respectful and affirming. Now, think of some situations you have faced over the past couple of months, or better yet, situations you know you will be facing shortly. Think of some things that are currently being asked of you that you would rather not do. Next, come up with an affirming "no" phrase. It might help to write it down. Next, practice saying no. Role-play (act out) your response as if you have just been asked the question. Write down a few different situations and role play until you feel like you have the hang of it. Practice makes perfect here; or at least it will make it a lot easier when you encounter these situations down the road.

Learning how to say no is an important part of being healthy and happy. It is one of the best ways we can be good to ourselves. It might feel foreign at first (like a lot of these ideas) but it is well worth the effort. Change is not easy, especially when it comes to changing the way you think and behave. And yet learning to live in a way that provides love, light, and joy -not only in your own journey- but to those around you, is truly beautiful. We are moving in the right direction.

BE GOOD TO YOURSELF

Self-Massage

Now, let's look at some simple, easy ways you can be good to yourself. One of these is self-massage. Massage is one of the best things you can do for your body. For those who are not familiar with self-massage, here is an example that you can follow. Give it a try. It is enjoyable, relaxing, and healing.

Choose massage oil that has a favorable fragrance. Beginning with your head, you will be working your way down to your toes, massaging your whole body in a steady, circular fashion…working your fingers steadily around in a downward direction.

Pour the oil right into your hair and begin by massing your scalp in small circular strokes. Work your fingers across you entire head and down to the neck area. Then, rub your neck in circles, especially at the base of the head where much of our tension is held. When you get to your shoulders, increase the size of your circles, making wider strokes until you work your massage into a straight and steady stroke from your shoulders to your hands. Keep stroking yourself across your arms in an outward fashion, moving all the tension from your shoulders out through your fingertips.

Continuing down your entire body, begin massaging your chest. Do not worry if you are stimulated. There is nothing wrong with self-stimulation; in fact, it can be very intimate and pleasurable. Resume the larger circular motions across your sternum and breasts and down to your stomach. Keep your mind free of self-criticism. Rub your skin with kindness and compassion. Love your body. Stroke your stomach with passionate, wide circles and eventually work this into a straight up and down motion onto your hip area. Now, rub your hips with large strong circles. Stroke your buttocks. Stay in each area as long as you can. Massage increases the circulation and helps improve metabolism. Your body will appreciate it.

Lastly, work your fingers down to your legs, changing your massage technique to firm, long strokes with your entire hand. Massage your legs up and down ending down at your feet. Here, you can sit down and end with the tiny, circular finger motions you began with. Rub the

YOU ARE WORTH IT

arches of your feet, the balls, even your toes. The total massage only needs to last about 5 minutes to be effective, but the longer the better. You will feel wonderful!

We are learning to touch ourselves with love and tenderness. Practice being mindful and really *feeling* the way you are touching yourself. At first, you might notice a general hardness or even "disconnect" in the way you touch yourself. Massage gives us the opportunity to stroke our bodies and touch our skin in a gentle, tender, loving way. While you are massaging your body, really focus on how much you love yourself. Pay attention to the small, sweet nuances. Be mindful of your beauty and gracefulness. We are transforming the way we treat our bodies. We are learning to love ourselves.

Aromatherapy

Aromatherapy is another simple way we can be good to ourselves. One avenue to enjoy is to light scented candles and be *completely* still and relax in their aroma. Totally relax your mind and your body. Let go of everything else. Close your eyes and breathe deeply. Take the scent as deeply into your body as you possibly can. Continue to breathe in and out, fully… peacefully. Clear your mind of all burden and worry. Focus on the light of the candles. Be conscious of your breathing. Feel your body relaxing and releasing. Just sit there as long as you can. Enjoy. Let your energy flow.

You can also experience aromatherapy on the go. Choose some nice lotions and body sprays in an aroma that makes you feel sensuous and vibrant. Bath and Body Works and Victoria's Secret have some especially inspiring scents, or perhaps there are specialty aromatherapy shops near you. Spend time finding the scent or scents that make you feel the best. Try them on. Spend an afternoon choosing perfumes, lotions, and sprays. You are worth it.

Then, take some extra time in the morning applying the aroma to your body before getting dressed. You will smell it throughout the day. It will be a breath of fresh air if you are cooped up in your office or somewhere else buried in paperwork. It will be an added delight if you are playing with the kids at the park or walking them through the zoo. It adds a little something special to your day, whatever your day looks like. It's all about being good to yourself. We are discovering self-love.

Vacation

Vacation is another great way to be good to yourself. We talked about taking time off work. We can also plan a getaway. It can be especially nice to find a favorite vacation spot, perhaps one where you can return regularly. It might even become sentimental. Remember my story about the beach in Cozumel? I brought my kids there several winters when they were growing up. I had spent a lot of time absorbed in career, so getting away for a week- just with them -became very precious and meaningful. We made special memories there.

You can also take a private getaway. Find a special place of solitude where you can go periodically to regain your energy and balance. It does not even have to be far away. Perhaps you can retreat to your deck or patio or a sunroom in your home or studio. The important thing is that it is peaceful and replenishing. You might choose a destination that is near the water or surrounded by thick trees and flowers. Or, perhaps just add a small fountain and some plants and flowers to your patio. The main thing is that you go there regularly to relax and enjoy. Spend time in your vacation spot. You deserve to get away once in a while.

We are beginning to build a new life. I hope you are discovering how good the journey can be. It is refreshing to realize we *can* build our lives around what makes us happy. We can speak to ourselves with loving kindness, practice daily affirmations, treat ourselves with affection and dignity, reward ourselves for a job well done, pause, relax, and enjoy. We can learn to make a new habit of being good to ourselves. You will discover a beauty so deep it will bring tears of joy to your eyes. Loving yourself with intimacy and passion is truly an amazing feeling. Keep trying until it feels natural. You're worth it.

References:

Stone, H., & Stone S. (1993) *Embracing your inner critic; turning self-criticism into a creative asset*, San Francisco: Harper.

Corey, Gerald & Marienne Schneider (2010) *I Never knew I had a Choice*, Brooks/Cole, Cengage Learning.

BE GOOD TO YOURSELF

Reflections

YOU ARE WORTH IT

BE GOOD TO YOURSELF

YOU ARE WORTH IT

BE GOOD TO YOURSELF

5

Discover your Beauty

In this lesson, I hope you will begin to discover your inner beauty. We can start *really* loving ourselves; in ways that are intimate, fulfilling, and satisfying. Self-love involves personal growth and change, but it is also about learning to appreciate your body, your essence, and your presence. We are all so very beautiful. We radiate love and light. Each one of us is miraculously and wondrously made, uniquely created to share the beauty of our inner light. We are all truly spectacular in our own, precious way. It is time for us to discover, see, and appreciate how beautiful we really are.

Many of us have spent much of our lives feeling less than beautiful-perhaps we have felt "less than" in general. Perhaps we have not reached deep enough to discover the magnificent well of beauty that lies inside. There is so much more to us than appearance, dress, and décor. Our inner beauty is the true essence of who we are. It is our crown. It is what makes us royalty in the eyes of the universe. It is what makes us precious in the eyes of our Creator.

Inner Charm

Part of what makes us so beautiful is our inner charm. We all have a realm of our personality that is enchanted. This is the part of us that giggles just a certain way, smiles with anticipation, and winks at just the right time. It is what makes us special. These characteristics are unique to us. No one can mimic our charm or replicate our cute idiosyncrasies. These make us special and attractive, even desirable.

We can embrace our inner charm and have the courage to express it. Some of us hold our inner charm below the surface. We disguise our enchanted selves under clothes of guilt, shame, embarrassment, walls, ego, and other false personas. We keep the best parts of ourselves in a compartment. We may not realize it, but we are suffocating. The charm within, our enchantment is longing to burst forward. We are created to let the light within us shine. We can show our beauty freely.

This all sounds good, but you might be wondering where to start. You may have never had the pleasure of discovering your inner charm. You may be feeling far less than enchanted. An exercise in meditation can help here. Find a quiet place outdoors in nature, somewhere beautiful and still. Make sure there is no traffic, no people, and no distractions; just you and the universe.

Then, take off your shoes and sit in a comfortable position. Try to sit in a place where you can feel the sunlight on your forehead. Close your eyes and breathe deeply. Feel the fresh wind sweep across your face. Let nature brush across your cheeks… your heart…your soul. Feel the earth. Listen to the breeze. Hear the crickets, the birds, the rustling of the grass and trees. Let these sounds and sensations fill your body. Try to let your energy blossom into the energy of the universe.

Continue in this stillness until you begin to feel your enchanted self. Sense your inner charm. Fall in love with your inner beauty. Feel how mighty and miraculous it is. It is far greater than anything you could ever hope or wish for. It is pure power and energy, the essence of the beauty of the whole universe within you. You are discovering your inner essence.

Hopefully, gaining a new awareness of your beauty and presence will make it easier to share your inner charm more frequently and freely. Just letting people get a glance of this magnificent part of you does much to brighten the world. Your smile can bring joy to a stranger. Your giggle can bring happiness to family members and friends. And your wink at just the right time can give confidence to someone who is in need of affirmation. Your inner beauty makes the universe a lovelier place.

Accept Yourself

Another important way you can embrace your inner beauty is to learn to accept who you are inside and out. We have already mentioned idiosyncrasies. We all have them. We each have parts of us we would change if we could. Perhaps you think your nose turns up too far or your hips are too wide. Whatever the case may be, we all have unique curves and various markings that distinguish us from others. In this lesson, the goal is to learn to accept yourself- *all* of you. After all, without each part you would not be you. And you are awesome, incredible, intelligent, and beautiful.

So where do we start?

Let's make another list. On the left hand side of a reflection page, write what you do not like about yourself, whether it is your laugh, your teeth, your hair, your eyes, your smile…whatever it is. Maybe it is even your attitude. Whatever you dislike, write it down. Then on the right hand side of the paper, write down things you do like about yourself. Then go a step further and add in how well the parts of your body function. (In the places where you listed features about yourself that you dislike). Such as, "I can see out of my eyes." (Some people are blind). Or, at least I have my teeth and can eat without any problems. Perhaps you have a bad attitude, but at least your mind functions normally.

It is not uncommon to focus on those parts of us we dislike, whereby losing a healthy perspective of our good qualities and gifts. You may think your legs are either fat or too skinny, but what a gift to have legs to walk on. You might not like your attitude (perhaps you suffer from depression and have the tendency to think negatively), but at least your mind works efficiently. Some people struggle with basic cognitive skills. Taking an inventory of your good qualities as well as your blessings is a great way to begin accepting yourself for who you are. It helps paint a brighter picture.

Feel your beauty

We are now ready to begin feeling our beauty. Let's go back to our experience in the nature meditation again. Close your eyes and remember how soft and fresh the breeze felt as it swept across your face. Reflect on the beauty of the universe surrounding you, permeating your body and soul. Visualize your own beauty seeping out into the universe. Remember the quantum analogy in lesson three? There is no tangible barrier between us and the universe. Our bodies appear to have a distinct outline, we appear to be made of mass, but we are mostly energy with nothing to block us from exchanging energy with the world around. We even exchange energy with people.

Picture yourself absorbing the beautiful nature around you. Visualize releasing your beauty into the universe. Now feel this beauty where you are. Illuminate… Radiate… Breathe deeply and smile. Feel the warmth. Feel the light. Feel the love… Know you are loved. Realize you *are* pure love. This exercise can prepare you to reach out and share your beauty with those you meet, even those you pass on the street. Smile at strangers. Make eye contact. Spread your love and light wherever you go, whatever you do.

We affect the universe in this way. We can advance love and make the world a better place. When we hide our beauty and attractiveness, we become dull and slated. We blend into the background of life. But when we smile and shine from within, our journey and the world around us is brightened with sparkling and radiant color. We truly make the world a more beautiful place with our presence. When we believe in our hearts that we can make a difference, we can freely express the best of who we are.

Love and beauty are one in the same. Love is pure beauty. It is what holds the universe together. We are made in love so we cannot help but be beautiful. We know this when we are connected to our inner essence. We can feel the power of beauty when we are in sync with our creator and the mighty universe. The greatest love affair we can have is with love itself. We begin to experience this as we fall in love with ourselves…

Focus on your Positive Qualities

Another way to feel your beauty is to focus on your positive qualities. When you think of yourself hold your best traits- those qualities on the right hand side of the list you made- in the forefront of your mind. Take inventory of your gifts regularly such as your good health, your eye sight, and the sharpness of your mind. Focus on your good qualities such as your smooth skin, your nice smile, or your bubbly personality. Our minds tend to magnify whatever we are looking at. It is almost like we have a magnifying glass in our head. Whatever we focus on becomes larger.

If you feel the inner critic creep back in, quickly turn your attention back to your strengths. Count your blessings frequently. You will begin seeing yourself in a new way, a more beautiful light. Hopefully, you are in the process of falling in love with yourself. It is truly spectacular. Other love affairs may come and go, and some may even stay a while, but your greatest love will be with yourself. Your journey can be beautiful in this way.

Show your beauty

Do not be afraid to look beautiful. Don't be embarrassed. This may sound odd, but many women are shy to express their beauty. Perhaps you are afraid of being judged harshly? Perhaps you are reluctant to expose the full reflection of your light and love. You may not be comfortable expressing your enchantment. Maybe you reserve it for special occasions or do not let it out at all. You hold it in its special compartment until the time is right or safe.

Instead, imagine living a life that is filled with enchantment. Dare to embrace and express your enchanted self. You can integrate the light and love within your personality and make a decision to let your beauty shine. You can wear nice things: pretty shoes, bright colors, flowers, lace, silk, ruffled skirts, cashmere sweaters…whatever makes you feel good about yourself. Smile. Sing. Dance. You're beautiful. You don't have to hide it.

Be beautiful for yourself. Put on a silky robe and light a candle just for you. Express your beauty because it feels good and you're worth it, not to impress or attract someone else. We can live enchanted lives for us. Those around will benefit too, and yet our energy is focused on our own spirit, beauty, and grace. Our greatest journey is possible through self-love.

Wear your prettiest clothes. Are you one of the women who purchase a pretty, perhaps even sexy piece of clothing, but then rarely wear it, or save it only for special occasions? Life *is* a special occasion. Each day of our journey is precious and can be spectacular. Time goes by too quickly to leave our prettiest clothes in the drawer or closet. It is alright to look beautiful. We do not have to feel awkward or ashamed. When we wear our prettiest clothes, we feel pretty. Our beauty radiates. We know we are special and deserve the best. We are developing an appreciation for ourselves and our beauty. We are blossoming.

Hopefully, you are also beginning to find passion. You may be gaining a zest for life and all the wonders that lie ahead in your journey. We can show our beauty along the way. We can lift the veil of illusion that clouds our minds with thoughts and feelings that we are not good enough. We can turn our faces toward the light we crave, feeling its warmth and love, and letting it become all of who we are. We are becoming one with beauty. We are discovering self-love.

Quit Comparing

We can quit comparing once and for all. Everyone is beautiful in their own way. Some are more outwardly beautiful, others possess inner beauty that can hardly be matched. Comparisons get us nowhere. They are forms of judgment that we can do away with. Instead, we can strive to be self-affirming. We can give up comparisons. When we compare ourselves to others, we almost always wind up with the short end of the stick. We tend to compare our insides with other persons' outsides. It just doesn't work if we want to feel healthy and whole.

We can feel most beautiful when we give up comparisons and all judgments for that matter. One of the greatest spiritual virtues is to give up our judgments entirely and try to live our lives in non-judgment or a state of complete neutrality. This can be difficult as many of us are used to forming opinions about everything we see. We tend to view the world and people dualistically as good or bad, attractive or unattractive, pleasing or displeasing. Imagine letting the universe and others be how they are. Imagine letting go of your perceptions and preconceived notions. It is not only healing, it is empowering.

This holds true with how we view people. We can appreciate the beauty of everyone we meet. We can enjoy their smile, join them in their presence; even participate in spontaneous conversations. We can acknowledge the beauty of other women and still feel beautiful ourselves. In fact, learning to appreciate the beauty of others ultimately increases our own sense of beauty. We feel more connected and less defensive. We come to realize the world is an amazing place made up of many diverse people. We can appreciate each and every one. We can enjoy their beauty.

Inner Confidence

This flows nicely into a discussion about inner confidence. When we feel beautiful, confidence naturally follows. A review of the literature on self-confidence indicates it is a strong prerequisite to feeling happy and satisfied in life. When we are confident, we make better decisions and take better care of ourselves. When we lack confidence, we waver. We are unable to follow a clear path. We are easily distracted. Our energy becomes scattered and faint.

How much confidence do you have in yourself? This might seem like a hard question to answer especially since your level of confidence probably fluctuates from day to day. Confidence is influenced by several factors such as how much sleep you are getting, your current stress load, and your latest luck. Our level of self-confidence is also dependent on how well we are taking care of ourselves. When we are eating right, getting enough sleep and rest, and achieving a proper balance between work and recreation, our level of self-confidence is higher. We are more confident and positive when our lives are in balance.

One way to answer the question of how much confidence you have in yourself is to consider how much faith you have in yourself. Consider the following question, "How strongly do you believe in yourself and your abilities?" Rank your answer from 1 to 10 with 1 being hardly at all, and 10 representing believing in yourself completely. I don't know anyone who is a "10" but I know many strong women who probably consider themselves an 8 or 9 based on their attitudes and accomplishments. I would say I range between 6 and 7 on any given day. How about you? Let's take some time to see where you rank on the confidence chart. We are discovering more as we go. Self-discovery paves the way to change, which leads to happiness.

Don't worry if you rank yourself low. We can all work on building self-confidence. You may consider yourself a 2 or 3. You may have experienced some rough times. Life has a way of beating us down at times. Unfortunately, some of us are also put down by people, perhaps even loved ones in our lives. But we all have the potential to build a higher level of self-confidence. We are capable and resourceful. All we need to do is believe in ourselves.

For now, let's consider what it would take for us to move just one step higher on the confidence chart. For example, if your confidence level is a "4", explore what it will take for you to get to a "5". You might consider such things as increasing your daily affirmations, reviewing your self-talk and changing your inner dialogue to be more positive, or even spending some time with a supportive, encouraging friend.

What other actions can you take to increase your level of self-confidence? It is worth exploring the answers to this question. When we possess inner confidence, we possess the freedom to live our lives in the best way possible. We have the courage to be who we are and do what we want. We can spread our wings and fly.

Inner confidence, like inner beauty is pure strength and energy. It helps our inner essence vibrate at a higher frequency. We can be creative, inspiring, and encouraging to the world. Inner confidence helps us know we are beautiful. It reminds us we are miraculously and wondrously made, created to shine our light and love. It is the beginning of an exciting and prosperous life.

Smile

The last thing I will suggest in this lesson is to smile. This is perhaps the simplest and most effective way you can increase your feeling of inner beauty. Smiling brightens the spirit. It makes you feel more beautiful. And it definitely makes you appear more beautiful.

Before we go any further, let's get a baseline. Begin paying attention to your facial affect, meaning your facial expressions. How often do you smile? Do you usually frown? Does your face feel tense? Perhaps you do not have much expression at all. Whatever the case may be, start paying attention to how often you smile. You should have a fairly accurate baseline after a few days.

Now here comes the fun part. Start smiling as often as you can, even when people aren't looking, and including when you are alone. You can cheer yourself up by smiling. If you catch yourself stressing or feeling discouraged about something, the simple act of smiling can be enough to raise your spirits and turn your mood around. If you feel your face tighten up and become tense, relax. Consciously release your facial muscles and let go. Turn up the sides of your mouth. Raise your cheeks. Smile. Try it. It's like magic.

Eventually, you can even include smiling in your meditation time. We will discuss meditation in more detail as the lessons progress. When you are sitting in stillness, you can smile from the inside out. You can picture your whole body smiling, your face, your heart…even your stomach and other internal organs. Feel all your body smiling. You will be amazed at how happy and healthy you will feel after completing this meditation.

Hopefully, this lesson has helped you discover your beauty. We are all beautiful women, delicately and magnificently painted by the tender brush of a mighty creator. We are his masterpiece. We are all beautiful children of a lovely universe, a wondrous God. The energy of our beauty combines and multiplies. Our individual beauty pales to the energy we project when we are participating in the universe and with others. We can appreciate the beauty of others for this reason. Together, we shine most brilliantly.

Relax. Let go. Smile. Keep discovering how very beautiful you are. You're worth it!

DISCOVER YOUR BEAUTY

Reflections

YOU ARE WORTH IT

DISCOVER YOUR BEAUTY

YOU ARE WORTH IT

DISCOVER YOUR BEAUTY

6

Take Care of Yourself

This lesson is filled with ideas about how you can take care of yourself. I hope you will be able to relate to some of these ideas and incorporate them into your daily living. It is very important for us to make a commitment to take care of ourselves. In the final analysis, we are all we really have.

Women are accustomed to taking care of others. We perform the art of raising children, balancing relationships, family, and career, perhaps taking care of our parents as they age, or contributing to community interests. We are involved in many affairs. We can effectively juggle many priorities and care for anyone and everyone around us if we have to. We are dedicated. We are tremendous. The question becomes how well are we caring for ourselves in the process? Have we put ourselves on the backburner?

As a warm up, let's explore the need for self-care. Why is it so important?

When we care for ourselves in an attentive and fulfilling way, we experience a greater degree of health, wealth, wellness, and joy; which are the main pillars that support the arch of self-love. If we are not taking care of ourselves, we are in no position to care for others. We will have nothing of true value to offer. We can learn to pay attention to ourselves including our needs: physical, emotional, and spiritual. We can direct and redirect our energy inward.

Before we go any further, let's look at a classic, popular psychological theory which continues to be a staple in the study of human development and growth today. It is Maslow's hierarchy of needs, which states our basic needs are physical or survival in nature such as our need for food, water, air, and sex. The next highest level is our need for safety and includes our need for order and structure, and protection from fear and anxiety. The next highest level, which happens to be in the center of the hierarchy, is our need for love. We long to feel accepted, loved, and wanted; and know that we belong. Close to the top but one step underneath, we find our ego and esteem needs, which include self-respect, competence, creativity, and freedom to be ourselves. At the top of the hierarchy is our need for self-actualization, which is our need to become "fully" ourselves. It involves developing our own autonomy and individuality.

Most interesting, this theory hypothesizes that to move upward toward satisfying higher level needs, our lower level needs must first be met. Extending this idea to the here and now, it stands to reason we must take care of ourselves physically and emotionally, which are at the base of the pyramid, in order to progress in self-growth, personal development, and spirituality. This lesson will talk about ways we can care for ourselves in basic ways.

It is especially exciting to realize how learning to love ourselves satisfies the love need found in the center of the pyramid. So many women expect others to meet their "love needs". It is refreshing and liberating to discover we can satisfy our own needs for love and affection simply by learning to love and care for ourselves. Self-love creates a solid bridge into a future that is filled with opportunities for self-actualization and "inner fullness."

We begin this lesson by going back to the most fundamental, basic needs. First, we will look at some ways we can care for ourselves physically.

Get Enough Sleep

The amount of sleep we need varies due to a number of factors such as age, gender, current work load, level of stress, and even the season. Most adult women need at least 7 hours of sleep per night as a bare minimum to maintain a full and healthy lifestyle. Ideally, we can try to get 8 to 10 hours of sleep per night. Sleep is replenishing. It is restorative. Although it varies by individual, generally more is better than less rest. Sleep gives us the vibrancy and energy we need for another day. It contributes to a brighter outlook.

Getting an adequate amount of sleep allows us to reach the REM stage where our minds release and dream. It is important for us to get enough REM sleep. Our brains need deep sleep. Our minds are so full and busy during the day. Consider your own life for a moment. How many ideas, plans, goals, and activities would you say you juggle from moment to moment throughout the day? 2, 3, 4, 5... Perhaps I have not even guessed a high enough number. We are definitely engaged in life. There is probably not a minute that goes by that you are not at least considering the step behind and in front of you. Sleep gives us reprieve from the constant business of the mind. It also provides needed rest for our bodies.

Rest is restorative. During sleep our physical body is regenerated, and dreaming enables us to explore our unconscious (George, 1998). He also says sleep helps us recover from the stresses we experience during the day, and it provides us the energy to cope effectively with challenges we will face tomorrow. If we sleep between 6 to 9 hours each night we are in the normal range. George reminds us that many of us disturb our sleeping cycle from taking its natural course by staying up longer to get more done and by jarring ourselves out of sleep by an alarm clock. He says restful sleep is vital for relaxation and we need to discover our personal sleeping cycle. "The key to quality sleep is being able to identify our natural sleeping pattern and then adhere to the required quota as much as possible." (George, 1998)

You may be wondering how you can get more sleep. Perhaps you work evening hours, or have two jobs. Maybe you have family members who keep you up late, or you have to get up very early in the morning to go to work. You might think 5 or 6 hours is as much as you can squeeze in. Well, think again. You cannot be effective unless you are well rested. You may be getting by, but eventually, you will wear down. If nothing else, you will not be as happy and satisfied in life. People who do not get enough rest are more stressed, irritable, and discontent. They may be getting by, but they are not feeling as good as they could. Taking care of yourself is about feeling good. You deserve it!

Get Plenty of Rest

Your body needs plenty of rest. Sleep is the primary way to provide yourself with the rest you need, but it is not the only way. We can also learn to take breaks during the day to rest the body, mind, and spirit. We can pace ourselves. Remember the lesson on balance, learning to balance work with play and relaxation. Let's apply this theory again here. When you are feeling tired at work, take a break. Grab a cup of coffee or a sweet latte and gaze out the window for a while. Take off early some afternoon if you are done with appointments and sit by a lake, park, or garden. Spend time in nature. Feel the breeze on your face. Meditate. Appreciate. Love yourself.

When we take the time to rest, we are replenished and renewed. Our energy is regenerated and we become more effective. Some of us spin our wheels without even realizing it. The harder we work, the further we drift from real solutions. We get overwhelmed. Things become foggy and confusing. This is no way to live. The world is so beautiful when we can view it clearly with a peaceful mind.

Rest promotes strength and clarity. The more tired we become, the darker things seem to appear. It is amazing how significantly sleep and rest affects our emotions. Two of the best ways we can take care of ourselves are to have a sleep routine that we stick to, and a commitment to resting when we are tired. These are two small, but wonderful gifts we can give ourselves to help us stay on the track of health and wellness. Our lives will be more meaningful, fruitful, and productive as a result of these simple actions.

YOU ARE WORTH IT

Eat Right and Exercise

 Another important ingredient to taking care of our basic physical needs is to eat right and exercise. It is important to maintain good health. We need to nourish and care for our bodies. Because this is so important, the next two chapters are devoted solely to this topic. Many women abuse their bodies by practicing unhealthy eating behaviors such as binging and starving. Others neglect their bodies by not eating very nutritiously or not exercising at all. Our bodies are precious. Our bodies are our temples. They house our strength and energy. It is harder to become all we can be- self-actualize- when we are not feeling well physically. Eating right (nourishing our bodies) and exercising are important parts of good health. They are both critical components to meeting our basic needs.

 A good way to make sure you are on the right track is to schedule regular checkups and receive preventative healthcare with your healthcare providers including your primary care doctor, dentist, and any other doctors you may see for specialized health care needs. Wellness is a foundational need. Although it may seem redundant, I will continue to emphasize that you deserve the best throughout this book. Healthcare is important and so are you.

 An appropriate assignment to follow this discussion is to pick up your datebook and make some appointments. Schedule your annual physical and pap. Make an appointment for teeth cleaning and a dental exam. How long has it been since you had your eye's examined? Have you ever had a mammogram? It is important to begin routine breast examinations no later than your forties. And especially as it involves special health concerns, are you overdue for any follow-ups? After all, life can be busy. Don't forget how precious your life is, or for that matter, how precious you are.

 Learning to care for ourselves in these basic ways paves the way toward higher levels of self-care, including self-love. It creates a solid foundation upon which we can build a happier, healthier life into the future. Some of us have spent many years meeting these needs for our children or loved ones. We know the drill. We had no trouble caring for them. All we need to do now is turn our attention back to ourselves. Just try to care for yourself as much as you do your loved ones. You are as precious as they are. And you're worth it.

Now, let's look at some higher level needs including suggestions to take care of ourselves emotionally, mentally, and spiritually. We will look at some basic, simple ways to practice and enhance our love for ourselves. These ideas are by no means exhaustive. My hope is they will become a good place to start on the road to self-care. Self-love is a lifelong process (like so many things). After all, it is not as much the "end" of the journey that we can look forward to as each beautiful step we will take along the way. Our journeys will be as beautiful as we make them, and pursuing self-love ensures that our steps will be bright and beautiful.

Read Encouraging Literature

One suggestion for attending to your needs for love and self-growth is to read supportive and encouraging literature on a regular basis. There are so many inspiring writers out there; authors who care about helping you build a better way of life. It is truly amazing just how much self-help or more appropriately personal discovery/spiritual growth literature is available. And many of these books can be checked out from your local library or purchased at substantially reduced costs through websites like Amazon, Half-price books, and Cheap books.

This goes back to our discussion on positive thinking and framing our mind in a positive light. The mind is never blank. It takes years of practice and experience in meditation to achieve a state of "no mind" or pure neutrality. We are always filled with thoughts. It is human nature. And like most things in nature, our thoughts are subject to the same polarities that exist in the universe. Our thoughts lean toward the positive or negative. Some people work very hard to rid their minds of the negative; but consider for a moment that if we focus our energy on maintaining a positive frame of mind, the negative will not have as much room (if any) to enter.

Focusing on the positive is empowering. If we habitually and systematically fill our minds with positive thoughts (like reading literature that brings wholeness and harmony to our lives), there will be little or no room for the negative. Our minds become healthy and vital. Our journeys and paths to wellness and success are made easier. It is the path of least resistance. Instead of fighting the bad we can embrace the good, which opens the door for a healing light to flow through us continuously and freely. It is an amazing personal politic to understand that sometimes less is more- the less we resist; the better we feel. We will discuss this concept in detail in the last section of this book. Learning to care for ourselves can help us discover the amazing gifts of love in the universe.

So set time aside each day to read and discover. For example, set aside at least 10 minutes each morning for reading and reflection. This fills your mind with positive, affirming thoughts that can become the pattern for the day. If you have limited time available in the morning, set your alarm a bit earlier. It is better not to be rushed in the morning. You are setting the rhythm for your whole day. Try to give yourself 2 hours before you have to go to work. Pace yourself. Try not to stress or feel rushed. Breathe. Relax. Prepare for your day calmly. And, include some time for reading meditations, reflections, scripture, and other passages…anything that you find comforting and encouraging. It is worth it.

Satisfy your deepest needs

Now, let's look at one of the broader ideas we will discuss in this lesson. Caring for ourselves involves learning to satisfy our deepest needs. You might be wondering what these are? Referring back to the hierarchy of needs, we discover that some of our deeper needs are for safety and security, order and structure, protection from fear and anxiety, love and acceptance, and self-esteem. Sometimes our deepest needs are lost in the rat race of life. We chase so many things: success, material rewards, recognition, relationships, power…the list goes on and on. Ironically, many of the items we pursue have nothing to do with our deepest desires. Worse yet, they might contradict our most precious needs.

TAKE CARE OF YOURSELF

Our deepest needs are the needs of our heart. They operate on a spiritual level more apparently than they exist on a physical plane. Examples are: a need for love and support, a healthy state of mind, self-confidence, and self-love. What are some of your deepest needs? This section of the lesson will take some time. It is not easy to identify our deepest needs. Some of them might be buried, beneath layers of guilt, shame, and ego-defense mechanisms. You can use the reflection pages at the end of this lesson.

So let's pause and begin exploring. Open your heart. Become aware. Ponder the following questions:

What do you hold dearest in your heart? What things can't you live without? What parts of your makeup do you consider precious, even sacred? What qualities make your life better? Consider some of these questions for a moment. Then, grab your journal and write a list of your deepest needs. Take your time. Do not be afraid. This list will become an invaluable tool for helping you care for yourself. We are edified in the process of self-exploration.

Now it's time to make a decision. Let's make a pact with one another to satisfy our deepest needs as we continue our journey through life. This is probably the best way we can assure a future of happiness and success. When we are attending to our greatest needs, we feel satisfied, fulfilled, and joyful. We feel a sense of serenity and ease, peace and contentment. We do not have to wait for others or hope they will make us happy. We can begin satisfying ourselves.

Surround Yourself with Love

Another important way we can care for ourselves is to surround ourselves with love. This includes loved ones, but in this lesson, we will discuss love on a more universal plane as well. We will talk about surrounding ourselves with the love of the universe, immersing ourselves in the journey and all the gifts that surround our time and space in life. It is amazing to become aware of the breadth and depth of love that is always within and around us. We are eternal. We are divine.

The first few lessons in this book introduced the concept of quantum energy. We have talked about the energy of the universe and how we can partake and exchange in its infinite presence. Love stretches this concept even further. Love is pure energy. It is pure light and inspiration, pure potentiality. Anything and everything that is truly important (and even possible) lies within the spectrum of love. We are love's energy. We help spread its light. We can share it with the world.

This has huge implications on a global level. This world is so deranged. We are out of sorts. Anxiety and depression are at the highest levels in centuries. Families are broken, people lonely and confused. We have so much to offer a world in need. Sometimes the simple act of talking to a stranger, offering a smile or words of encouragement is all we need to do to surround ourselves with a love that transforms. We not only add hope to the universe, we are participating in transcendence and healing. And as we share our light, our love…we grow. We change. Our lives become more abundant.

You can surround yourself with love wherever you are, whatever you are doing. Express your creativity. Inspire someone. Help a family in need. Volunteer. Chant. Sing. Say a prayer. Recite a mantra. We can pause and notice the love around us whether we are at work, at home, in the car, or in a foreign land. We can open our hearts to the love of the universe and be filled with an energy that is purely electrifying, wildly exciting, and radically comforting. We begin exchanging energy with the world. We discover we are all sojourners in faith. We are united in love.

When you meet people and interact in your daily life, search out their positive energy. Pay attention to their beauty, glory, and divinity. Salute their spirit. Embrace their soul. This is how we make love our journey. It is what leads to the deepest and most satisfying existence imaginable. The world becomes a friend. Resentment, anger, and fear disappear. We are filled with pure love and forgiveness. It is spectacular.

Another great means for self-care is to surround ourselves with loved ones. Hopefully you have family or friends whom you enjoy spending time with. I love spending time with my kids and most recently, my grandson. I also appreciate the time I share with my partner.

Make time for your family. Spend quality time with your children. Play with your grandkids as much as you can. Life is short. Relationships are precious. You never know when they will end.

It is also encouraging to surround yourself with friends. Friendships are priceless. They fill the gaps. There is something about friendship that makes life complete. We can tell friends things we may not be able to share with our family members because they are too close. We can laugh, talk, and share in recreational activities; even just sit quietly over a cup of coffee. It is amazing how wonderful it feels to share the power of silence with someone. Friends provide us with sacred moments in which we can learn more about ourselves, others, and the beauty of love. They enrich our journey.

So have plenty of friends. Do not limit yourself in this area of your life. I have many good friends and they all have unique qualities. They all satisfy different needs along the journey. You may be consumed in a primary relationship. Perhaps you spend all your time and energy on a significant other, a lover, perhaps your husband or wife. Alternatively, we can look at our love life and compare it to a flower. Our closest relationship is in the center- the soft, colorful heart of the flower that holds it together. The flower also has many petals which make it complete, in fact, without the petals; the flower would not be as beautiful. Our friendships are the petals that surround our core relationship. They complete us. They enhance the love found in the center. They help us blossom in our fullest beauty.

Ask for what you need

Another important ingredient in caring for ourselves is learning to ask for what we need. Many women are self-sufficient. Some are single mothers. We are familiar with balancing career, family, and numerous other responsibilities. It is good to learn to ask for what we need. It may be as simple as asking for some extra vacation time when we are feeling burned out. Perhaps we need to ask for help around the house? Maybe we need help with the children, either a nanny or an occasional babysitter. Many of us neglect our needs. We just keep going and going, and do not recognize that we need help. We may be too independent to ask. We may be too prideful to accept assistance from others. Whatever is standing in the way, it is time to recognize our limitations and begin asking for what we need. Our journeys will be less burdensome and difficult.

What are some of the things you have needed that you have not been asking for? Let's take some time to consider this question. Reflect on a normal day. What is it like? Have you been exhausted, stressed out, worried, or even depressed at times? It could be time to ask for what you need. Decide what some of your needs might be, and then start asking for help. It will get easier with practice. Before you know it, you will wonder why you didn't ask for what you needed all along.

A wise old gentleman once said that we cannot truly give until we learn how to receive. It took me a while to understand this philosophy, and yet I now believe the universe contains a delicate balance of giving and receiving for us to discover. The universe supports us as we give to others. We can partake in the abundant flow of gifts available to us each and every day when we allow ourselves to receive. It all starts with asking for what we need. It begins with our surrender of ego, pride, doubt, and self-reliance. Open yourself to the gift of receiving. Embrace abundance.

Do at least one thing each day that makes you happy

We have already begun the discussion on what makes us happy and we will continue to explore this topic throughout this book. Tending to our happiness is another simple way we can take care of ourselves. We can do one thing each day that makes us happy. It can be as simple as taking a walk, a nap, or going to a park. Other examples are listening to music, hiking, spending time with family and friends, and dancing. Try to do at least one thing each day that brings you joy. If nothing else, listen to some soft music before bed. Look out the window and let the music sooth your spirit. Perhaps you can gaze upon a field as the sun sets, and watch the tall golden rod bow in the wind. Relaxation and visualization are also good ways to discover happiness. They help us replenish and find our center.

Taking care of ourselves requires paying attention to *us*, including what makes us happy. Doing at least one thing that brings us joy is a good place to begin. It does not have to be huge, although it can be. Be creative. Be courageous. It is alright to take a nap in the middle of the afternoon if you are tired. Or, grab a suitcase and pack just enough for a weekend; hop a plane or hit the road. You do not always need a plan. Explore. Enjoy. Venture out. Let go…

Take care of yourself emotionally

The last topic we will discuss in this lesson is taking care of your emotions. Many of the strategies I have already suggested are great ways to take care of your emotional health. This last segment builds upon the concept of self-care by discussing skills such as monitoring our emotional landscape, tending to our emotional needs, and especially making sure to take care of our thoughts and feelings. Referring back to the hierarchy of needs, we are not able to pursue our greatest selves unless our physical needs as well as our emotional needs are met. A big part of this is love. Thankfully, we are learning to love ourselves intimately and unconditionally.

So let's look at the make-up of our emotions. I will begin with a basic flow chart that represents how our personalities operate: *Thoughts▯ feelings▯ behavior*. You have maybe seen this before. Many therapists and psychologists subscribe to this idea of the flow of energy throughout the human mind and body. This demonstrates how powerful our thoughts are. When we are thinking negatively, we generally become depressed and/or anxious, which in turn has physical manifestations such as sleep disturbances and irritability. Perhaps we begin taking our negative feelings out on those around us. Or maybe we hold them inside, but feel as if we could explode.

We can stop this negative cycle when we take care of ourselves emotionally. If you catch yourself feeling sad, worried, challenged, angry, or just plain discouraged, take a step back and consider the following poker analogy. Before the game begins, the shuffler sorts the cards.

YOU ARE WORTH IT

We can apply this to our emotional health. It's time to sort things out in your mind. Sort out your thoughts like you would sort a deck of cards. Look at all of them, good and bad, the high and low cards. You can write them down on the reflection pages at the end of this lesson. Then begin choosing the cards you would like to play with. Build the best deck you can. Throw out the bad cards. Pass your low cards to the kitty. Keep your high cards, your best thoughts.

Of course there will be days when all your cards are low. We all encounter hardships. Nothing in life is perfect. You may be dealt cards that just will not make a good hand, no matter what you do. That's OK. We can bluff. We have already discussed the strategy of "acting as if". It comes in handy here. We can try to simply get through the day, the hour, the moment; and act as if life was better. We can take care of ourselves through our struggles, try to do at least a few things that make us happy, and treat others *and ourselves* with loving kindness. This too shall pass. We will make it through. In fact, sometimes the flow of energy works the opposite way: *Positive behavior can lead to better feelings, which in turn lead to more positive thoughts.* Bluffing or "acting as if" can be a good skill to learn. It can help us cope in difficult situations.

We have discussed many ways to take care of ourselves, some requiring more change than others. If you are feeling overwhelmed, just hang in there. We have covered a lot of territory. Self-discovery and personal growth are not easy. Hopefully you are beginning to discover self-love on a deep and meaningful level. My wish is that you are starting to trust in the loving flow, abundance, and energy of a powerful love within yourself. We do not have to worry so much or work so hard. We can relax and enjoy. We can learn how to take care of ourselves in the process. We are worth it!

References:

George, M. (1998). *Learn to Relax: A Practical Guide to Easing Tension and Managing Stress.* San Francisco: Chronicle Books.

YOU ARE WORTH IT

Reflections

TAKE CARE OF YOURSELF

YOU ARE WORTH IT

TAKE CARE OF YOURSELF

YOU ARE WORTH IT

7

Nourish Your Body

Good health is the integration of mind, body, and spirit in a way that promotes wholeness, wellness, and harmony. The foundation for caring for your physical health is nourishing the body. As a society, many of us have drifted away from the basic principles of eating for nourishment. Food has become the enemy for many women. We use it to gorge, we withhold it to starve (dieting), and we abuse it or at least do not appreciate it for the gift that it is. It is time for us to restructure our thoughts concerning food.

In this lesson, we will look at surrendering to the foundational principal of nourishing our bodies. We will discuss nourishment as a regular practice in loving and caring for ourselves. We will consider some of the basic ways we can make food our friend. Eating right is one of the best things we can do for ourselves. Not only does it contribute to our health and protect us from disease, it gives us the energy we need to make the most of our journey. It helps us perform at our best level. Proper nourishment even affects our level of happiness.

Before we begin our discussion, let's return to the concept of energy. We will continue to refer to our connection with the universe. We are empowered beyond belief when we are exchanging energy with the universe- creating love, and appreciating the divinity within us. When we eat fresh foods, we are directly partaking in the gifts of nature. We are allowing the universe to nourish and care for us in an intimate and sacred way. Eating in this regard can be looked at as a special event. We can learn to hold reverence and praise in our hearts when we eat, instead of eating "unconsciously" without paying attention. We can be mindful of our connection to God and the universe and be grateful when we nourish our body with the food it needs.

It is important to become conscious of our eating patterns. There are many people who suffer from various forms of eating disorders, whether they are diagnosable such as in the cases of anorexia and bulimia, restricting and bingeing; or a disorder more commonly as known as "run-away eating", which is eating habits that have spiraled out of control. Many women eat for emotional reasons rather than to satisfy their instinctual hunger. This can become a vicious cycle, in which food becomes the enemy rather than our sustenance. Food is designed to be enjoyed in moderation. Food is our closest ally in nature. It keeps us alive. It nourishes our bodies.

Reflecting upon eating from the perspective of nourishment, we will look at various ways we can develop a healthy relationship with food. The main goal is to learn to listen to your body and what it needs. Hopefully, you will learn to eat when you are hungry and stop when you are full. This sounds so basic and yet eating can be challenged by things such as stress, emotions, hardships, depression, even boredom. As you read this lesson, try to separate your desire to eat from all the emotional circumstances that surround your eating habits. Surrender your fears, your anxiety, your worry, and your disappointments and really *separate* all the junk from your need for nourishment, good health, and well-being. The word junk is purposeful here. It seems some of us eat junk in an effort to get rid of the junk. Food can be an ineffective survival skill.

When you begin listening to our body, perhaps you will hear how hungry you are for the first time in years. Your body may be longing for proper nourishment and care. Or, perhaps you just need to fine tune some fairly good eating habits you have already developed. Most of us are at different stages, and yet this lesson can be applied to everyone.

NOURISH YOUR BODY

Whether you have gorged or restricted, become skinny or fat, or have outright avoided food for fear of gaining too much weight; the common thread is food. It has been the enemy rather than the friend it is intended to be. It is time to change our relationship with food.

This lesson presents numerous ideas on varying ways you can nourish your body. It may seem overwhelming, so as a guide simply try to incorporate some of these ideas into your daily eating routine. Find out which ideas work for you. This chapter is designed in a way that presents many different strategies for healthy eating; but I recommend integrating these ideas in a way that is tailored to fit your individual needs. I would also suggest releasing perfectionism as it is unrealistic to expect you will eat nutritiously or "properly" all the time. The strategies presented here are guidelines and should not be used to condemn or judge yourself negatively.

Eat Right

Let's begin by simply discussing the importance of eating right. The USDA, United States Department of Agriculture recently updated the food pyramid. It is a good place to begin when considering what it even means to eat right. Their website, www.MyPyramid.gov, illustrates your ideal intake from the five main food groups: grains, vegetables, fruits, milk, and meat. It may be surprising to discover the quantities recommended in each group; especially vegetables (2 ½ cups per day). This provides a wonderful baseline for us to begin discussing more positive strategies for befriending food and eating healthy. It gives us a basic idea of how near or far we are from getting proper nourishment at this point in our lives.

Fruits and Vegetables

There are many other formulas for healthy eating beyond the basic food pyramid. The first strategy in this lesson is balancing your diet with fresh fruits and vegetables. As you can see in the food pyramid, getting enough vegetables and fruits is crucial to good health. We will discuss the importance of eating fresh because canned and packaged foods are often processed and treated with many additives such as excess sugar, high fructose corn syrup, salt, fillers, and dies. When we choose fresh fruits and vegetables, we not only avoid harmful byproducts and artificial ingredients, we are also eating pure energy, full of vitamins and minerals that are immediately digested, metabolized, and blended with our own energy in ways that are uplifting, strengthening, and satisfying. Food not only nourishes our body, it also affects our emotional landscape. When we eat fresh foods, we benefit psychologically as well as physically.

Try eating more fresh fruits and vegetables each day and see how much better you feel. Your spirit and emotions will be higher and more positive. You will also have more mental and physical energy. Good nutrition leads to a better outlook. It not only improves on physical health, it also improves our cognitive, emotional, and spiritual health. I have found this in my clinical practice with clients and patients who have improved their nutrition during therapy, as well as in my own personal experience. Other therapists have reported similar discoveries. Several research studies support the positive correlation between eating nutritiously and mental wellness.

One research example comes from Lederer (1983), where in his marital therapy research project he reports that over 50 percent of the couples studied presented with symptoms of fatigue, depression, or insomnia and were eventually diagnosed as having some nutritional basis that either caused or exacerbated their marital distress. Lederer found that when couples began eating more nutritiously, symptoms abated and marital therapy was either not needed or was greatly facilitated.

Another example comes from Kintner, Boss, and Johnson (1981) who conducted a longitudinal research project and reported that families with poor diets tended to experience high levels of conflict. He found that husbands and wives used food as a way to relate to conflict in the family environment. For example, the dependent or the controlled spouse tended to have a poor diet, whereas an independent spouse tended to have a good diet. The implications for family, individual and even group therapy are astounding.

On an individual level, therapist Karen Wall LMHC, ACADC describes the connection between mind, body, and spirit at the beginning of her sessions with women with eating disorders by drawing a tri-modal diagram to depict what happens when we neglect nourishing our bodies. She begins by illustrating three circles to represent mind, body, and spirit partially overlapping one another. She relates this illustration to the functioning of a fully congruent and healthy self- image. When we are nourishing our bodies and eating properly, our mind, body, and spirit are all interconnected in a way that helps us feel integrated, satisfied, and whole. She states when we are not eating properly, the mind begins to fight against the body, pulling the three circles apart in a way that causes us to lose connection with our spirit. As you can see from this example, eating well is a foundational part of emotional and spiritual wellness, and increases our sense of wholeness and harmony.

Proper Portions

The benefits to eating right are numerous. Eating the right food groups is important, but another key ingredient to good nutrition is eating in proper portions. Ideally, it is best to eat smaller amounts of food more frequently throughout the day. Many nutritionists suggest eating five times per day- 3 well balanced meals and two healthy snacks. This is ideal for our metabolism. It provides just the right amount of nutrition and calories for our bodies and minds to function at optimal levels. We are highly energized and not weighed down by excessive quantities of food.

When we do not eat regularly, the metabolism loses its natural rhythm. It can even shut down in more extreme cases. Take for example restricting or starving (even crash dieting). When we do not eat for long periods of time, our bodies go into starvation mode where the metabolism actually slows down and quits working properly. When we decide to eat again, our metabolism responds more sluggishly than if we had been eating regularly all along. What is worse is when starvation or restriction leads to bingeing and gorging later. A weakened metabolism is left to face larger quantities of food than would normally be consumed and digested in one sitting. This is when food really becomes the enemy. It becomes a battle against good health.

The best way to avoid the vicious cycle of overeating and starving is to eat frequently, regularly, healthily, and in proper portions. Start paying attention to your level of fullness when you are eating and between meals. It generally takes your body 3 to 5 hours after a meal to become hungry again. Try only eating when you are truly hungry. Also pay attention to your satiety level (your level of fullness) while you are eating. It is ideal to quit eating before you are stuffed (or 100% full). Try eating to ¾ or 75% of your stomach's capacity. Quit eating before you become uncomfortable. This will help you avoid feeling like you should starve or deprive yourself of food later.

Avoid Emotional Eating

Perhaps the most important thing to avoid is bingeing. Do not let overeating become or continue to be a habit. Avoid emotional eating. Some of us eat for "emotional nourishment". When you are upset, bored, stressed out, depressed, empty, discouraged, frustrated, disappointed…you name it; resist turning to food to sooth your emotions. Gorging your body will only make you feel more miserable. As we discussed previously, it is another way of hurting yourself. It is a subtle form of masochism. Try not to over eat when you are extremely upset. Relax. Be mindful of what you put in your body. Increase your awareness of your consumption. Nourish your body in healthy portions. Be mindful of your satiety level. Be good to yourself.

Eating fresh and well balanced meals in healthy portions is the best way we can nourish our bodies. I mentioned the word "surrender" earlier. It is beneficial to consider surrendering to nourishing your body as a foundational step toward eating healthily and regularly. Many women try to control their food intake. We use food to manipulate our emotions, rather than for nourishment. We use food for reward and punishment, control, and stress relief. We might even use eating to alleviate boredom. We may be uncomfortable when our lives are quiet and still. It might be hard to relax. We try to fill the void.

We can all learn to nourish and empower our bodies with food. We are worth it. We are worth the very best, which includes caring for our body, mind, and spirit. We can surrender our mental struggles against food and allow our whole selves to connect, integrate, and be restored...

Eat Colorful Foods

Another strategy for eating healthy is to eat colorful foods. A general rule of thumb is the darker the better. Foods that are darkest in color are richest in vitamins. Some examples are spinach, berries, and beans. Purchase the garden salad that includes dark purple spinach leaves. Choose fruits that are deep red, purple, and orange. Pick vegetables that are the darkest greens. There are plenty of colorful options in the fresh sections of most grocery stores. Fresh foods provide the most color. Packaged and processed foods are relatively bland and lower in vitamins and minerals.

When it comes to preparing your meals, think "color". Not only will your meals look great when you serve them, they will be naturally balanced when they include many colors. It is nature's way of helping us get proper nutrition. Different colors of food contain different vitamins and minerals. Try including fruits, vegetables, wheat, chicken, and salad. You can be especially creative in the way you display this meal in that these foods provide a lot of contrast. It can be a fun way to express yourself and nourish your body at the same time. Or even better, share the meal with family or a friend.

But even when you are eating alone, remember to include color. Take an extra few minutes to search the refrigerator and pantry to find fresh foods that offer variety. It will be worth the added time and attention in that you will be giving your body all the vitamins and nutrients it needs to thrive. And as we discussed earlier, you will also feel better emotionally. Darker foods such as berries and spinach help alleviate depression. They literally elevate the mood when consumed. It is amazing how sensitive we are to what we put into our bodies. All the more reason to take some extra time and preparation in serving ourselves a well- balanced plate of assorted colorful foods.

Antioxidants

Another way to nourish your body is to eat foods that are high in antioxidants. This is especially important for women. Antioxidants protect against the aging process, reduce stress, and can even increase our level of cognitive functioning. They help us feel more vibrant, energetic, and beautiful. They help reduce wrinkles, increase the vision and clarity of our eyes, strengthen our bones and hair, and help us feel more healthy and happy. Some examples of these foods are: blackberries, strawberries, blueberries, raspberries, prunes, acai berry, broccoli, asparagus, brussel sprouts, spinach, pomegranate, avocado, dark chocolate (preferably with 60% or more cacao), almonds, foods containing omega like salmon, and green tea.

It is beneficial to add even just one item that is high in antioxidant content to each meal you consume. It can be as simple as adding a handful of berries to a cup of yogurt, or placing some asparagus beside your main entre at supper time. You can even spread some spinach beneath your egg for breakfast which is a tasty way to add greens. Most of the foods high in antioxidants are also rich in color, so this will fit nicely with the idea to use more colors in each meal. Again, we are nourishing our bodies, treating ourselves with love and care. It is so much better than using food to punish or reward ourselves. We are coming along way and it feels very good.

Protein Linking

Another good strategy to keep in mind as we consider and plan eating more nutritiously is protein linking, which involves "as a guideline" trying to eat at least 50% the protein that you do carbohydrates in any one sitting or meal. This guideline is simply an ideal and not as easy as it sounds. Many foods are high in carbohydrates, even healthy foods. A beginning goal can be to try to get as much protein as you can to offset your carbohydrate consumption. Some ideas are: eating cottage cheese or peanut butter with your fruit, or meat with your noodles or potatoes. Basically, keep enough high protein items in the kitchen so that you can mix and match protein with carbs as often as possible. Many foods have protein and carbohydrate content right on the labels. The food groups highest in carbohydrates are fruits, bread and wheat, and the milk group. Keep staples available in your kitchen that are high in protein such as meat, beans, peanut butter, cottage cheese, carrots, yogurt, and nuts. This is another basic way you can make sure you are nourishing your body the best way possible.

Homeopathic Health

Another simple way to nourish our bodies is to take vitamins, herbs, and supplements. This is a great way to compliment the good eating habits we are establishing. It is important not to substitute vitamins and minerals for eating right; however, they are highly effective for supplementing your diet. We can treat our bodies with special care by giving ourselves highly concentrated health remedies like herbs and vitamins. Homeopathic remedies provide ways for us to value our bodies and care for our health.

There are several nutritional enhancements to choose from. The simplest way to decide which vitamin is right for you is to do some research. An infinite amount of information can be found on the worldwide web. There are many factors to consider such as age, the level of energy you desire, how active you are, your metabolism, how sensitive you are to various minerals such as iron, whether or not you have any allergies, and what your overall health goals are. You can also consult your physician. Once you choose a vitamin that best fits your needs, make a commitment to take it regularly every day.

One supplement that enhances emotional and physical health is Omega including Omega 3, 6, and 9. Omega has numerous benefits such as heart health and anti-aging properties, but the biggest advantage to taking Omega is its neurochemical benefits. Omega balances the psyche. It literally compliments our brain chemistry in such a way as to reduce depression, anxiety, mood swings, negativity, and irritability.

Numerous studies indicate that Omega has several balancing effects on the brain's neurochemistry. The recommended dose to effectively balance mood is 1 to 9 grams. (Preston, 2010) Generally over 1 gram or 1000 milligrams works well to achieve emotional balance. Listen to your body as you experiment to find your optimum dosage. Consult your doctor. You will be amazed at how much better you feel!

Herbs are another great natural remedy. There are so many and they vary a great deal in purpose and desired effect. They can help you in areas such as memory, brain function, hormonally, emotionally, physically; they can slow down the aging process… the list is endless. A good place to begin is to make a list of your needs such as more energy, a better memory, or stress relief- and then do some research on the herbs that best satisfy these categories. A good source is Ayurveda medicine, which we will talk more about next. They recommend various herbs according to the needs of your body, mind, and spirit. Good physical health involves the balance of all three components.

Ayurveda

Ayurveda medicine comes from the heart of eastern India. The basis of Ayurveda is achieving a balance between our bodies and the universe. Returning again to our analysis of energy, we are most healthy when we are interacting harmoniously with the energy of the universe, working with it rather than against it. According to this ancient Vedic doctrine, there are certain times of the day that are ideal for certain activities such as eating and exercise. One example is they recommend noon is the best time to eat our largest meal because our metabolisms are at their highest levels when the sun is at its highest point in relation to the earth.

The more we do to align our energy with the energies of the universe, the more succinct our lives will be. This is not only true when it comes to eating and nutrition, it is also important when considering expending energy. We are part of a lovingly orchestrated universe. Flowing in harmony with nature can become a guiding force that makes our lives more peaceful, serene, and healthy.

NOURISH YOUR BODY

Another good Ayurveda technique is to drink hot water. This is a natural way to flush toxins from your system. It might seem odd at first as we are used to drinking hot beverages such as coffee and tea, or hot chocolate- not plain water. And yet when we drink hot beverages, our metabolisms are at work digesting the minerals and additives in the beverage and are not able to fully engage in cleansing the body. When we drink (or sip) very hot water, it works to flush our metabolism and organic system. It is a very simple remedy to optimal health.

Drink Plenty of Water

Speaking of water, another important way to maintain good health is to drink plenty of water in general. As a rule of thumb, we need to drink 8 glasses of water per day (preferably about 8 ounces each). That is 64 total ounces of water per day. It may not seem possible at first, so begin by drinking as much as you can, increasing your intake of water daily until you reach this goal. Stay with it, as you may be tempted to give it up. If it becomes too difficult, try squeezing fresh lemon in your water or adding just a hint of flavoring such as Crystal Light. Slowly add fewer flavors until you are able to drink the water plain. The water works especially well to flush the system without additives. Your body will thank you as it functions more seamlessly and effectively.

Spice up your Life

This last strategy is perhaps the most fun… spice up your life! Spices are good for us. Not only do they add flavor to our food, they also contain benefits such as increasing the metabolism, improving digestion, helping the immune system, and even improving cognition. They definitely make eating more fun. And when our foods are tastier, they are also more satisfying. We will be less likely to eat before we are hungry again. Spices help to fully satisfy our taste buds and therefore our appetite. They reward our pallet.

Trying foods from other cultures is an excellent way to spice up your menu. Foods from countries like India and Cuba are especially flavorful. Experiment by eating new things. You can experience eating

YOU ARE WORTH IT

and nourishment in ways that are creative and exciting. Nourishment does not have to be a strict schedule of certain foods. Think outside of the box. Explore. Discover.

In this lesson, we reviewed numerous strategies for nourishing our bodies. I hope you can find a creative way to integrate the ideas that fit your personality and apply them in your life in a way that works for you. The main goal is to learn to love yourself enough to *want* to nourish your body. My hope is that you will quit bingeing, restricting, gorging, and/or starving as a means of trying to manipulate yourself or cope with your environment. It is time to heal and be healthy. We can love ourselves enough to treat our bodies with care, respect, and kindness. We can learn to value and appreciate our bodies and food. We are worth it.

Before we end this lesson, let's practice an exercise that will solidify the most important idea mentioned in this chapter, which is learning to nourish our bodies instead of eating for emotional nourishment. Although the many food strategies presented can be helpful, changing our patterns of emotional eating is the foundation to making the rest of these suggestions happen in our lives.

Here, we will practice a technique called Mindfulness Meditation and we will apply it to our eating habits to learn the art of Mindful Eating. First, close your eyes and picture yourself at a table with a colorful plate of food in front of you. Picture all of the food groups. See the nourishment and vitamins in the healthy foods you have selected to consume. Feel you hunger. Feel your body craving the taste and textures of this healthy, colorful pallet of food.

Now, picture yourself slowly taking each bite, enjoying every bit of nourishment and taste. Each bite offers a different flavor and an important array of vitamins and minerals. Your mind is happy. Your body is satisfied. Your soul is fulfilled. You feel content. Continue to picture yourself nourishing your body. There is a warm glow around you. You are illumined in this reflection. You feel comforted. You feel nourished.

This provides a vision for nourishing our bodies. It is an example of mindful eating. The goal is to begin practicing an increased awareness and consciousness while you are eating. Be mindful of your food and yourself. Be aware of your satiety level. Take the time to taste *and appreciate* each bite when you sit down at the table and eat. Focus on the gift of food. It provides us with the basic energy of life. It gives us strength and nourishment. It is a friend, not the enemy.

*The suggestions in this lesson are broad based and basic. The strategies are not individualized for specific health concerns. The best way to improve your health and eating habits involves consulting a nutritionist.

References:

Kintner, M., Boss, P., & Johnson, N. (1981) The Relationship between dysfunctional family environment and family member food intake. *Journal of Marriage &Family,* 43, (3), 633- 641.

Lederer, W. (1983). Marital choices: Forecasting, assessing, and improving a relationship. New York: Norton.

NOURISH YOUR BODY

Reflections

YOU ARE WORTH IT

NOURISH YOUR BODY

YOU ARE WORTH IT

NOURISH YOUR BODY

8

Stay Fit

This lesson will explore and emphasize another key component of good health - exercise. Exercising your body is one of the best things you can do to increase your energy level. We will consider the multi-dimensional advantages of staying fit. It is far more than keeping our bodies in shape. The largest benefit of exercise is the positive impact it has on emotional wellness, not to mention it enhances our psychological and spiritual wellbeing.

The benefits of staying fit are remarkable. First, let's look at some of the more obvious benefits. Exercise is one of the best ways we can care for our bodies both in the present and for the future. It strengthens our muscular skeletal system and our major organs such as the heart, lungs, and circulatory system. Recent studies in human development even indicate that exercise contributes to the longevity of cognitive functioning.

Whitney, DeBruyne, Pinna, & Rolfes (2007) provide a complete list of the benefits of being physically fit including: more restful sleep, better nutritional health, improved bone density, enhanced resistance to illness, lower risk to some types of cancer, reduced risk of heart disease, stronger circulation and lung functioning, lower risk of type 2 diabetes, lower incidence & severity of anxiety and depression, longer life and higher quality of life in later years, releasing anger, tension, and anxiety, increased feelings of well-being, self- esteem, and improved self-concept, preventing hypertension, providing a buffer against stress, improving work efficiency, decreased negative thinking, and providing a source of enjoyment.

The benefits of staying fit are apparent and numerous, but how can we apply this information to our lives? This lesson will look at some simple strategies to help you incorporate fitness into your everyday life. First and foremost, we can continue listening to our bodies… increasing our awareness of what we need to be healthy and vibrant. We learned to nourish our bodies in the previous lesson. Now, we can expand our vision to include taking care of our needs for physical activity and exercise.

The main goal is to learn another important aspect of loving and caring for ourselves. Exercising is much more than weight loss, the shape or size of our bodies, or even how we look. Staying fit is a foundational component of self-care. It is part of the beautiful tapestry that makes up not only our physical, but also our emotional, intellectual, psychological, and spiritual health.

Exercise, like any activity, takes practice; and sometimes it takes a while to develop endurance. Be patient with yourself. Don't give up. The best things in life require dedication and motivation. We are helping our bodies be the best they can be, which in turn will help us live our journeys to the fullest. As mentioned above, the benefits of physical fitness extend into all other dimensions of our life. They enhance every aspect of our inner landscape, especially our minds and emotions. Exercising releases chemicals in our bodies like endorphins, dopamine, and serotonin that help us feel good about life and who we are. Physical fitness releases positive energy that helps us maintain a healthy equilibrium and balance.

Getting Started

My recommendation is to start realistically if not modestly, but make a commitment to be persistent. It is better to exercise every day for 20 minutes, than to exercise for 1 or 2 hours and then skip the rest of the week. Balance and moderation is the key, but also consistency. Set an achievable goal for yourself. It will not do any good if you get burned out right away. Then, gradually increase the amount of time you exercise each day. Ideally, it is recommended that we exercise 30 to 50 minutes per day, at least 4 to 5 days per week. This may sound like a lot, but once your body gets used to exercising, you will enjoy the activity. You can begin to feel the numerous benefits right away.

Find a form of exercise you enjoy

The first helpful suggestion is to find a form of exercise you enjoy. It is highly unlikely you will continue to do something you dislike (or even hate). So many people view exercise as a burden or at least a negative chore. When we repeatedly force ourselves to do things we don't want to do, we eventually give up and end up feeling defeated. This can lead to self-criticism and self-blame. We may be left wondering what happened to our initial level of resolve. We might feel incompetent and incapable. The key is to find a form of exercise, or variations of fitness that are rewarding and fun. We needn't give up altogether; we just need to find out what works for us.

Some people get caught in the rut of hitting the gym and working out on the same machines, or the same pieces of cardiovascular equipment day in and day out. Exercise soon becomes mundane and tedious, more like a chore than an adventure. It is liberating to consider that exercise can be exciting and fun. We can add creativity and variety in order to let physical fitness spice up our lives. All we need is the motivation and courage to try something new. There are so many ways we can stay fit.

Many gymnasiums and fitness centers offer numerous classes several days of the week such as boot camps, circuit trainings, aerobics, body sculpting, spinning, yoga, Tai Chi, and Pilates, which are sometimes free to members. Trying different exercise classes can help add variety to your workout and also will help you strengthen and improve your physical fitness in new and challenging ways. Not only does this help break up the routine, it can be a fun way to meet new people and learn things about yourself and your body.

Tai Bo

One of the most enjoyable classes offered in fitness centers is Tai Bo. This form of exercise combines martial arts, aerobics, and kick boxing. It is invigorating and challenging. It is extremely high energy. The class usually lasts 45 minutes to an hour, but it moves so fast that it is finished before you know it. It is fairly easy to learn the various punches, kicks, and moves as the routines build upon each other. After a couple of times, you'll be a pro!

Other fun sports can also challenge your fitness level like tennis, soccer, volleyball, and swimming. Even lower intensity sports such as bowling and golf have some fitness benefits. It is better to get your body moving in a minimal way than no way at all. Sports that demand a lower amount of energy may be better to begin with when you are first trying to get in shape. Keep an open mind. You might surprise yourself by trying something new.

You may even enjoy competitive sports. You might consider joining a softball, volleyball, or basketball team. There are many sports teams organized for casual enjoyment. They are quasi competitive, and the majority of teammates consist of people of average to even below average physical capability. Many of them are simply playing for fun. This is not only a great way to stay in shape; it is a good way to meet new people and friends.

Relaxation and Exercise

There are also many relaxing forms of exercise to choose from. It is a myth to think that exercise needs to be rigorous to be beneficial. Some of the best forms of fitness activities are slow and controlled, utilizing the core muscles and deepest areas within the muscular skeletal system. Lower intensity forms of exercise can be utilized alone, or as a supplement to more aggressive routines. They can also add variety and enhance the normal routine, especially when you feel the need to do something different for a while.

Yoga and Pilates

Two popular forms of lower intensity workouts are Yoga and Pilates. Both of these are great ways to improve your mind/body connection while increasing your level of fitness. They encourage mobility, range of motion, flexibility, coordination, concentration, relaxation, connection, integration, and strength. These are especially beneficial for middle aged women who want to strengthen and slim their core muscles in the stomach, hip, and glutei areas. They are great for increasing overall muscle tone while increasing energy and peace of mind. Generally, the music is inspiring and meditative. You can release your mind and get in tune with your body. It is a great way to focus on love and self-care. It is also a good way to get in touch with your spirituality and the universe.

Interpretive Dance

Another form of exercise that is relaxing and creative is interpretive dance. This is a fascinating way to just let yourself go and enjoy your body, soul, spirit, and experience- together with the beautiful sounds and rhythm of music. We can move our bodies in complete freedom, without an agenda or boundaries; and express our deepest feelings and emotions, putting them into motion. Many times we need to be creative and freely associate in order to express ourselves most fully. Interpretive dance is excellent for combining physical, emotional, and spiritual health. The energy released in this form of exercise is phenomenal and healing.

Since you might not be familiar with interpretive dance, we will go through some of the steps that can help you begin learning this beautiful form of expressive art. First, choose music that best suits your mood. If you are feeling somber, depressed, anxious, or even frustrated, find music that is highly artful and beautiful, soft and eloquent, such as classical (Mozart) or light contemporary. If you have been feeling angry or despondent, perhaps some stronger instrumentals would be better such as Beethoven or classical rock music like Alanis Morissette. The main idea is to choose a particular genre that will help you translate your emotions into movement.

Close your eyes and begin listening to the music. Open your stance, your mind, even your hands as the music begins. Be still for a moment and absorb what you hear. Let the music flow through you until your body begins moving with the sound. Move freely, uninhibited. Let down your walls. Discover your feelings and emotions and let them captivate each movement. Let your body flow and move in exaggerated, full, and overextended motions. Escape confinement. Test your boundaries. Feel the freedom, release, and spirit in your expression.

Interpretive dance can last as long as you want or need it to. You will know when you are finished. Try to give yourself as much time as you need to fully express the wide range of emotions within. Women tend to suppress emotion much of the time. Dance is a great way to express what we have been holding onto (especially anger) in a safe, comfortable environment. It is also a great way to stay fit. The exaggerated movements of emotion work all parts of the body in ways that are toning and strengthening. Dance until you're tired. Dance until you feel cleansed.

Belly Dancing

Belly dancing is another form of dance that has numerous benefits including helping you stay in shape. Like interpretive dance, it can be an excellent outlet for self-expression, and yet belly dancing differs in its structure and routine. It is a great way to exercise, but its largest advantage is it makes you feel very sensual and whole. It involves large and graceful moves contrasted with small and quick, controlled movements of major muscle groups such as the hips, abdomen, shoulders, and arms. It takes time to learn and perfect the various movements, but the challenge is well worth the effort. Formal instruction is recommended.

Many cities have dance studios that offer belly dance class. It is amazing how wonderful a group of women can look and feel together. The combined energy is beautiful, graceful and eloquent. Women of all shapes and sizes expose their center and wrap themselves in trinkets and jewels. They move together in romantic, passionate ways including belly rolls, figure eights of the hips, snake arms, shimmies, and full body waves. The energy and sensuality these women experience collectively is incredible. This dance is especially good for women who struggle with self-confidence and body image. By the time you are done, you will feel amazing and beautiful. It is one of the best things you will ever try.

A last form of dance we will discuss is exotic dancing, which has become more popular in recent years. This used to be reserved for places like exotic dance clubs, but increasingly, women are dancing exotically for themselves. It is empowering. There are studios opening up all over the nation that teach numerous forms of dance. Women can learn various movements and styles of dancing that not only make them feel sexy and vibrant; they can also increase their level of fitness. This not only provides a good work out, it is very strengthening and empowering. It is a great way to increase self-confidence and self-esteem. Most importantly, it is a lot of fun!

Power Walking

One of the most basic, effective forms of exercise is walking. Brisk walking for just 30 minutes a day helps your heart, lungs, and circulatory system; walking also controls body weight, relieves stress, and invigorates your body and mind. (Corey, 2010) You can take it up a notch by power walking, which simply involves taking wide strides with your legs while swinging your arms vigorously back and forth. It is a great way to elevate your heart rate for an extended period of time, which not only builds endurance and stamina; it burns calories and increases your metabolism. Many cities and towns have walking trails carved in the midst of great scenery. One of my favorite places to walk is a 3 mile trail through a thick forest surrounding a lake. It is magnificent to see the sunlight dancing through the tall twisting trees and bouncing in shimmers of light across the placid, calm lake. You can really feel the energy of nature. It is invigorating.

Whether you find a nature trail or hit the track, power walking 30 to 60 minutes per day, 4 to 5 days per week will help you achieve similar results to running or jogging, yet it is easier on the joints and not as challenging to the cardiovascular system. The wider the strides and the faster the pace you are able to maintain, the better the benefits. It is more involved than strolling, although once you get used to the higher intensity, you will be able to enjoy your surroundings just as much. It only takes about 3 to 4 weeks to get in the shape required to maintain the "power" behind your walk for an extended period.

Power walking like all the other forms of exercise we have discussed increases your energy level, which is the biggest advantage of staying fit. I strongly believe in the presence and power and energy in the universe and within us. Anything we can do to increase our positive energy is well worth the effort; and exercise is one of the best ways to increase your level of positive energy flow. When we obtain adequate levels of physical activity, the molecular structure of our bodies vibrate at a higher energy frequency. We feel better emotionally, physically, and even spiritually. We can more fully connect with others, ourselves, and the universe. Walking outdoors is a simple way to increase your energy level. The energy exchange is truly amazing!

You might even consider challenging yourself a bit more and plan an outdoor vacation that involves exercise and fun. There are so many activities to consider from camping and river rafting to hiking and kayaking-perhaps even walking or running in a marathon. Many of these activities require some practice to build up endurance, but preparing for the adventure is almost as fun as the activity itself. We will end this lesson by discussing just a few of these options and some ways you might prepare and plan for these excursions.

Hiking

One of the most spectacular ways to have fun and stay fit is to plan a hiking trip. There are many places to hike. Most of the national parks and many of our landmarks and tourist attractions have hiking trails designed and marked for the enjoyment of walkers and hikers alike. Some of the most beautiful trails are in the mountains. My son and I hiked the most incredible trail imaginable at Mt. Rainier National

Park. It took us up 1000 ft. in altitude, past two magnificent, sparkling lakes of aqua blue, and toward our ultimate destination which was at the top of the nearest foot hill of Mt. Rainier. We passed endless fields of wildflowers on our way up the trail, including fresh fields of lavender. When we reached the top of the trail, we just sat there and enjoyed the beauty of the earth around. It was as if all the colors of the universe just hung from the sky in front of us. It was the most beautiful scene I have ever enjoyed.

To prepare for a hike such as this, it is good to make sure to walk (preferably even power walk) for at least 30 to 60 minutes per day for a period of 1 to 2 months. Hiking trails are generally rated according to difficulty and also marked for distance and altitude. Push yourself, but try not to overdue. It is not always possible to turn around once you get started, so it is better to know how many miles and the level of difficulty of the trail before you begin. If you are new to hiking, try to choose a trail that is no longer than 3 miles. You can work your way up from there. Especially when steep altitudes are involved, a maximum of about 8 miles is plenty. There are longer hikes available, but 6 to 8 miles is an adequate challenge.

Kayaking/River Rafting

Kayaking and river rafting are other ways to have fun and get a good work out. To prepare for trips like this, it is good to build upper body strength. Weight training is the ideal way to prepare, or a nearby gym might have rowing machines or other cardiovascular equipment that include upper body strengthening. Most resorts near water such as lake and mountain resorts have kayaking and river rafting available. Again, the routes are generally rated according to level of difficulty (and in the case of river rafting also according to the level of danger). For beginners, select a lower grade adventure. You can always work your way up from there.

We have discussed many ways to stay fit in this lesson. Most importantly, we have explored different ways to make exercise enjoyable

STAY FIT

and fun. Staying fit is much more than working on our shape or forming our figure. It is about feeling healthy, vibrant, and wonderful about ourselves inside and out! It can be challenging, exciting, and adventurous; or relaxing, soothing, and releasing. If we dare to try new things and be creative, we can experiment with different ways to stay fit and feel good about ourselves. Try some of these ideas for yourself and see what you like. By all means, treat yourself to regularly participate in the activities you enjoy. You will have more strength and energy. You will feel better physically and emotionally. So why wait? Get started. You're worth it…

- The suggestions in this lesson are basic and broad based. For more specific information on an exercise program that is best for you, consult a personal trainer or exercise physiologist.

References:

Corey, Gerald & Marianne Schneider (2010) *I Never Knew I had a Choice, Explorations in Personal Growth.* Brooks/Cole Cengage Learning

Whitney, E., Debruyne, L. K., Pinna, K., & Rolfes, S.R. (2007) Nutrician for health and Health care (3rd ed.). Belmont, CA: Wadsworth, Cengage Learning

STAY FIT

Reflections

YOU ARE WORTH IT

STAY FIT

YOU ARE WORTH IT

STAY FIT

Section Two
Wealth

9

Get to Know Yourself

This section of the book is titled wealth, but we will not be discussing wealth in the typical context, although the suggestions in the following lessons may well lead to wealth in a more popular sense. The purpose of this section is to help you discover the infinite source of wealth you already possess. There is an unending reservoir of strength, intelligence, and creativity within each and every one of us. We can learn to discover and maximize our inner wealth. It is our greatest asset.

Have you ever felt limited by what you have or don't have? My hope is this section of the book will help you become more aware of your inner strengths and resources. I hope you discover that all you really need to achieve your dreams is within. We do not need to wait for something or someone to happen to us. We can begin the journey to success right now for we are gifted with everything we will need to achieve our goals. All we need is a little confidence. We hold the future in our hands.

The best way to begin cultivating our inner resources is to get to know ourselves. What I mean here is really exploring our inner landscape including our interests and abilities, our disinterests and limitations. We are not all designed to succeed in the same areas. If we were, we would have a dull and monotone society. Life would not be as rich or fruitful. We are all uniquely and powerfully gifted with wondrously miraculous abilities, some big and others small, and yet neither one more or less important. The irony is sometimes it is the smallest of gifts that make the largest difference in this world.

This lesson can be likened to evaluating your investment portfolio, but you will be considering your intellectual, emotional, spiritual, and psychological assets instead of your stocks and money market accounts. Hopefully you will begin to see that there is a wealth of opportunity and an endless supply of success within your very being. We can quit looking around and reach within. Empowerment begins here.

We will begin this lesson by exploring a series of questions. These are all designed to help you get to know yourself better. Consider each one as openly and honestly as possible. It may be difficult, but it is well worth the effort. The best changes in life can happen through self-exploration. Simply try to keep an open mind and heart as we ponder the following topics. Getting to know yourself is a great gift. It will prepare you to utilize the infinite amount of wealth you already possess.

What makes you Tick?

We will begin by considering what motivates you. What makes you tick? Many effective therapeutic strategies are built on the foundation that human behavior is motivated by wants and needs. We behave the way we do to fulfill certain needs and/or achieve a certain level of satisfaction. So, what motivates you? Is it getting along with others? Perhaps career or family drives your actions? Maybe you enjoy traveling or leisure and recreation activities? Whatever it is, when you begin to discover what motivates you, you will be in a better position to harness your energy.

Some of us get diverted with many things. We are less than motivated, and yet we find ourselves maintaining the same schedules and routines day in and day out. We may feel very productive (or at least we are expending a lot of energy), but perhaps we do not really enjoy all of our tasks and responsibilities. Or maybe we just don't have enough time to do the things we enjoy the most?

A good way to sort things out is to make a list. What really motivates you? That is, what are you truly interested in doing? This is a key to helping you discover your inner storage of wealth. We tend to be good at those things that we are truly interested in. For example, I love to write. I am very inspired to write books, even though I spend a great deal of time in psychotherapy and counseling work. I have written for several years. It has been my passion for a long time, especially in an effort to help women overcome challenge.

So grab your notebook or the reflection pages and make a list of the things you value. You might be surprised at what you find on your list. Some people get so busy with handed down roles and routines, they forget what they really enjoy. Not everyone knows what makes them tick. Take your time. Don't hold anything back. Do not stop to think too hard, just make your list. It is amazing what we write down when we are uninhibited and uncensored. When you are done, look it over. These are the things you can do to improve your future. They will lead you to success.

What are your inner resources?

Next, let's consider our inner resources. As mentioned earlier, you are your #1 asset. All you need to succeed…the talent, ability, intelligence, creativity, and confidence lies within you at this very moment. It is up to us to tap into the inner source of our strength. You might be wondering how? We will look at some ways you can begin to explore your inner landscape and discover your resources. The main idea to keep in mind is that we all have an abundance of ability. Be patient with yourself. It will come.

Discovering our inner strengths and abilities involves a process of self-discovery that is ongoing. We continue to discover more of our talents as we try new things in life. We might even amaze ourselves. The key is willingness. We can stay open minded as new opportunities arise. We do not have to sell ourselves short. We can guard against preconceived notions that we are not good enough or smart enough or whatever the obstacles in our minds might be. And the more we try, the more we learn.

Another tool to begin acquainting ourselves with our inner resources is to explore our past and note all of the accomplishments and achievements we have experienced. Go back as far as you can remember, even back as far as grade school if you can remember that far back. Find a quiet room where you will not be disrupted. Give yourself plenty of time for this exercise. If you feel rushed, complete it another time when you have fewer obligations. Sit in a comfortable position. Close your eyes. Open your heart. Explore your past.

Some examples of what you might find are earning good grades, being a good athlete, becoming a parent, raising children, solving a problem at work, helping a neighbor, supporting a family member, volunteering, building a career, or being a dedicated partner. Don't stop at just one or two accomplishments, try to remember them all. Some of us have more achievements than we realize.

Then, with your heart and mind still open, reflect upon the positive qualities you possess that led to these accomplishments. Using the examples listed above, some of your inner resources might be intelligence, motivation, compassion, creativity, self-discipline, empathy, perseverance, dedication, and commitment. Whatever your particular achievements are, it is guaranteed your inner resources led to these. Do not limit your exploration. Maintain a kind and loving attitude toward yourself as you explore your gifts and talents. This is not a boastful exercise, rather, it is empowering. It will help you discover your inner wealth.

Finding our inner strengths and resources is the beginning of making our journey's more successful and fruitful. It gives us a roadmap so that we can better direct our efforts in the future. Our energies are often limited. We are finite beings. Some of us get caught up in so many things, our energy becomes fragmented. Knowing ourselves in a way that provides knowledge of our inner gifts and talents can help us utilize our energy in the most effective way. We maximize our experience. We make our journey the best that it can be.

GET TO KNOW YOURSELF

What are you good at?

Continuing our self-exploration, we now turn our attention to another question that can help you discover your inner wealth. We are continuing to get to know ourselves better. Ask yourself the simple question, "What am I good at?" Some of you might find this question silly or even redundant, but keep an open mind and seriously consider this for a moment. Some of us have been working against our grain and not even taken the time to realize that life may be a struggle. We can get trapped in society's idea of who we should be or even the expectations of our friends and loved ones. Here, we will take the time to honestly consider what we are truly good at. It might be technology or design; it might be cooking. It could be singing or sewing or building or excavating. You might not even know what you are good at, but just give this exercise some time and space in your mind. We are all good at something. Discovering what we are good at paves the way to a brighter, more successful future. We can focus our energy on our natural abilities, which helps success come more naturally as well.

So, what are you good at? Take a moment to list at least something; if not a few things you are truly good at. Write these down on the reflection pages. Take as long as you need. Be patient with yourself, kind and confident. Talents will surface. You can reflect as they do. What has really worked in your life, and what has not? Be honest. It's OK to admit our limitations in the process of realizing our strengths. It is all part of the process of self-discovery.

Hopefully, you will discover at least one thing you are good at, if not a few things. Hold onto the reflection section at the end of the lesson. This can be a roadmap to help you fine tune your journey as you continue through the rest of this book and the rest of your life for that matter. We all need little guides and reminders to keep us on track. Life can become busy and complicated. Lists can simplify the process.

What do you need?

Now, we turn our attention in another direction, away from our inner resources and toward what we need. Another important aspect of getting to know ourselves is to realize what we truly need, deep down. This section will encourage you to reach beneath the surface to a place where you will find your most genuine needs and desires. When we get in touch with our truest, deepest needs; we get in touch with ourselves. This is one of the best ways we can learn who we really are and what we truly want our journey to be.

Perhaps the best place to start is to look at this as a sorting out process. Most of us have a lot of wants and "what we consider to be" needs. Maybe we have been hoping for something to change in the workplace. Perhaps we are praying that our partner will change, or that our financial position will improve. Maybe we would like to lose weight, worry less, or travel more. Many of us can list several things when asked what we need. But let's try to put our usual lists aside and dig deeper into our genuine needs. When these are met, the rest miraculously falls into place.

To begin, let's close our eyes and open our hearts as wide as possible. This exercise involves preparation. First, cleanse your mind of everything that has been cluttering your thoughts. Let go of all your worries, doubts, fears, even your hopes and dreams. Release your goals and struggles. Clear your mind of everything, good and bad. Focus on becoming a blank slate. Try to find a place of pure neutrality, where nothing affects you. You are completely free, entirely peaceful. Nothing is bothering you. You are not judging, criticizing, even evaluating. You experience utter comfort and relaxation.

When you feel as if you are at complete peace and neutrality, ask yourself the question, "What do I truly need?" Stay with this question a while. Meditate upon it. Reflect on its deep and healing presence. Allow the answers to come in their own time. Do not construct the answers. Do not judge or criticize what comes to mind. Simply let it be and stay with the answers as they appear seemingly out of nowhere. Continue to relax and let go. Take stock of your needs lovingly, compassionately, and objectively.

You may discover that you need more rest, relaxation, fun, or social activity. Whatever it is, it's OK. Don't fight these needs or for that matter, do not reject any of the needs that reveal themselves during this meditation exercise. You may find you need more love in your life, perhaps you would like to spend more time with your loved ones. Another common need is our need for safety and security. You might discover you need more faith in God, yourself, others, or the universe. Perhaps you have been running on self-will or self-sufficiency and you need to let go and trust in the energy and abundance of the universe. Whatever comes to mind; just let it be. Accept your thoughts. Embrace your needs.

When you have given this meditation adequate time, (generally about 30 minutes, but longer if possible), open your eyes and reflect upon the needs you discover. How are you already meeting these needs in your life? Where do you need to change or improve? These are important follow up questions in that it does not usually come easily or naturally for women to meet their own needs. We are accustomed to taking care of others. Many of us juggle numerous responsibilities and goals. Our multitasking may be eclipsing our most tender psychological needs. Hopefully, this lesson will begin changing this for you.

What makes you smile?

Another important question to ask in getting to know yourself better is "What makes me smile?" The answers will probably be surprisingly simple. Maybe it is spending time with friends, having coffee and visiting about old times. Perhaps you remember smiling at the park as you played with your kids or grandkids. Or maybe you were on vacation and tried a new activity such as snorkeling or scuba diving. Some of us do not smile very often. We have become a pretty serious society.

In any case, it is important to consider what makes you smile as you can start doing these things more often. Many of us are on a one way track and we are travelling very fast. We do not always take the time to pause along the way and enjoy the things that make us smile. We might pass our friends and loved ones by along the way. We might not think we have time for leisure activities. And yet, we need to smile.

Two of our most foundational needs are for relaxation and fun. We can take the time to laugh and play. We are worth it!

Know your limits

Another important aspect of knowing who you are is discovering your limits. We explored our inner resources earlier in this lesson. Now, we will look at our limitations. This might not be as easy for you. It can be challenging to admit our weaknesses. Some of us are reluctant to accept our limits. Perhaps you hold on to the belief that you can do anything you set our mind to. But there are times when motivation only takes us so far. We all have limits to our talents and abilities. We may also face environmental constraints. We cannot all achieve the same things based upon our individual circumstances and the context in which we live.

Exploring your limitations honestly and realistically can help you learn what to avoid in your future. We can learn to optimize our energy. Acceptance is the key to helping us work through this process. We learn to accept ourselves the way we are, including our weaknesses. We can embrace ourselves and love the strengths we do possess, without judging or criticizing ourselves for our limitations or even our shortcomings. The gift of self-acceptance makes the journey more joyful and meaningful. We are provided the strength and energy we need to focus on what we can accomplish. We can quit fighting against our fiber.

So let's give it a try. From a noncritical mindset, a frame of mind that is kind and loving, consider your limitations. A good starting point is to index your failures. Ouch. The word failure hurts, believe me I know, so let's hold our minds in a light that is loving, kind, and accepting as we begin indexing our downfalls. What has not worked in your life the way you wanted or expected? We can learn to look at our weaknesses and failures from a point of reference that is supportive and compassionate. If you feel your body becoming tense, consciously pause and "soften" your disposition. We will use the art of softening as we consider many uncomfortable topics in the following lessons. Intentionally and consciously softening our emotions, feelings, thoughts, and attitudes can help us through the most difficult times.

Within each failure that comes to mind, you may find some of your limitations. Try to focus only on your part in each situation. Although it is generally easier and perhaps more natural to blame others or factors beyond your control; for the purpose of this exercise, attempt to focus on the only thing you have direct control of, which is your own behavior. Give yourself some time with this exercise even though it may be uncomfortable. You are clearing the way to a more successful journey in the future.

You may discover that many of the failures you index consist of similar limitations. Generally, people have a set of limitations that tend to unmask themselves throughout different scenarios in life. It may be you passed up the opportunity to apply for a promotion. Maybe you missed the chance to go on a spontaneous, romantic vacation with your significant other. You may have wanted to enter a poem, story, or article in a local literary competition. When considering what lies beneath these failures to act, you may discover low self- esteem, a lack of self-confidence, or maybe procrastination. Whatever you find, simply take note of your limitations in a nonjudgmental and compassionate way. You are learning a lot about yourself.

The goal is to become more familiar with your limitations, so you know what you need to work on, or simply avoid altogether. Some of our weaknesses lend themselves to self-help such as increasing self-esteem or self-confidence. But others, such as a lack of ability in certain academic areas or a lack of talent for music, art, or dance- these are some of the things we can grow to accept and learn how to live with. We are not all created to succeed in the same areas of life. We are each gifted in unique, yet spectacular ways.

The most important, overriding idea here is to love yourself completely for who you are the good and the bad, your inner resources and weaknesses and limitations. Getting to know yourself is much easier in the light of self-acceptance and is especially easier with the gift of self-love. Hold on. Be patient. Learn with ease. We do not have to be everything to everybody. We only need to find contentment with who we are. This is the goal of the journey.

Feel when you are depleted

Similar to this topic, we can learn to feel when we are depleted. Some of us are used to running on empty. We go and go and go and do not realize how tired we have become. We chase goals and follow plans, sometimes to the point of exhaustion. It is good to take a step back and realize when we are depleted. Sometimes we need to recharge our battery. This does not mean we need to give up or quit what we are doing permanently; it might simply mean it is time to take a break. We may be in need of replenishment and rejuvenation. There is no harm in resting. The world will not quit spinning on its axis. Our lives will not fall apart. In fact, sometimes the best thing we can do to further a project is to give it a rest for a while. Often times when we take a little time away, we come back fresh with new ideas and renewed creativity.

Learning to realize when we are depleted in order to rest and rejuvenate is a critical skill as we strive to discover our inner wealth. It increases our effectiveness and helps us avoid burnout. We do not have an endless supply of energy. We have talked in previous lessons about managing and conserving our energy. Getting in touch with our energy supply allows us to apply our best energy when it is needed and in ways that are most fruitful and rewarding. We know ourselves well enough to admit we need rest and replenishment. We are not afraid to take a break.

Search out your Destiny

To end this lesson, we will begin our discussion on destiny, which is a theme we will readdress throughout this book. It is impossible to become our "best selves" to discover the great wealth that lies within each and every one of us, without exploring the topic of destiny. Our destiny is the ultimate way of expressing our self. It is what we are born to do. It is who we are and what we are meant to bring to this world.

A major part of getting to know ourselves is exploring our destiny.

GET TO KNOW YOURSELF

We can contemplate and explore what we are meant to do with our lives. We can use the information we have discovered about our inner resources and limitations to formulate a plan to make a difference in the world. Whether it is by teaching, practicing medicine, singing, writing, mothering, participating in missions work, or involving ourselves in community service, we are all born to make a difference. We travel this earth for a reason.

Some of you may already work in a field that is your heart's desire. You may have found your purpose and decided to journey within your calling. That's great. There is no better way to live than in the heart of your destiny. Others may wonder if they will ever find their passion or for that matter, if they have a destiny at all. Hang in there. We all have a miraculous purpose, an amazing journey created for us (and only us) to complete. You will find it as you continue to get to know yourself better.

Be patient with the process. Self-discovery is incremental. You will eventually get to know yourself better, especially as you practice some of the meditations and exercises in this book. This is only the beginning. We still have much to learn about self-love. Finding your destiny is only part of the beautiful masterpiece, which is what you are. We are all precious and magnificent works of art, designed by the master creator of the universe. The One who painted the sky and hung each star is also creating a masterpiece within each and every one of us. May we all come to know these great facts about ourselves. We are beautiful. We are worthy. We have a purpose. Get to know yourself and you will find out what that is. You can start today!

YOU ARE WORTH IT

Reflections

GET TO KNOW YOURSELF

YOU ARE WORTH IT

GET TO KNOW YOURSELF

YOU ARE WORTH IT

10

Invest in Yourself

This lesson emphasizes the importance of investing in yourself. Building on the last lesson, we learned that we are our #1 asset. We hold the potential for our future within us. As we live this philosophy, we begin to realize that we need to invest in ourselves to succeed. We can intentionally build our future in a way that is personally enriching and rewarding.

Many women are well invested in others. We have had numerous responsibilities such as motherhood, partnership, career, community service, or at least a combination of many roles. We have spent much of our journeys outwardly focused and rightfully so. Women are incredibly supportive, resourceful, compassionate, intelligent, and dedicated. Our emotional makeup provides us with the ability and desire to help and care for others.

This lesson will discuss balancing caring for others with self-care. It will show you how to invest in yourself like you do in others. The goal is to help you realize you are worth your time and attention, even your resources. Some of the ideas and exercises may seem foreign at first, but consider them openly in any case. Change is never easy and investing in yourself may be an unusual concept to explore. Patience and open-mindedness will assist you as we look at various ways we can invest in ourselves as valuable women. Again, we are laying a foundation for creating wealth in our personal journeys. So let's look at some suggestions.

Read, read, read

One of the simplest, most inexpensive ways you can invest in yourself is by reading. There is a wealth of information available at our fingertips thanks to the modern day explosion of publishing and literature. It is estimated as many as 160,000 new books are published per year. And with internet access to discounted books as well as free distribution through libraries and other institutions, reading is becoming increasingly affordable and practical.

Reading keeps the mind fresh, active, and engaged. Our brains, like any muscle, need exercise. They weaken with complacency. Reading stretches and strengthens the mind by encouraging us to consider new concepts, process new information, learn new strategies, techniques, and ideas, and further organize and synthesize what we already know (just to name a few benefits). Basically, reading keeps us abreast of new discoveries, current events and issues, and either challenges or solidifies various outlooks and ideas in our existing knowledge base.

We can strive to make more time in our lives to read. Perhaps you already read regularly. But if you are one of those who struggle to find the time to read, here are a few suggestions that will help you find the time:

1. Block at least 1 hour per day for reading. It does not necessarily have to be one consecutive hour, perhaps you can schedule up to four, fifteen minute segments in your day. Perhaps you can read during break at work, or before bed in the evening.

2. Turn off the television or better yet, do not even turn it on. We live in a society of instant gratification and this applies to entertainment. Americans on the average spend 14 to 20 hours per week watching television. One way to have more time to read is to read instead of watching TV. It is just as relaxing, more enriching, and very enjoyable.

3. Read a couple to a few books over the same period of time. This adds variety to your reading. Sometimes, we get sick of a book before

we are finished. Simply book mark your page and set it aside for a while. Hopefully when you come back to it at a later time, it will be interesting and entertaining again.

4. Keep a book available wherever you are. Consider keeping one in your car, bedroom, in your purse, office, at work, wherever you frequent. This will help you squeeze reading time in spontaneously and sporadically throughout the day. Simply reading between appointments or during times when you are waiting in between activities can be enjoyable and relaxing.

Reading is definitely one of the best ways you can invest in yourself. Take the time to discover this for yourself. You will not be sorry. You will feel sharper, younger, brighter, and more efficient. And like all the other ideas in this book, you can start today.

Never stop learning

Another great way to invest in ourselves is to continue to learn new things. We do not ever have to stop learning, in fact, it is better if we don't. Many people continue their education far into adulthood. Learning is not only for young people and the phrase "You can't teach an old dog new tricks." is a myth. One of the greatest gifts in the world is the fact that we can learn our whole life long. It is one of the gifts that make the journey so exciting.

There are many learning options available. Of course there is formal education. Increasingly, people are earning advanced degrees and reinventing themselves later in life. Several people in this economy have had to retrain, involving earning a higher or alternative degree or certifications. It is never too late to further your education. This is an excellent way to invest in yourself. And, it provides unlimited opportunities for added wealth in your future.

Less formal ways of learning are also available. The fastest growing avenues are workshops, conventions, and seminars. Self-improvement and educational workshops are flourishing all over the country. Many are very affordable. These provide great opportunities to further education, training, skill level, and even increase levels of happiness and life satisfaction (especially in the case of self-help and personal growth workshops). They are usually offered over the course of a single day or weekend. They are fast and efficient ways to increase your base of knowledge, awareness, and self-contentment.

Life's experiences and lessons are also an important source of learning. We can try to keep an open mind and willingness to experiment and live life to the fullest. We learn so many things simply by living out our journeys. Life is designed to teach us. A perpetual attitude to remain teachable can take us further than any degree or formal education, lecture, or seminar. In fact, the most highly intelligent and successful people in this world have remained teachable and had a heart for learning up through their last day on earth. Many wealthy people deeply appreciate the importance of perpetual learning. They maintain humble hearts.

The last (and perhaps the most important) component of learning we will discuss is willingness. This is the thread that runs within the fibers of everyone who maintains a capacity for learning. You might already participate in advanced or continuing education. Maybe you attend lectures and workshops regularly or at least attend a yearly conference. But for those who are not in the practice of continued education, let's complete an exercise in willingness. Hopefully, this will help get you started on the road to wealth through learning.

First, find a quiet room where you can sit or kneel in privacy and silence. Next, close your eyes and clear your mind of any and all obstacles and thoughts. Breathe deeply. Become completely conscious of your breath as it begins to consume your thoughts. Focus on your breathing until you feel as if your mind is free and clear of all thoughts and obstacles. You are now ready to begin.

We will begin by saying a Mantra. Say, "I do not know everything. I have much to learn." Repeat this several times in a loving and kind way. If you feel yourself getting tense or tightening up, discontinue the Mantra and return your attention to your breathing. When you feel relaxed again, restart the Mantra, "I do not know everything. I have much to learn." When you are comfortable with this chant, introduce

INVEST IN YOURSELF

a new Mantra. Say, "The universe will continue to teach me as I am willing and open." Repeat this phrase several times in the same loving, kind way. You might even feel as if you want to sing this. That's alright. Mantras are powerful patterns that can be spoken or sung. When you feel like you have completed this exercise, open your eyes. Reorient yourself. How do you feel?

Becoming a student of life is a transformative gift. It is definitely worth considering. It is phenomenal how much we can learn simply by maintaining a heart and mind of openness and willingness as we travel along our journey. It is a long term investment in yourself that pays innumerate dividends. Seriously consider this challenge if you have not already. Believe me. You're worth it.

We will dedicate the rest of this lesson to discussing some of the other ways we can invest in ourselves: financially, personally, and on a larger socio-cultural scale. Again, the goal of this chapter is to help you discover that investing in yourself is one of the best ways to increase wealth in your life. We are our greatest asset. All the things we will ever want and need can be cultivated within us.

First, we will look at some financial aspects of investing in ourselves. We will start with a simple rule of thumb. Spend as much (if not more) on your insides as you do your outsides. This can be rephrased and expressed as make sure to spend as much on your mind as you do on your body (including appearance). Some of us focus our resources on appearance: clothes, accessories, facials, beauty products, salon services- the list goes on and on. Some of us do not invest nearly as much in books and education; perhaps we have not given ourselves the privilege of earning a basic degree. When we begin spending as much (if not more) on our insides (the mind and spirit) as we do our outsides, life begins to change. We feel more satisfied, rewarded, and successful.

Build a nest egg

The next suggestion is save for your future. You never know when life will hand you a different set of cards. You might be forced to retrain or start over in the future due to changes in the economy or business.

On a brighter note, you may make a personal decision to change occupations or careers, which involves relying on your nest egg. It is nice to have the funds available when the need arises. Keep in mind; you can't lose by investing in yourself.

A nest egg provides safety and flexibility for the future. It is advisable to diversify as you save and invest. Develop a nest egg, but do not put all of your eggs in one basket. You may keep some funds in a simple savings account, invest a portion of your income in a portfolio of stocks and mutual funds, or develop a part-time home based business to provide you with extra cash. The point is plan for the future. Do not spend 100% of your earnings and especially, do not overspend. So many Americans are upside down right now. It is prudent to keep some reserves, especially for changes that might come along in your future. If nothing else, you will have more freedom down the road to do what you want. We all owe ourselves at least that much!

Buy gifts for yourself

We can also invest in ourselves in smaller, more personal ways. One of these ways is to occasionally buy gifts for yourself. This might seem odd, but just think about it for a minute. When is the last time you got yourself a gift, something you have been wanting for a long time, or even just a simple gift such as a new hat or scarf? Maybe you are already in the habit of taking care of yourself. If so, wonderful! But for those who have never considered gifting to themselves as part of a self-care plan, let's look briefly at how this works and most importantly, the benefits.

The way it works is simple. At least once a month, but preferably once a week, buy yourself something special. This might seem like a lot, but small things count such as candles, hair accessories, panties, lip stick, and soothing air fresheners. Some women resist their own needs in an effort to provide for others. We are used to self-sacrifice. Perhaps you will not have the cash available when you run across something you like. Give yourself a rain check and keep it in mind. The next time you get paid or have some extra cash, treat yourself. This is one of the best ways you can love yourself. It will increase your feelings of inner wealth and abundance. You will be amazed at how some of the smallest gifts can make a mark toward your happiness.

Take yourself on a date

Another idea for investing in yourself is to take yourself on a date. This too may seem odd, but allow me to explain. A date can include taking yourself to the movies, out for a latte, or even an eloquent little lunch. Most of us are under the false impression that we have to reserve outings for when we are in the company of others. Not many may have considered the notion that you can take yourself on a date and yet, this is a great way to invest in yourself, primarily by building your feelings of value, self-worth, and happiness.

The exercise involved with this idea is simple, just schedule a date. The main challenge might be resisting any feelings of embarrassment. It might feel awkward at first, but you will quickly get used to the benefits of going on a date all by yourself. You can start slowly by going for a latte or Chi. Advance to the movies and dinner as you get more comfortable with yourself and being alone in public. Some may have a hard time overcoming this stigma, but it is well worth the effort. When you take yourself on a date there is no compromise, no need to sacrifice or worry, just 100% of what you want and need. It is a beautiful practice in self-care.

Develop your talent

We now turn our attention to some of the broader scale ways we can invest in ourselves. One of the best of these is to develop your talent. We all have unique and incredible talents and abilities. You may or may not be familiar with your talents, which is why the next chapter is dedicated solely to helping you discover your talent. For the purpose of this lesson, we will discuss how important it is for you to develop your talent. It is the key to finding success and happiness in your future.

Let's face it; we are not all doing what we desire in life. We are not all blessed with a dream job or for that matter even the time to pursue our dreams and talents. We can change this. Our talents encompass our greatest potential. They are what lead us to success and happiness. The best way we can invest in ourselves is to develop our talents, if not full time, at least part time in a hobby fashion. There is no better way to live than to follow your dreams!

This takes courage and faith in our abilities. We all have varying degrees of self-confidence. It takes a lot of faith to try something new, even if we think we have the talent. Where are you with your level of self-confidence? On a scale from 1 to 10 with 1 being not confident at all, and 10 being extremely confident, where would you rate yourself? The better question follows. What would it take for you to increase your level of self-confidence by just 1 or 2 points? If you rated yourself a "4" in self-confidence for example, what would it take for you to get to a "6"? Perhaps you could read a book or attend a workshop on increasing faith in yourself. Maybe group therapy is the answer. You could even attend a self-help group or empowerment group. These ideas can help you get to a place where you believe not only in yourself, but also in your talents and abilities. Again, the wealth of your journey lies inside you.

You can begin on the path of developing your talent, whatever it is, once you gain the confidence. If you like to dance, dance. If you like to sing, sing. If you like to write, write. There may be a dozen voices in your head trying to discourage you from doing what you like to do. Ignore them. You cannot go wrong by doing what you like to do and developing your talent. It may not pay immediate dividends, but you are guaranteed a more fruitful and satisfying life in the long run. The benefits will be there. Just hang on and believe!

Pursue a career that is rewarding

This brings us to another important suggestion, which is to pursue a career that is rewarding to you. As we mentioned earlier, many women get caught up in careers and other activities that they do not really enjoy. A good way to avoid this discouragement is to pursue a career you enjoy. The words enjoyable and rewarding are interchangeable. It is impossible not to enjoy that which is truly rewarding, and vice versa; that which is enjoyable is also rewarding.

So let's take some time here to consider our career. Granted, nothing is perfect so a good place to begin is to make a pros and cons list concerning your career. What things about your job do you like? What aspects do you dislike? On the pros side, list all the ways your present career is rewarding. Conversely, on the con side, list ways in which you are not rewarded in your career the way you hope to be. Putting things down on paper is always a good place to start when you are analyzing an important aspect of your life rather it be a career, a relationship, or even an upcoming decision. It will help you view it more holistically and objectively.

When your list of pros and cons is complete; look at it as a whole before breaking it down into segments. First, look at everything on your reflection page. Which side of the list is longer, the pros side or the cons? Hopefully you found the pros side to be greater, but even if the con side is longer, at least you are beginning to see that change may be worth considering. Now, look at the various comments you have listed, especially those that pertain directly to your career either being rewarding or lacking reward. A question to ask is, "Do I want to spend the rest of my life doing these things?" If the answer is no, you may explore the option of changing careers. Who knows how long the rest of your life will be?

Speaking of how much future is ahead of you, it is never easy or comfortable to consider the finite nature of our existence. Many of us live as if we are immortal, or at least we seldom live each day as if it could be our last. Existential concepts such as these have evaded the consciousness of a great majority. We live in a world of illusions and one of the greatest of these is that we can always do it tomorrow (i.e.) make the change, pursue our dreams, develop our talent, or spend more time doing the things we enjoy. How many plans do we have for after we retire?

Hopefully in reading this lesson (and this book for that matter), you will decide that life is too short to postpone your dreams, desires, and happiness. We can and deserve to work a career we enjoy. Work is such a major part of life. If we are not happy with what we are doing, we will not be happy in general. Give yourself a break. Find a career you enjoy. Find one that is rewarding. You're worth it!

Find your purpose

This leads to our last discussion in this lesson on finding your purpose. We will touch upon this issue many times in the lessons throughout this book because self-love ultimately includes discovering your purpose in life. A guide to self-love that did not emphasize purpose would be incomplete. We are all created to find a purpose in life. We each have something to offer this world; rather it is big or small. Some of the smallest acts of kindness contain the greatest potential to change this world. The earth is in need of our gifts. Society in general is ready for transformation and healing.

The greatest investment in our lifetime is to find our purpose. Some refer to this as our higher calling or destiny. It is what we are meant to do, who we are meant to be. It is why we were put here in this world! Many times developing and pursuing our talents leads us to our calling naturally. Other times, it is a process of trial and error. In any case we can hang in there and persevere. Good things do not generally come easy. Usually, they take a lot of hard work and dedication.

This may seem overwhelming, so we will simply begin by considering the concept of finding purpose or meaning in life. From an existential perspective, finding purpose and meaning can actually alleviate much of the anxiety people experience from facing the reality of the finiteness of our existence. It can offer comfort and life satisfaction not only to us, but also to others. Working in the heart of our destiny allows us not only to make a positive difference in our own lives; it helps us bring hope and healing in the lives of others. It could be through writing a song, a book, or a poem. Maybe you are called to be a doctor or nurse, teacher, counselor, or minister? Whatever the case may be, we are all called to serve a higher purpose in this world. We are called to an individual, yet miraculous mission.

INVEST IN YOURSELF

Just begin pondering the idea of finding your purpose at this point. Rest in it. Trust, accept, and allow all the thoughts flow in as you contemplate your higher purpose in life. You may be following your destiny already. Perhaps you have tried to pursue your calling and became frustrated, discouraged, or you gave up. Or, maybe you have never even considered the possibility that there is more to life than the 24 hours we juggle in a day. Whichever category you fit in, join with me in the following prayer as we end this lesson:

My Creator, you have made me for a reason. You placed me on this earth to make a difference, to somehow bring the world closer to love. Show me your ways. Show me my path. Help me trust in your love and the love and guidance of the universe. I release my motives and fears. I surrender my future to you. Build in me the confidence to succeed, to trust, and to work in your love. These things I pray.

Amen

YOU ARE WORTH IT

Reflections

INVEST IN YOURSELF

YOU ARE WORTH IT

INVEST IN YOURSELF

YOU ARE WORTH IT

11

Discover your Talent

We all have special, innate talent. A unique purpose and destiny lies within the heart of each and every one of us. The previous chapters have built up to this point. We are all created to be someone special, to do something spectacular; and that someone and something is absolutely incredible and miraculous. Part of finding the magnificent treasure of who we are involves discovering our talent. We each have valuable, personal talents, and our talents affect the world. When we discover and utilize our talents we illuminate the space around us, which in turn illumines the lives of others. This gives our journeys meaning. It leads us to wealth and happiness.

It is up to us to discover our gifts. Although you may encounter friends and loved ones along the way that try to point you in the right direction, ultimately, we need to be the ones who uncover our gifts. We choose who we will become. No one knows us better than we know ourselves. Self-discovery is a personal process. It is both intimate and expressive. It unleashes our gifts and leads us to a pivotal place where we can share them with the world.

The best way to discover our talent is to take a hands-on proactive approach, rather than passively accepting the direction of others. This is not to say feedback is unimportant or that we should not consider what others have to say. It simply means our own heart will best reveal our talent if we search it out. We can trust in the process of discovery. We will not be let down.

So where do we begin? We will explore ideas on the following pages that will help you discover your talent. But before we begin, let's ponder the following question.

What are you naturally good at? You might be able to list some things in your mind right away. Examples such as homemaking, career, cooking, speaking, or perhaps playing an instrument might come to mind. Maybe you are good at singing, dancing, teaching, public relations, daycare, arranging flowers, painting, or playing tennis. You have heard the expression, you're a natural. This may sound simplistic, but many of us ignore our natural talent, or at least we do not take the time to develop it.

Exploring and reflecting on what you are good at creates a backdrop for the suggestions to follow. We can begin to turn our attention toward making more room in our lives to pursue our talent. We can give our gifts space in our lives. We can honor our strengths and abilities. We can treasure them as our greatest assets! Most importantly as noted in this first suggestion, we can create time for our talent.

Surrender Busyness

Busyness is one of the largest obstacles that interfere with the ability of women to discover and develop their talent. We take little time to do what we enjoy or what we are good at because we are so busy trying to attain other goals. Let's face it. Many of us are swamped. We are up to our ears in appointments, responsibilities, and other obligations. We may not be able to remember spending much time pursuing our talent after high school, or maybe as far back as grade school. Remember talent shows? We sang and danced; we played instruments and acted in plays. That was before we were handed our official roles in life.

What did you like to do when you were younger? What were you especially good at? Let's take a minute and reflect on our childhood years. What came easy to you?

When you are done reflecting, take another moment and consider how you are integrating these talents into your present life. Hopefully, you are lucky enough to be able to express these talents in your profession or in some other fashion that is congruent with your daily life. It is wonderful to be able to express yourself along the journey. You are already brightening the world with the colors of your talent.

This lesson is also written for those who have yet to discover the beauty of expressing their gifts. If you feel unhappy or dissatisfied in life, or even if you sometimes wish things could be better, it may be time for a few changes. Don't worry. They do not have to be big. You can make very small changes in your life to begin expressing your talents. Just find a small portion of each day to fit in time to do what you're good at. Make time for the things you enjoy. If it's dancing, dance. If it is singing, sing. If it is painting or writing, paint and write. Even if you sing and dance in the mirror or take up an acting role with a small community theatre, you are expressing a precious part of who you are. Believe me. You are worth it.

The rest of this lesson will look at more specific strategies for helping you get started toward finding your talent. The main idea is to be flexible. It is helpful to be willing to experiment and learn. Many get caught in the comfort of familiarity. We may not realize how much the false security of stability can cost at times. We know what to expect, there are few surprises, but what about spontaneity and passion? Are we seeing all of the dimensions of who we could be? Are we truly complete and satisfied? Hold these questions in the back of your mind as we explore the following strategies.

Experiment and Learn

Sometimes the easiest way to get pointed in a new direction is to experiment with new experiences. Challenge yourself. Place yourself in situations that are new and unique. This may consist of an immersion in a different culture, taking classes in a subject that interests you, or attending a creative workshop. More opportunities exist today than ever before. A huge variety of seminars and retreats are available on topics of spirituality, finding joy and happiness, personal growth, empowerment, finding love, relationships, creative writing, and all the other arts (just to name a few). The simple act of attending some workshops that interest you may be all you need to discover your talents.

Another idea is to attend exhibits and art shows, visit local art galleries, or if you have the means, schedule a trip and tour international homes to the fine arts like France, Italy, and Persia. There are also cities here in the US, with art galleries and museums rich in creativity, seasonal art tours, and local talent displays. Do some research. Surf the internet and find some exhibits that interest you. Even if you never get there, exploring and planning can peak creativity within. I guarantee it is more enriching than checking email and face book.

Another way to stir interest is to attend festivals. From music festivals to drama and other fine art festivals, even food festivals are unique experiences that can spark the creativity within you. They generally have a theme such as medieval, renaissance, Japanese, Greek, postmodern, and jazz, just to name a few examples. Not only will these events stir your creativity, you can also experience different cultures, beliefs, and rituals. You can expand your horizons. The more willing you are to reach beyond your boundaries, the more you can discover about who you are. This is a great way to discover your talent as well.

Just remember, do not be afraid to try new things. Some of us have become rigid in our patterns of living. We may not realize the extent of our inflexibility until we start pushing ourselves outside our normal boundaries. It's OK. The key is to remain willing to consider experimenting and exploring. The further you push yourself, the more fulfillments are possible. It is amazing when you begin opening up the different compartments of who you are. You may not have even fathomed that you would enjoy new experiences so much. Surprise yourself! Treat yourself. Expose yourself to new things. It's worth it.

Rekindle your Dreams

Another strategy for discovering your talent is to remember your dreams and rekindle your desire to pursue them. Think back to the last time you had a strong dream or desire. Maybe it was as far back as childhood, and you wanted to be a doctor. You gave your dolls medicine, listened to their heart, and checked their ears, nose, and throat. Maybe you played school and you were a teacher. What were your dreams? What are your dreams now? Consider both big and small. Some of our smallest dreams are the most endearing. Maybe you wanted to be a poet. Perhaps you pictured yourself participating in missions work overseas. Or maybe you ponder completing a genealogy of your family or assembling a scrapbook of special memories.

Whatever your dreams have been, consider embracing them again. Some of us became too busy to dream somewhere along the way. Well, times have changed. We are learning to slow down and live more intentionally, in ways that are congruent with who we are and what we need. Let's make a resolution now. Let's rekindle our dreams and follow our heart. This may involve significant change. It could be as drastic as changing careers, changing locations, or going back to school to further our education. Don't let anything be an obstacle. It is time to go for it. It might seem scary, but things have a way of working out when you follow your heart. This is the magic of God's universe.

Discover your Inner Strength

Another way you can assure your talent is to discover your inner strength. Each and every one of us has a reservoir of unlimited energy and infinite strength. We can tap into this mighty source within. You might be wondering how. The channel to connect with our inner strength manifests when we are silent, still, and mindful. Sometimes the less hard we try, the further we evolve. We talked about the universal law of least resistance. We can sit somewhere quiet, peaceful, tranquil, and serene, and let our inner strength find us. It will. It is like a beautiful oasis within.

With inner strength comes creativity and this paves the way to discovering our gifts and talents. They may even rush in on us like a raging river. Prepare yourself to be inspired. The energy you will receive can feel overwhelming at first. It is exciting and exhilarating, enlightening and healing. We have longed to express ourselves. We have held so many things inside. How refreshing to feel the winds of change upon our face, to consider living a life that provides happiness and satisfaction. Inner strength gives us the confidence to pursue our dreams. It fortifies the journey. It helps us reach toward destiny.

Discover your Natural Poise

Inner poise is another valuable trait we all possess. We each have a perfect rhythm that naturally supports our strivings and talents. You may be afraid that you can only pursue your talent clumsily. You may fear scampering, making mistakes, even failing. Don't worry. We are blessed with the natural poise to support our desires. Your efforts will be smoother than you dare to believe. Just trust. Believe in yourself.

Connecting with our natural poise is similar to connecting with our inner strength. It requires calm, silent, intentional, and mindful concentration. We can find a quiet place and focus our attention within to experience the infinite reservoir of energy and inspiration that lies in the heart of our present centeredness. An unending stream of unfaltering guidance flows from this place. We discover balance. We are poised to pursue our talents and desires here.

Try making a little time each day to connect with you inner self. Find a place of solitude, where you can get away from everything and everybody. Turn off the noise inside and out. Turn off the television, radio, or any other electronic devices in the room. Or better yet, find a tranquil place in nature. Next, turn off the noise in your head. Clear your mind. Consciously let go of all worry, all concern, and release all thoughts completely.

Breathe...
   Deeply
      Mindfully
         Beautifully
            Peacefully

Let all your worries and thoughts drift as if they were drifting off to sea. Watch your thoughts roll away upon the waves. They flow further and further away. If you find yourself taking them back, simply take notice and release them again. Be gentle, kind, and loving with yourself as you experience this exercise. You are clearing your mind and opening your heart. It is a gentle process and requires patience and care. It will happen for you, stay with it.

Eventually, you will begin feeling connected with your innermost self. This is where you can feel balance and poise flow in. Bask in this feeling. Do not hurry or end this meditation abruptly. Let it soak in for a while. You are filling yourself with natural poise. It is like drinking a glass of water. The taller the glass and the more water you drink, the longer you feel refreshed afterwards. Think nourishment. You are nourishing your mind, body, and spirit to perform and express yourself in the best way possible.

Having discovered inner strength and poise, your talents will begin to flow naturally. You will find more energy and confidence for self-expression. Your journey will be enriched as you begin exploring your strengths and exercising your capabilities. We become lights to the world. It is how we make a difference.

Be Patient

A helpful hint is to be patient with yourself while discovering your talent. Good things do not happen overnight. It is like trying on new hats at a boutique. Not everything you try on will fit. The same is true when you experiment with your talents. You will discover that not everything works, at least not at first. That is why patience is a virtue. You might shift gears many times before something truly feels right. You might go back to school and experiment with various courses of study until you finally discover what interests you the most. Or, you might try several instruments before you find the one that truly makes your heart sing. Whatever the case may be, hang in there. Don't give up. Be patient. Do yourself a favor and stick with it. It's worth it.

And if at first you don't succeed, try, try… again. Great things are worth the effort. It might take several practices and many more rehearsals before you master an instrument, a trade, or other pursuit. Chances are you will not be perfect in the beginning. Beauty and talent evolve over time. Becoming is a process. Just because we do not get it the first time, or even the second or third, does not mean it is not meant to be. You will know soon enough, but at least give yourself ample room for success. It is a gift.

You can spend the rest of your journey uncovering your talents. This is the beauty of self-discovery. There is no better way to live than in the heart of your interests and desires. Discovering your gifts is a process worth investing in. It paves a path for success and creates a life filled with joy, adventure, love, and satisfaction.

I challenge you to take the plunge. Begin experimenting. Start believing. Try new things. Uncover new ideas. Push yourself. Challenge yourself. You are worth it!

DISCOVER YOUR TALENT

Reflections

YOU ARE WORTH IT

DISCOVER YOUR TALENT

YOU ARE WORTH IT

DISCOVER YOUR TALENT

12

Inventory Your Strengths

All successful businesses take inventory periodically. Whether the inventory takes place once a year, once per quarter, or even monthly or weekly, taking stock is a necessary ingredient for success. This sets the stage for the upcoming lesson. We are learning how to be successful. We have explored our assets and talents and learned the importance of investing in ourselves. We are beginning to see the great wealth that lies within each and every one. Our gifts are truly amazing.

Now, we turn our attention to our strengths and the best place to start is to take an inventory, similar to that conducted by a business. Taking stock of our strengths is a major part of realizing our own personal success. We can begin by taking stock of our advantages, aptitude, abilities, achievements, even our thoughts and ideas. The best inventories are exhaustive and thorough. We leave no stone unturned. This is how we take complete inventory and realize the full extent of our strengths and gifts.

Brainstorm

The best way to get started is to brainstorm. Open your mind and begin reviewing anything and everything that might be a strength. If you have trouble getting started, consider the following questions: What do others say you are good at? What things have gone well for

INVENTORY YOUR STRENGTHS

you in the past and how did you contribute to these successes? Try not to close your mind to any of the strengths that surface. Sometimes we sell ourselves short.

As you brainstorm, turn to the reflection pages and begin listing your strengths. This is your personal inventory. Write down whatever comes to mind. Do not censor your thoughts. I suggest you put a bookmark in this page and spend at least an hour journaling in the back of this chapter. This may seem like a long time, but taking inventory can be a time consuming process. It may take you a while to get started, but when your ideas, memories, and recollections begin to flow, an hour may not seem long enough. Take this time for you. Your strengths are the best of who you are. They are worth uncovering and discovering.

Inner Strengths versus External Supports

Now that you have created your inventory, let's review it. Most of our strengths can be divided into two categories, inner strengths and external supports. They are each worth counting and considering. Some of you may have listed positive internal qualities you possess such as intelligence, compassion, flexibility, and insightfulness. You have also listed external strengths; supports around you such as family, friends, your church or other spiritual organizations, maybe your home or community. Thank God for our support. It can help us immensely, especially in times of need.

We will be focusing on developing our inner strengths in this lesson, our internal locus of control. It is all we can truly influence and change. We will focus on our inner qualities; those things that govern our psyche. They are like gold. Discovering and acknowledging our inner strengths is like discovering a garden within. We will be amazed at the beauty of the many colors and the variety of plants and flowers. We are becoming aware. We are blossoming.

Taking an inventory of our inner strengths is only the beginning. It gives us a baseline of our potential. Our inventory provides a starting place, a foundation upon which we can grow and develop, learn and mature toward becoming whoever we are meant to be. We can be anyone we would like to be, the person we have always dreamed of. No limits exist to our becoming whoever we wish we were. Our time is now.

Be Optimistic

Another important aspect of building our strengths is to be optimistic. Do not limit yourself when taking inventory of your good qualities. If you did something well in your past, even once, write it down. Have you ever heard of someone failing for being too confident? More often it is a lack of confidence that defeats us. A positive spirit goes a long way toward success.

Optimism highlights our strengths. We may have several abilities, yet be pessimistic about our ability to achieve. A lack of belief in our strengths and abilities holds us back. It is as if we are viewing ourselves through a clouded pair of lenses. Our vision is blurred. We do not see the beautiful creations we are, let alone our many gifts. Our perceptions are skewed. This distortion leads to a journey of compromise. We do not realize the many gifts we are created to enjoy.

I am sure you have heard the dichotomous expression "glass half empty or glass half full". Many women take a glass half empty view of themselves. We focus more on our limitations than our strengths. We criticize ourselves for our weaknesses, and minimize our talents and abilities. Well, it is time to correct our vision. We can begin to see ourselves through the "glass half full" perspective. We can renew our self-perceptions and recognize and embrace our strengths. A positive, confident view leads to a journey that is rewarding and fulfilling. It leads us to the path of destiny.

Strength in Limitations

Here is something that may come as a surprise. You can add to your list of strengths by brainstorming your limitations as well. Some of our greatest challenges and weaknesses can lead us to new, unrealized strength. Some of the hardest trials we face contain hidden strengths

INVENTORY YOUR STRENGTHS

within for us to discover about ourselves, others, and the universe. Perhaps not right away, but as we struggle to overcome, new strength is born in the victories we find. It may seem like an oxymoron to consider that many of our greatest strengths are actually born through challenge. This is just one of the many features of the universe that diverge and enlighten.

So let's add to our list again by brainstorming and listing our challenges, weaknesses, limitations, and trials. Beside each challenge, list some of the triumphs that have appeared. Perhaps you have struggled with physical illness: cancer, chronic pain, diabetes, or another ailment. What have you discovered about yourself? How have you persevered? How has your faith evolved? How about your appreciation for life? Or maybe you have faced a mental or emotional condition. What have you learned about yourself? How has your view of life changed? What about your trust in God?

You can add all of the victories you have discovered through weakness to your list of strengths. By now, your list is probably getting pretty long. Remember, don't be shy. Be confident and give yourself every benefit of the doubt. We have spent enough years in self-doubt. It is our time to shine now. We are building a new self, one who is proud, grateful, and self-assured. These are the building blocks for discovering the infinite wealth that lies within us. We are becoming who we have always wanted to be, confident and beautiful, content and at peace with who we are.

Preserve your Strength

We have discussed the concept of energy throughout this book. We talked about balancing our energy in Chapter 3. Learning to balance our energy becomes especially important as we consider our strengths. We have listed them and they are many, and yet without a pace or rhythm that is healthy for us, our strength can be depleted. We can learn to balance our efforts so that we do not get burned out.

Women are amazing. We juggle multiple tasks and handle many responsibilities simultaneously and successfully. We do it because we can. We have multiple capabilities including intelligence, compassion, creativity, and determination (among other strengths). These alone and in combination make a recipe for achieving about anything we set our minds to. The only problem is we risk burnout and this can be troubling indeed. When our energy is depleted, our strengths begin to fade. We are more susceptible to negative feelings like despondency and defeatism.

One of the ways we can guard against burnout is to make sure not to expend too much energy in dead-end endeavors. Life presents many opportunities. The journey blossoms to provide many paths that we can take. Learning to carefully choose the roads we travel is a skill of discernment that takes practice and experience. We discover the activities and commitments that are most gratifying and rewarding not only for us, but also for those we share our lives with (on all different levels and in many dimensions). We often learn the hard way when we get caught up in activities that ultimately provide little or no reward. We can guard against these in our future.

Avoiding expending our energy on needless endeavors might involve saying no. Some women fall in the trap of doing too much because of a lack of assertiveness. We can learn how to protect ourselves and our precious reservoir of energy by saying no when necessary. It might feel unusual or even selfish at first, but protecting our energy allows us to fully utilize and share our strengths with ourselves, the universe, and others. Ultimately, balancing our energy is the most efficient way we can help others and ourselves. Consciously managing our energy helps us to share our inner wealth with the world.

We may still feel off balance at times. The perfect formula for preserving and expending your energy does not exist. More often than not, it is the process of trial and error that leads us to discover our greatest strengths and abilities. The good news is whenever you begin to feel your energy level decreasing; you can go back to the meditations we have learned in this book. Remember the meditation from the last lesson on discovering your inner strength and poise? Relaxation techniques and moments spent in peaceful tranquility are perfect for restoring energy.

INVENTORY YOUR STRENGTHS

Mindfulness Meditation

One of the best strategies for regaining your energy is mindfulness meditation. It involves connecting in the energy within your body and the universal energy directly surrounding you. The body itself is made up of highly concentrated bundles of energy. We perceive our bodies like we do other objects; they appear to be formed of mass, however, from a metaphysical perspective everything on this earth is pure energy, even the most solidly appearing objects like rocks, chairs, tables, even stretches of earth as large as mountains. Enlightening your mind to experience yourself as part of a greater universe will help restore and renew your energy during the following meditation.

Sit in a comfortable location with your legs in a lotus position. If you are not able to cross both of your legs; simply cross your left leg over the right. This allows your energy to be most concentrated, your body will vibrate at its highest frequency, which allows you to open up to, enter into, and be charged, by the energy of the universe. Place your hands on your knees and hold your fingers open and palms upward toward the sky. Sit in this position calmly and quietly until you feel the surge of energy from within. Feel yourself transmitting energy from your body into the space directly surrounding you. See this energy rippling and sailing across the universe in your mind's eye.

If you find it difficult to clear your mind and relax, practice thought stopping, which involves becoming aware of your thoughts and gently stopping them as they interfere with the focus of the meditation. Try to maintain a complete consciousness of the energy your body is exchanging with the universe in the space around you. Protect your thoughts as you monitor the intensity of your energy level. You are replenishing. You are transcending. You are healing.

Practice this meditation daily until it becomes more natural. It may even take several times before you can experience the energy exchange. That's alright. It has taken many people years to experience the gifts of enlightened meditation. Simply trying this relaxation strategy alone will reduce stress and help you regain much of the energy you expend in a day. You have discovered a great treasure, even if you are only able to relax for a little while. We all deserve to relax and replenish.

You are your Strength

Your strength is the best of who you are. You *are* your strength. We have listed our strengths on paper. Now, we can embrace their reality in our heart. We can believe in them. We do not need to hide them in fear of failure, nor do we need to keep them hidden in modesty, embarrassment, or feelings of low self-worth. Our strengths are what make us shine. They lead us to a life that is fruitful, successful, and fulfilling. They are the inner fiber that makes us happy, healthy, worthy, and satisfied. We can look at our inventory and be satisfied with who we are. We are strong and intelligent women, ready to take on the world. We can let our light shine!

It is your strength that leads to a successful journey. It provides the means to accomplish all that we wish for in life, all that we dream and desire. It is the heartbeat of inner wealth that lies within each and every one of us. Our positive qualities enrich our journey and the journeys of others whose paths we cross. Life is full of twists and turns. We brush across the lives of countless people, some for only a split second. Our inner strength is contagious. When we share it with those around us, we enrich the world. A mere smile to a stranger can make a difference. It displays the strength of love.

Strength joins us to Destiny

Our strength is what joins us to our destiny. Look at your list of strengths on your paper. Let your eyes settle for a while on each one. Accept them. Embrace them. Prepare your heart to confidently display these qualities in all you say and do. Then, hang them somewhere in your home or office. These are the fine qualities we possess that will lead us to our destiny one day. They equip us to accomplish anything we set our mind to. They are our roadmap to happiness, peace, and fulfillment.

Perhaps you are already pursing your heart's desires. If this is the

INVENTORY YOUR STRENGTHS

case, you are probably familiar with many of your strengths already. Many are beginning to work their destiny. The world is changing. We are changing. We are embracing the best of who we are and ushering in an age of healing and empowerment. And yet, we continue to evolve. Discovering all of our strengths is a lifelong process, one that does not end until we move to the next phase of our journey. We can all continue adding to our list. The more we discover, the better equipped we are to share our gifts and talents.

For those who have not yet considered your destiny, I challenge you to begin by reflecting upon the strengths you have discovered in this lesson. I have said it before and will say it again; there is no better way to live than in the heart of your destiny. It is the most beautiful place you will ever experience. Let your strength lead you there. You do not need to know exactly where this is, just trust the process. Allow your inner resources to guide you to a place beyond imagination, a place that exceeds your wildest hopes and dreams. Others will meet you there. You will not be alone. You can join the beauty and abundance of the universe. You can enter the ecstatic realms of love.

YOU ARE WORTH IT

Reflections

INVENTORY YOUR STRENGTHS

YOU ARE WORTH IT

INVENTORY YOUR STRENGTHS

YOU ARE WORTH IT

13

Nourish your Mind

This lesson discusses the importance of nourishing the mind. We began discussing some strategies for taking care of our minds in lessons 4, 6, and 10 such as positive self-talk, reading, and continuing education. In this lesson, we will look at some of these ideas in more detail; as well as outline other strategies for nourishing the mind. We might be more accustomed to the importance of caring for our bodies. Much literature exists on exercise, nutrition, and proper diets. It is just as important to take care of our minds. Our intellect is another reservoir of inner wealth.

Before we begin our discussion, let's look at the concept of intelligence. A person's intellectual abilities were once viewed in unilateral terms. The earliest cognitive theorists proposed singular intelligence factors. We know today that intelligence is multidimensional. Howard Gardner suggests our intellect is made up of eight dimensions: verbal-linguistic, musical-rhythmic, logical-mathematical, visual-spatial, bodily-kinesthetic, intrapersonal, interpersonal, and naturalistic. (Gardner, 1983, 1993, 2000)

Women of all cultures fit this multidimensional model. We are highly gifted, incredibly creative, lovingly logical, challengingly verbal, inspiringly visual, authentically natural, and both intra and interpersonally successful. We can learn to treasure our multiple intelligences as gifts. Nourishing our minds will help us expand our lives. We can continue to grow in all of these areas, whereby furthering our reservoir of inner wealth. Most importantly, we can share our gifts with others to affect the world.

Now, let's look at some strategies we can utilize in order to fine tune and nourish our minds. The ideas on the following pages are not inclusive by any means. Use these strategies to grease the wheels so to speak, to get the ball rolling. Perhaps you are already engaged in challenging yourself intellectually. In this case, these strategies can serve as reinforcement for what you are already accomplishing. But for those who have not invested much in nourishing your mind, the following strategies should help you get started in the right direction. Here we go.

Challenge Yourself Intellectually

The basic premise to nourishing the mind is to make an ongoing commitment to challenge yourself intellectually. Some of us get stuck in the same patterns. We become comfortable in life. We have a routine that works well. Perhaps you have been in the same career for years. Maybe you have spent your life raising a family and are just beginning to consider new possibilities. Whatever the case, many of us get caught in ruts. We quit challenging ourselves. We neglect expanding our knowledge. After all, we are content. Or are we?

Sometimes the very things we need in life are those challenges we avoid. Growth is usually uncomfortable. It seldom comes easy. It probably seems more predictable and safe to keep doing what you are doing and getting what you're getting. But what happens when you consider gaining more in your journey. How does it feel to imagine bigger and better possibilities? What are some of the opportunities you have passed up over the years? What have you always dreamed of doing?

Let's take some time to reflect upon these questions…

A commitment to challenge yourself can help you realize these possibilities, opportunities, and dreams. The world is full of information, from local workshops to the World Wide Web, from your local library to international databases of information. Take advantage of all the learning opportunities you can. Push yourself. Go beyond the comfort zone. Experiment and grow. You won't be sorry. Your efforts will pay huge dividends in your future.

A simple way we have already discussed to challenge your mind is to read regularly. Whether the material is online or in print, reading is an excellent way to nourish your intellect. You will encounter new ideas, perspectives, research, theories, and discoveries. You can learn a lot from books. They can be the best teachers. One of the major advantages is you can read at your convenience. Unlike attending a lecture or class, which generally meet at scheduled times, you can pick up a book any time you want and read as long as you like. The flexibility is wonderful and makes this a good learning option.

Another way to challenge the mind is to write. We all have good ideas. A great avenue to express ourselves is through writing. You can decide later whether you would like to publish or not. Some people develop their ideas into books. Others write for newspapers, magazines, or trade journals. Some people enjoy writing short stories and poetry. Many women write in journals, which is a creative, personal means of self-expression. Some write blogs as an avenue for sharing their ideas. No matter what outlet you pursue, writing is an excellent tool for developing the mind. It helps bring thoughts and opinions into fruition. It is a great way to synthesize and express your creativity and knowledge.

Yet another way to challenge your mind is to do research. This is a less commonly utilized tool for learning, none the less one of the most effective. Conducting research provides higher level challenges in that there are multiple variables and factors to consider simultaneously. Research challenges us to think outside of the box. It brings us out of the comfort zone. Another great aspect of conducting research or studies is your findings can be used to help others learn. We can share our ideas and discoveries with fellow learners. You can also contribute to your professional field or any field that interests you for that matter. It is a great opportunity to make a difference.

We have already discussed other methods of exercising and nourishing the mind like continuing education opportunities, workshops, advanced degrees, and other certifications in your field of interest. Many people end their education after high school or college. The thought of furthering your education, especially through formal academic programs such as Master's and PhD degrees may seem frightening. Some of us give up before we even start. We stay content with our current level of achievement.

We can confidently push ourselves beyond where we are. No matter if it involves taking advantage of local seminars, attending classes at a technical college, or pursuing a highly advanced degree such as a PhD or Medical Degree, we can believe in our efforts and ourselves. The next lesson will be solely devoted to learning to believe in yourself; and we will take this topic up in more detail. The main point here is not to be afraid to challenge yourself intellectually. You will reap many benefits for your efforts.

Stay Open Minded and Flexible

Another strategy for nourishing the mind, perhaps one of the best ones, is to stay open minded and flexible enough to incorporate new ideas into your current way of thinking. We all have schemas. A life schema is a way in which we view ourselves, the world, and our experiences. We develop our schema as we live our lives, from as early as we can remember to the present day. Patterns develop. Attitudes and behaviors form. We become set in our ways. We establish patterns of thinking, feeling, and behaving that are deeply ingrained.

Learning to be flexible and stay open to new ideas and ways of thinking helps us evolve and grow in new directions. It is one of the most nourishing gifts we can give our mind. We learn to look at life, ourselves, and the situations we experience differently, in a fresh new way. It is amazing what a difference a renewed outlook can make. We may find the answers to lifelong struggles. Perhaps we will solve a problem that has been getting in our way. Or maybe we will finally make a decision that we have needed to make for a while. Whatever the situation, considering new dimensions by becoming open minded and flexible is a truly remarkable personal strength. It pays great dividends.

Consider Alternatives

Another strategy for maintaining a healthy mind is to consider alternatives. Some people think dualistically. They view situations and people as good or bad, positive or negative, and they have the tendency to think in black and white terms. A great way to break up this rigidity is to consider alternatives. Nothing is black or white, good or bad. The universe is complex and so are we. We can apply this complexity to our experiences. Our journeys are multidimensional. Clear cut answers seldom exist. A right or wrong outcome is usually unrealistic.

Learning to consider alternatives is an excellent way to liberate the mind. When situations arise, especially those we are unfamiliar with or uncomfortable in, we can pause and consider various options before we draw conclusions and decide on a particular thought, feeling, action, or direction. It may be a family dilemma. Perhaps a loved one has let you down or challenged you in a particular way. Before jumping to conclusions, you can stop and consider the different factors that may be affecting his or her behavior. Another example can be found in the work setting. You might be asked to complete a project that you don't feel equipped to handle. You could try to accomplish it using the same skill set and knowledge base you are familiar with, or you could explore other avenues to complete the project. You could even collaborate with others and get ideas from your colleagues and coworkers.

Daring to step outside of our familiar perceptions and preset notions and consider alternatives is not always easy, but the more we practice the better we get. Before you know it, pausing to consider options will become second nature. All you need to begin is to make a commitment to catch yourself when you feel stuck or set in your ways. You will know it. When you begin feeling stubborn, irritable, discontent, or even hopeless; pause and relax. These are the signs it is time to open your mind to alternatives. You turn your mind to potential solutions and discover the value of options. You will see the beauty and success they bring to your life.

Learn from Everyday Experiences

Another simple strategy for nourishing the mind is to learn from everyday experiences. We can consider each situation we encounter holistically and ask ourselves what we have learned through the process. Everything happens for a reason. We might not understand right away, but we are assured that all our experiences are leading us to a better understanding of our journey, ourselves, others, and the world. We learn as we go. We gain wisdom. We can learn at least one thing from every experience in our life, even the painful ones end up serving a purpose in the long run. In fact, sometimes we learn the most through challenging times.

Appreciate the Simple Lessons in Life

We can develop an appreciation for the simple lessons in life as well. Sometimes the smallest lessons lead to the greatest expanses of knowledge, especially self-understanding. Take for example a homemaker who tries to bake from scratch, knit, crochet, or sew; maybe even decorate the home. Perhaps her pie crust is tough, her cakes flop, and her cookies don't turn out as well as she would like. She may find her thread or yarn in knots and her home décor may require an interior designer to unravel. It will not take her long to learn she may not be designed to perform homemade baking, sewing, and decorating at all. She may be inspired to seek training in some of these areas. She may even learn it is better to hire these tasks out and work a profession that affords these amenities.

The most precious lessons in life are also simple. It could be discovering your heart swelling with joy when you reach out to comfort a stranger. Or maybe you learn that when you smile at others, even strangers, they often smile back, even if they appear angry or bothered to begin with. We learn a lot about ourselves, others, and the world when we practice simple deeds of kindness and experience what happens. We discover the beauty, divinity, and love that permeate the universe, including the hearts we meet along our journey. These lessons are truly miraculous.

NOURISH YOUR MIND

We have discussed many strategies for nourishing the mind. I hope you will be able to incorporate some of these ideas into your daily life. Just remember, it's worth investing in yourself.

We will wrap up this lesson by exploring how positive thinking provides a constant source of nourishment for the mind. I cannot emphasize this concept enough. It is truly remarkable how substantially our thoughts impact our lives. If you choose just one of the suggestions in this lesson to begin applying to your life, focus on the following proposal. You will be amazed at how your life can change for the better, simply by concentrating on positive thought.

The Power of Positive Thinking

The best way to nourish the mind is to exercise the power of positive thinking. It is amazing how much more effective we are cognitively as well as in all other areas when we maintain a positive frame of mind. Positivity brings precision, clarity, serenity, and peace. We are more intuitive, creative, efficient, and successful. Positive thought is brilliant. It is illuminant. It leads to real problem solving and solutions. It can even lead to helping us achieve our destiny.

You may be wondering where to start. Many women have spent many years in negative patterns of thinking. We are used to catastrophic cognition, thinking the worst case scenario in most situations we face. Or perhaps we have been apathetic, not really caring for fear of getting hurt. The first step in moving toward positive patterns of thinking is to free your mind of all negativity: resentment, regret, disillusionment, fear, frustration, and discouragement. Clear your mind of all these obstacles to prepare the space you need for positive energy to flow in.

We have already experimented with energy meditations. We have also done a meditation on releasing negative feelings. For the next exercise, we will combine these two meditations in order to free our minds from negative thought. The main goal is to release all the negative energy from your mind and allow the positive energy of the universe and your creation to flow in.

So find a seat, somewhere quiet and peaceful. Try to find a tranquil place in the direct sunlight. Sit there for a moment, legs loosely crossed with your hands resting on your knees, palms facing upward. Cup your hands as if you are catching the sunlight within your fingers. Now breathe deeply, in and out. When you feel completely relaxed, begin releasing your negative energy. Let go of any disturbing thoughts you have, anything causing pain or discomfort: all anger, resentment, and frustration. Release self-doubt. Search your heart. Clear your mind of all self-condemnation, critical self-judgment, and self-reproach. Try to picture these negative thoughts and feelings radiating out into the universe. You might visualize negativity rolling away from you like waves washing away from the seashore. Or, picture the negative emotions floating away like bubbles. Experiment with guided imagery and see what works best for you. Utilize the image that helps you release this negative energy.

Remain still in the sunlight, breathing deeply and visualizing the negative energy projecting away from you and into the universe. Continue to relax and let go until you feel your energy clearing and cleansing. You will begin to feel a great sense of enlightenment and renewal. Be patient with yourself. It will come. A positive, delightful energy more magnificent than you have ever felt will begin electrifying your body. You can feel your skin stand on edge. You will begin to experience pure joy, happiness, and sheer contentment.

The more often you practice this meditation, the better you will get at releasing negative energy and embracing the positive healing of the universe. As you gain experience with this technique, you will be able to stop negative thoughts throughout the day when you catch yourself slipping back into a heavy mindset. Be patient and persistent. We are changing patterns that are well ingrained. The process of restructuring our cognitions from negative to positive takes time, patience, and practice. Stay with it. Remain faithful. It will happen. Your thoughts will change. Your mind will become brilliant and creative. You will be inspired. You are worth it and so is the world you will touch with your brightened outlook.

NOURISH YOUR MIND

Soften and Brighten your Outlook

Hopefully, this lesson is helping you begin softening and brightening your outlook. Consider the descriptive adjective "soft". It is the opposite of hard. Some of us have spent too many years with hardened attitudes. We may even feel brittle. Now, we can soften our minds, bodies, and spirits. Soft is subtle. It is comforting and enriching. Soft is compassionate, tender, and kind. It feels like silk brushing across our tired bodies. Soft is healing. It is beauty at its finest.

Our thoughts become brighter when we nourish the mind. A positive outlook will help you conquer any challenge you face, whether it be a family problem, a financial crisis, a personal devastation, loss of your job, or health problems. You name it, with a positive attitude, it will get better. In fact, our thoughts create our lives. Our perceptions become our reality. If we think things will only get worse, they will. If we dare to believe things will get better, a miracle comes our way. It is the law of attraction and it is definitely operational in the universe.

Lastly, let your thoughts be illumined. We all need replenishment and renewal. It is during quiet times of rest, relaxation, and tranquility when our minds can be illuminated and restored. We need these breaks. It is hard to stay positive when we are pushing ourselves too hard. Take some time to meditate this week. Just sit in a still and peaceful place. Release all of your worries, fears, disappointments, and hardships. Before you know it, it will become a well-deserved ritual. It will help you have a brighter outlook, and subsequently, a brighter journey. Give it a try. You're worth it!

YOU ARE WORTH IT

Reflections

NOURISH YOUR MIND

YOU ARE WORTH IT

NOURISH YOUR MIND

YOU ARE WORTH IT

14

Believe in Yourself

This section of the book has been dedicated to the topic of wealth. Hopefully you are learning and discovering the abundant source of inner wealth you possess. We have looked at our strengths, resources, talents, gifts, assets, and abilities. Next, we will focus on the importance of believing in ourselves. No matter how much strength you possess or how smart you are, how regularly you nourish your mind, how much you learn, or how much education or training you have or the number of credentials- it is all of little value unless you believe in yourself. That is why we now turn our attention to self-confidence.

Building Self-Confidence

Like building anything, it is usually best to start from scratch. We will first look at preparing to build inner confidence by comparing it to a demolition project. Sometimes we need to tear down old, worn out, existing structures before we can build something new and more valuable. It is similar when establishing confidence. We may have to prepare our inner landscape first, clearing away such obstacles as self-doubt, self-criticism, and self-persecution. Some of these words may sound too strong, but reflect for just a moment on the main themes that run through your head. What types of messages are you giving yourself? How are you affirming or devaluing your hopes, dreams, and efforts? Consider these questions as we begin the excavation process.

Excavating the Obstacles

The first major obstacle we consider excavating is self-doubt. This is probably the most detrimental and cumbersome. Let's face it. Doubting ourselves can be a constant nuisance. It's like having a little devil on your shoulder whispering, "No, you can't". No matter how many opportunities come your way, you may continue to question your ability to succeed. Even more perplexing might be the fact that no matter how many successes you have had in your past, you continue to doubt your talents and capabilities. When will we realize we are amazing? We can accomplish numerous projects in several arenas simultaneously and still wonder if we are good enough. It is our most fundamental challenge.

The time has come to surrender self-doubt. In fact, the first part of this lesson will be built around surrender. Sometimes we need to let go to prepare our hearts to receive. Similar to excavating a broken down landscape, we need to excavate our hearts to prepare to receive the amazing gift of self-confidence. We can become willing to release all of our questions, inferiorities, feelings of inadequacy; and prepare to be changed and healed. It is time. We are ready.

The next obstacle to surrender is self-criticism. We have already talked quite a bit about removing this from our inner-dialogue. It is critical to release our negative self-judgments once and for all if we are to build confidence. It is time to level negative self-talk. We need to finally do away with it entirely. We have been practicing and working toward this goal, and now it is time to put an end to self-criticism. It must be demolished.

We accomplish this through surrender. We can resolve with utmost intention that we will no longer beat ourselves up. No more negative self-talk, no more personal criticisms. Our new journey does not leave room for these obstacles. We are clearing the way to a brilliant and joyful future. We will need self-confidence to attain our goals in life, especially those that are closest to our heart.

A third major obstacle that must be surrendered is self-persecution. So many women punish themselves. They do not think they deserve the very best whether it is success, achievement, celebration, or even a fair chance. Self-punishment is perhaps the most harmful obstacle of all. It can be likened to a ball and chain. We carry it around our ankle, dragging it behind us wherever we go, which makes each of our steps heavy and cumbersome. Let's begin excavating our spirits by demolishing this worn out structure first. It is the first step in clearing the way toward healing and growth. We can begin this process through an exercise in guided imagery.

Picture a ball and chain that has weighed you down. Now picture yourself unfastening it from your ankle to release yourself. Feel the weight lifting away from you. Picture this burden you have carried finally being removed. Now visualize the weight being lifted, rising up from a crane. The chain that once held you in bondage is now supporting the heavy ball in the air. It is now a wrecking ball and begins destroying the negative strongholds in your spirit: self-doubt, self-criticism, self-persecution, loathing, despondency, and self-degradation… all these obstacles are being leveled and flattened in preparation of rebuilding. We will be starting with a clear and beautiful, new landscape.

We are creating an empty canvas and we can paint a new foundation upon which we can build self-confidence. We are all familiar with the term confidence, but let's look closely at what it really means. Self-confidence is stark inner faith. It is accepting who we are and what we are. It is feeling lovable and worthy, beautiful and desirable. It is holding onto the knowledge that we will be alright, perfectly cared for by a God of the universe who will never let us down. It is seeing ourselves for who we really are… precious, miraculous, awesome, intelligent, inspired, and magnificent creations of a Master Creator. Self-confidence allows us to stand side by side with others and the universe.

Self-confidence facilitates the energy flow that we have been talking about. It helps us maintain a positive outlook. It illumines the psyche, helping our minds, bodies, and spirits to be radiant and beautiful.

YOU ARE WORTH IT

Self-confidence is the handmaiden of inner peace and freedom. It is the foundation of a fruitful and joyful journey. It is the ingredient necessary to begin believing in ourselves.

We will not realize the great wealth that lies within unless we learn to believe in ourselves. That is why we will spend the rest of this lesson looking at ways we can nurture our self-concept, meaning improve how we view ourselves and how we feel about ourselves. One of the greatest gifts you will find along the journey is an ability to believe in yourself. Inner confidence sets us free from self-doubt. It knocks the pesky devil off our shoulders. It helps us follow our path with less reluctance and more inner faith.

Encourage Yourself. Be Your Own Cheerleader

A great way to start believing in you is to offer yourself regular encouragement. Become your own cheerleader. This idea might sound unusual, but it is truly effective. You do not have to cheer out loud, so you don't have to worry how the people around you will react. All you need to do is begin cheering for and encouraging yourself privately. It is like personal coaching. Give yourself accolades for a job well done. Talk yourself through difficult situations. Tell yourself things like "You can do it." And "Go ahead; give it your best shot." Encourage yourself in all your endeavors. It will produce amazing results. You will gain a new lease on life.

Have Faith in Your Abilities

We all have special talents and gifts. Women are incredible. I cannot say enough about our strengths. It is true. We are kind, considerate, passionate, genuine, generous, smart, creative, resourceful, inspiriting, and inspiring. Our potentials are endless. I believe there are no mountains too high for us to climb. No sea is too wide for us to swim. No valley is too deep for us to cross. And no stars in the sky are brighter than the love that beats within our heart and soul. Let these thoughts become a new reality for you. Dare to believe you are incredible.

We took stock of our strengths in lesson twelve. We will build upon our inventory in this lesson by utilizing guided imagery again. Let's take a moment to identify our abilities. Picture yourself in a marketplace. The market is our inner landscape. In the market, we find goods we would like to purchase, foods and other items that are nourishing, attractive, and seemingly helpful. Let's search our inner landscape the same way we browse a market place. What are your goods? What qualities do you possess that are attractive, nourishing, and helpful? What characteristics or goods do you have that you would purchase if they were not already yours?

If you need help getting started, simply consider some of the good qualities already listed in this lesson. Are you compassionate? Do you help others? Maybe you operate a home daycare and provide for children's needs while their parents are away at work. Perhaps you volunteer at your church, or in the community, or reach out to support missions work. These are all valuable qualities to possess. So what does your marketplace look like? What goods do you possess that you are proud of? Take a moment to explore, discover, and reflect…

Now comes the hard part, developing faith in our abilities. This separates the women from the girls. Developing faith in our qualities or (goods) is a large part of learning to believe in ourselves. Remember the wrecking ball that removed the obstacles. It excavated self-doubt. We can apply it again here. Self-doubt prevents us from affirming and expressing our abilities. We can level it now. We are moving forward with inner faith and confidence in who we are and what we stand for.

But what if you are still reluctant? Here are some things that can help.

Dare to try new things

Daring to try new things can help you gain faith in yourself. Do you ever wish you could do something, but you just don't have the courage to try? Are there things you have dreamed about, but never pursued for fear of failure? Are you reluctant to try something new? It could be as simple as taking a fun class like Zumba or Yoga. Or it could mean trying something more adventurous, like traveling to a foreign country. Whether big or small, trying new things can help you gain self-confidence. You will be surprised at the things you can do and discover.

We have already mentioned routines and how easy it is for us to get stuck in familiar patterns. Hiding behind the comfort zone is a habit to guard against if we would like to create new experiences. We will be reluctant to try new things if we cleave to predictability. Rather, we can break away from habit. We can develop the courage to step outside the box and enter the realms of the unknown. It may sound scary, but it is actually quite liberating. You will be amazed at how much you can discover about yourself, the world, and others. You may meet the best friends you will ever have. You might find the love of your life. Hopefully, you will discover the best parts of who you are!

Live Courageously

Believing in yourself will help you live courageously. You can live beyond your wildest dreams. You will have joy beyond imagination. You can dare to be *all* that you are. You can live your journey without fear and insecurity, without shame and regret, without guilt and feelings of inadequacy. You can live a life free of the obstacles that hinder your inner landscape. Living courageously allows you to walk the most brilliant path you can dream. It will lead to pure peace, happiness, and satisfaction. Most importantly, it will help you find your destiny. Courage illumines the journey.

Living courageously might seem impossible to you. Here, we will utilize a tool we have already learned. Sometimes the best way to find courage is to "act as if". You may be wondering how you can ever become brave enough to believe in yourself, try new things, or even make a new friend. You can begin overcoming your reluctance by acting as if. We have done this before. Act as if you are brave. Pretend you are courageous. Ignore your resistance and try to behave as if you believe in yourself, as if you are excited to try new things; and go ahead and smile at those you encounter along your way.

Living courageously actuates self-confidence. It involves saying good-bye to worn out habits, deeply ingrained patterns, and the same old routines and outcomes. It is saying hello to adventure, pleasant surprises, and beautiful new horizons.

Develop a network of support

Another helpful strategy for maintaining self-confidence is to develop a network of supportive people. Choose friends who really care. It is easy to be part of a crowd. We can readily disappear in the company of friends, even if we are not especially close to them. You may attend happy hour after work on Fridays. Perhaps you are part of a community organization or social club. You might belong to a church or a book club. These are all good activities, but consider the following questions, "How many people are you really close to?" or "Who are your best friends?"

These questions are important because one of the best ways you can maintain confidence and believe in yourself is to surround yourself with people who really care about who you are. It is sometimes easier to have surface level friendships. It is a risk to let people know who you really are. But the risk comes with so many rewards. When people know us personally, they can be supportive, encouraging, and uplifting. Close friends can pick us up when we are feeling down. They can help us smile and have fun.

When we surround ourselves with supportive friends, their encouragement affects our thought processes. Humans are contextual. We are affected by our surroundings. We affect each other. Our environment influences our thoughts, emotions, feelings, and actions. Our self-esteem increases when we spend as much time as possible in encouraging environments, interacting with people who care about us. We are better able to believe in ourselves and our capabilities. A bright future becomes clearer and we see that we can attain it if we work toward it. It is harder to doubt ourselves when our friends are affirming us and helping us see our gifts. Close and intimate friendships are enriching and empowering.

Believe in your Dreams

Another successful life strategy we can practice is to believe in our dreams. This naturally follows from learning to believe in ourselves. Once we have achieved a confident state of mind, we can embrace our dreams. Just reflect for a moment on some of the dreams you have had in your lifetime. Like most, you probably started dreaming at an early age. You maybe began by playing Legos and pretending to be an architect or a builder. Maybe you played with stuffed animals, hoping to be a veterinarian. Many of our dreams have come through fantasizing. It is a great way to be inspired.

But you might also discover that your dreams began to fade sometime after childhood. Perhaps your early dreams were met with disappointment. Worse yet, maybe your basic needs were crushed. Many women come from broken homes, abusive environments, and have suffered from neglect and abandonment. And yet if you really search your heart and soul, you can rekindle the dreams you have had throughout your lifetime. Even if they did not last long, they made a mark in your memory when they were present. Search. Reflect. Reminisce. Dream again…

As you are reflecting, begin writing some of your dreams on the reflection pages. Before you forget or as you move from one to another, write each one down. Your dreams and desires are important. They are the most precious part of who you are. They might have once been forgotten, but we are renewing our hope. It did not die; it has been preserved for the day of rediscovery. We are ready now. We can dream like it is yesterday.

We can also believe in our dreams again. Like we once did when we were children playing with toys, fantasizing about our futures, imagining we could do anything. We are finally discovering we can. Our childlike faith is returning. We have reached a special time along the journey when we can believe like we used to, or maybe for the first time. Our dreams *are* our future. They lead us to destiny.

You are created with an incredible destiny. You might not know it yet, but you are. We are all born to fulfill a special purpose in life.

BELIEVE IN YOURSELF

It is a great joy to discover the ultimate meaning of our journeys. It is spectacular to begin to discover why we are here. We can believe in ourselves, our journey, our abilities, and our destiny. We can have faith in ourselves and confidence in all that we can do.

So follow your heart. Live out your dreams. Once you begin, you will never want to turn back. Live courageously. Love wholeheartedly. Reach for the sky and know you are as brilliant as the stars. A season of great wealth is upon you now. All the treasures of the universe are available within and around you. Go ahead. Grab them one by one. Put them in your pocket and run with the wind. Believe in yourself. You *are* worth it.

YOU ARE WORTH IT

Reflections

BELIEVE IN YOURSELF

YOU ARE WORTH IT

BELIEVE IN YOURSELF

YOU ARE WORTH IT

Section Three
Wellness

15

Live with Ease

This lesson will focus on one of the most fundamental features of wellness, living with ease. We begin here because so many women suffer from the syndrome of "trying too hard". We push ourselves beyond our limits. We expect perfection in ourselves and others. Some of us do not know when to slow down and relax. It is hard for us to simply enjoy.

Before we continue discussing this topic, let's look at the definition of wellness. Hales captures the essence of wellness when she writes, "Wellness can be defined as purposeful, enjoyable living or specifically, a deliberate lifestyle choice characterized by personal responsibility and optimal enhancement of physical, mental, and spiritual health. (Hales, 2009).She highlights the multidimensional nature of wellness, which I believe is a key to creating wholeness and harmony. Wellness is so much more than nutrition and exercise. It exceeds strategies for positive thinking. It is more comprehensive than practicing relaxation techniques. Wellness is an inner wholeness. It is finding harmony within and around. It is physical, cognitive, emotional, psychological, and spiritual. It encompasses and radiates around our entire being.

One of the signs that we are discovering wellness is we will begin living with ease. Have you ever known anyone who does not let anything or anybody bother them? They never seem to get annoyed, irritated, or angry. They are able to accept what comes their way and deal with it with grace and poise. Have you ever wished you could be more like them and just let go? We will look at some of the factors in this lesson that can help each one of us develop an attitude and lifestyle of ease. You will no longer envy these people. You will be one of them!

Lighten Up

The first suggestion of this lesson is to lighten up. But before you read any further, consider the following questions:

How do you react when things do not go your way? Do you feel like it's the end of the world?

Are you uptight, tense, or do you worry often?

Do you try hard to control everything around you including people and situations?

Are you easily frustrated, agitated, and annoyed?

Are your feelings easily hurt?

Are you overly sensitive or do you take things very seriously?

Are you a very serious person in general?

Is it hard for you to accept circumstances beyond your control?

Are you a perfectionist? Are you hard on yourself when you make mistakes?

If you answered yes to some or all of these questions, it may be time to lighten up. After all, we are meant to enjoy the journey. It is hard for some of us to comprehend this fact, but it is true. *We are created to enjoy life*. We will discuss this in detail in the last section of this book. We are all born to live a fulfilling and satisfying life, not to toil over stress and frustrations. We can find peace and tranquility by lightening our minds, bodies, and spirits. So where do we start?

We begin by looking at the mind. Enlightening the mind involves acceptance and letting go. We let so many things bog us down: worry, remorse, confusion, regret, sorrow, and agitation. It is liberating and refreshing to simply accept the things we cannot change in life. Think about it for a moment. We are surrounded by people, situations, happenings, and events in life that we have no real control over. Sure, we might try to take control, but many times this only leads to frustration. Instead, we can learn to practice mindfulness acceptance, which is a soothing technique that allows us to relax and let go. We can focus our attention on our inner body, our breath, movements, thoughts, feelings, whatever is present in our innermost being. Our inner landscape is our center, our essence. Healing happens when we draw our attention to our inner being and seek to accept the people, places, and situations around us for what they are. We find peace and happiness.

Meditation is an excellent way to lighten the mind. Most mindfulness techniques consist of various forms of meditation. We can increase our awareness of ourselves, the universe, and what is happening around us; and at the same time embrace an open attitude of acceptance, kindness, and love. We can also turn our attention to self-acceptance and offer ourselves compassion, forgiveness, and love. This illumines the mind like no other remedy. It is healing and empowering.

As we continue onward, we can also lighten our bodies. Relaxation techniques work well here too. First, learn to monitor your body. How does it feel? Are you tense? Is a particular muscle group tired? Are you weary? Or maybe you are feeling energetic and happy. Take notice of all of your emotions and sensations. It will be easier for you to lighten up as you become more aware of your body. You will begin to notice when you are tired or tense.

We can attune to our physical wellbeing. When we feel weighed down, we can make a conscious decision to lighten up. We can take a few deep breaths, have a cup of tea, spend some time outdoors, or even take some time to enjoy the beauty of a picture. We are learning to care for ourselves. We are attuning to our needs. Many times all we really need is to lighten up. After all, everything has a way of working out in the end.

Perhaps most important is to lighten our spirits. We can even become free spirits. It is spectacular to consider the possibility of letting your spirit be your compass and guide. We can let go of all fears and insecurities and begin to explore and discover. Your journey will reach new dimensions when you dare to listen to your heart and follow your dreams.

Do you have a heavy spirit? Have you felt a sense of burden or have you been feeling gloomy? If so, it is time to lighten up. You were not created to struggle. Life is more than the challenges you face. Wondrous experiences can be discovered. Brilliant memories can be created. We can live like there is no tomorrow and appreciate the beauty of each of our moments. You can begin today. After all, it is the first day of the rest of your life.

The Law of Least Effort

In his book the *Seven Spiritual Laws of Success*, Deepak Chopra writes about the law of least effort, which he likens to the path of least resistance. We touched upon this earlier. Chopra describes the energy of nature and how effortlessly nature flourishes. If we look at a blade of grass, it does not appear to struggle to grow taller; it simply grows in the field toward the sunlight. Similarly, a flower does not struggle to blossom, neither does a bird strain to soar in the sky. It simply spreads its wings and glides effortlessly in the sunny breeze. We can learn a lot about the energy of the universe by observing nature. It can teach us how to utilize and preserve our own energies. Nature provides the perfect example when we consider living with ease.

The principle of seeking an attitude of little or no resistance- living life with acceptance and ease- is a foundational concept to begin lightening up and enjoying life. Like we discussed earlier, acceptance involves accepting the persons, situations, events, and happenings in your life as they are, without trying to change them. (Note: this may not apply in cases of abuse.) It is also the art of accepting yourself as you are. You can quit exerting needless energy trying to accomplish that which is beyond your control. You do not have to work overly hard to see the manifestation of your efforts. You can release your greatest hopes and desires to the universe and watch as they become what they are meant to be. In this way, we blossom and grow. So how do we get there? Some of you may be wondering where to begin.

A large part of walking the path of least resistance is learning how to appreciate the moment at hand. We have discussed this concept in earlier lessons, but here the emphasis is on learning to relax and let go in the moment- knowing everything is happening exactly as it should within and around you. The world is moving in perfect time, impeccable rhythm; and you can join in this harmony by simply attuning your spirit and attention to the present. The art of present mindfulness will change your world. It will bring you joy and a new understanding. Present moment awareness will connect you to the deepest love you will ever experience. It is where we find self-love.

Chopra describes this as follows, "If you embrace the present moment and become one with it and merge with it, you will experience a fire, a glow, a sparkle of ecstasy throbbing in every living sentient being. As you begin to experience this exultation of spirit in everything that is alive, as you become intimate with it, joy will be born within you, and you will drop the terrible burdens and encumbrances of defensiveness, resentment, and hurtfulness. Only then will you become lighthearted, carefree, joyous, and free." (Chopra, 1994)

Have you spent much of your life on the defense? Have you expended energy needlessly seeking the acceptance and approval of other people? Do you suffer from resentment, pain, and hurt? We all encounter these obstacles. We would not be human if we didn't struggle. But now we have an awesome tool to take the pain and struggle away. We can apply the law of least effort to our lives and allow the journey to carry us along its peaceful stream. We can relax and let the universe guide us in its loving arms of care and protection. We do not need to fight any longer. We do not need the approval or acceptance of others. We can accept our life exactly as it is in this moment, including ourselves. Aw. Peace… sweet serenity. It is like a fresh breeze.

YOU ARE WORTH IT

Retire from the Guilt Committee

Another suggestion that will help you live with ease is to retire from the guilt committee. This means resigning from the negative thoughts in your head that hold you painfully accountable for everything, rather it is actually your fault or not. Perhaps some of you can identify. Do you ever find yourself mulling over regret after you make the wrong decision or don't quite hit the mark you hope to reach? You know what I mean. We can be so hard on ourselves. Perhaps you forgot to pick up the dry cleaning or worse yet, the kids. Maybe you didn't get the promotion at work or even more disappointing, you were laid off. Self- blame is a negative form of egocentrism. Some of us think we are to blame for everything. We place ourselves in the center of all happenings. It is refreshing to realize that many things are beyond our control. We are part of a great universe, not the center of it.

Do you feel guilty often? When is the last time you picked yourself up and brushed yourself off? Living life with ease requires we lighten our perspective and give ourselves a break. We will make mistakes and that is alright. We will make wrong decisions and our choices will not always be for the best. We will forget things, inadvertently disappoint people, and move in wrong directions. This is all part of being human. It is comforting to keep in mind we are learning through it all. In fact, sometimes our greatest lessons come through the mistakes we make. We can relax and cut ourselves some slack. We can retire from the guilt committee.

Let go of Regret

Another suggestion that will help you live with ease is to let go of regret. When you view the past, it is helpful to realize you did the best you could at the time considering where you were along your journey and the resources you had during that time. We are always growing. We continue to learn and adjust. It is unfair for us to look at our past and judge ourselves harshly for "not being better than we were" or "not doing better than we did". We have done much changing and maturing- besides, hind sight is 20/20. Some women are consumed with regret. We ruminate in what could have been. Or maybe you yearn for something you have always hoped for. Rumination can lead to depression. There comes a time along the journey when we need to let go. We need to move on if we hope to discover the peace and joy that awaits our future. It is not easy, but it is necessary. We can release the old and experience the new.

Regret holds us down, it does not change anything. We do not need to punish ourselves or pay penance for our mistakes. Nobody's perfect. We all have challenges and issues. We can recognize our limitations and simply resolve to do better next time. Maybe you have struggled in a relationship and it ended in divorce. Do not let it stand in the way of loving again. Perhaps you lost your home, family, job, or business. Do not let bad fortune steal your zest for life. Everyone gets a second chance, and third, fourth, and fifth chances if we need them. Some spiritual teachers even believe we are presented with the same lessons over and over until we finally learn them. Hang in there. No one said life would be easy. It is a whole lot easier when we are not so hard on ourselves.

Only look back if it makes you smile

We can ultimately learn to only look back if it makes us smile. So many precious memories lie in the crevices of our past. We do not usually spend enough time treasuring the good times, those beautiful moments created with our loved ones that are now priceless and timeless. These moments are our greatest treasures. We will have them forever. We can hold them dearly each day. We can learn to treasure the good times we've had and savor all the golden memories we have created.

So adopt the motto of only looking back if it makes you smile. You can begin today. Starting now, do not look back on your mistakes. Don't ruminate on wrong decisions or poor choices. Instead, only look back if it makes you smile. Perhaps you recall precious memories of you and your children when they were small, like watching movies and eating macaroni and cheese. Maybe you remember a time when you and your partner enjoyed a sunset together, or better yet, gazed upon the sunrise after tenderly holding each other all night. You might have precious memories of your parents or grandparents. Whatever these treasures are from your past, place them in a golden frame so that when you look back you can smile. These are the best parts of your life. They have made you who you are today.

Release the heavy weight

We began our discussion about the unnecessary weight many of us carry in the first lesson of this book. In the last lesson, we discussed the ball and chain that some of us drag behind, obstacles such as self-criticism and self-persecution. Much of the unnecessary weight on our spirits comes from guilt and shame, feelings of regret and remorse. We have begun to deal with these feelings in various places throughout this book. The purpose of this lesson is to become even more aware of how heavy these burdens are in preparation of finally letting them go. Letting go is a process and it is often not until we realize the full extent of our pain that we become ready to release it completely.

The purpose of the following section is to teach you an exercise in feeling, so that whatever you are experiencing can be fully recognized so that you can intentionally perceive and release your feelings and emotions- especially the painful ones. The goal is to release negative emotions from your psyche and into the universe. It is a process of exposure and intensification that leads to peace, contentment, freedom, and release. It involves allowing your feelings to envelop you, accepting your circumstances exactly as they are, by fully affirming your pain. It can be difficult in that many of us are used to blocking our pain. We dissociate or at least detach. This exercise creates the opportunity to be fully present in your pain- to finally experience your emotions completely. In this way, you are prepared to let go of pain and discord. It will no longer fester just beneath the surface. You can clear the way to become happy, joyous, and free.

Feelings Exercise

We begin by searching our hearts. What has been weighing you down? What has been hindering your joy, haunting you, or robbing you of self-confidence? Could it be a mistake you made that cost you the trust of a good friend? Perhaps a poor decision you made early in your life has continued to present stumbling blocks along your journey. Take some time here to discover the source of your guilt and shame. Allow your feelings. Let the pain flow in.

This exercise can be overwhelming, so if your feelings become too intense, take a break. Do something relaxing and fun until you feel comfortable again. Go for a walk, sit outside on your patio, or call a close friend. Breathe. It is alright. Be patient. We have carried our pain for a long time. It will take some time to release it back to the universe. Eventually, you will reach a place where you are able to stay with your pain long enough to allow it to be fully present within you. You have reached the time of healing. You are finally ready to embrace it. Accept it. Prepare your heart to release it.

Then, feel the light of healing. When you are experiencing the full extent of your pain, whether it is sadness, shame, remorse, regret, or any negative emotion that weighs you down; it is time to lift your arms and open your hands so that you can release your pain into the universe. You can pray to your higher power, asking for your pain to be taken away. Pray for comfort, healing, and peace. Even though this is one of the most challenging exercises in this book, it offers great rewards. It is a renewing experience. Trust in the process. Be patient and persevere. Embrace healing. You are worth it!!!

You can't change the past

Another helpful and simpler strategy that can lighten your journey is to keep in mind you cannot change the past. We have heard this phrase many times, but now it is time for us to let these words solidify in our hearts and minds. Say it out loud, "I can't change the past." Let this phrase resonate for a while…stay with it. Sing it as a mantra. Accept it. Embrace it. Prepare to move forward. In fact, it is not until we become willing to release the past that we can even begin to change and move forward.

Times change… People change. We change. We are different than we once were. We cannot change the past, but we can change ourselves. If you have made mistakes you have the rest of your life to live out your amends. You can walk in a new light through better actions day by day. This is how we heal.

You are alright just the way you are

Another good thing to keep in mind is you're alright just the way you are. We will talk more about this in lessons sixteen and seventeen. For now, let's begin warming up to the concept that we are OK "as is". This idea might cause disequilibrium at first. It may be confusing to consider the notion that you are alright precisely *where* you are, exactly *how* you are, and without making any revolutionary changes in your life. Do you think in "if only" terms? If only I was smarter, prettier, faster, more graceful, more social, more confident...the list might be endless. It is liberating and empowering to surrender to the fact that you are alright just the way you are. That doesn't mean there is no room to learn and grow, it simply allows you to accept and enjoy yourself each step along the way.

Let's begin a new routine to help us warm up to the idea that we are alright just the way we are. Starting now, whenever you catch yourself thinking in "if only" terms- stop yourself and substitute the "if only" message with an encouraging and edifying self-statement. We have already talked about restructuring our cognitions, changing our internal dialogue from negative to positive and turning self-criticism into affirmations. If you find yourself thinking "if only" thoughts such as "if only I had taken that job" or "if only I hadn't made that decision" or "if only I was a little bit smarter", stop yourself as soon as possible. Replace these thoughts with self-affirmations like "I am good at my job" "I made the best decision I could at the time with what I knew back then" or "I am intelligent and will continue to learn new things each day." Practice this exercise daily. Your life will change and you will begin to see that you're worth it.

LIVE WITH EASE

Surrender Perfectionism

One of the single most valuable strategies for living with ease is to surrender perfectionism. Our desire to be perfect is the common thread that runs through many of the struggles and dilemmas we face in life. Perfectionism is the opposite of accepting ourselves and our lives as they are. It is an illusion that makes us believe there is any such thing as "perfect". We are all beautifully unique. Our imperfections are endearing and enchanting. Have you ever seen someone with a cute button nose like Meg Ryan, or striking eyes like Alanis Morissette, or a uniquely large smile like Julia Roberts? All these celebrities have one thing in common. They have a distinct feature that sets them apart from the rest. Their imperfections are darling.

Another ingredient for change is to surrender trying to do everything perfectly. All we need to do is the best we can. So many women decline new opportunities in fear of failure. If we cannot do it perfectly, we may not want to do it at all. It is time to remold our expectations for ourselves. We do not have to do everything perfectly. We do not have to do *anything* perfectly. We can lighten our path by lowering our expectations and simply do the best we can. We find the courage to embrace our dreams and follow our heart. We might not succeed the first time, we may make mistakes and learn as we go, but we will be navigating closer to our destiny. We will no longer be paralyzed by our mistakes. We will use each step to learn and grow.

Before we move on to the next lesson, let's prepare our hearts further by finally giving up our need to be perfect. We have no time for pretending. We are embarking on a new and brilliant future. We will accomplish new things, actuate new ideas, try new activities, discover new plans, and realize new goals. We may even decide to follow new dreams. Whatever it is, perfectionism will only hold us back. Let it go. Remember, it is only an illusion. We are making room for new realities. We are preparing to discover happiness and joy.

YOU ARE WORTH IT

Practice Unconditional Love

Lastly, the best way to assure living with ease is to practice unconditional love- not only toward others, but also self-love. Love is the gateway to happiness. It is the passageway to freedom. Let it run free in your life. Let it capture you. Let it rapture you. Give it away *and keep it*. It is the greatest treasure you will ever know. Discovering love, especially self-love is a gift that makes the whole journey beautiful. Love makes you beautiful. It makes you shine!

Women are caring. We are nurturing. We are giving by nature. You may have no problem offering unconditional love to others, the love that expects nothing in return. If that is the case, keep it up. We cannot give enough. We cannot love enough. But if you have struggled to love people unconditionally, if you put expectations on relationships, or if you manipulate and hinge your relationships on what's in it for you; it is time to change. You're missing too much. When you learn to love unconditionally, your heart runs free. It is filled with peace and harmony. You become happy and whole.

Living with ease requires that you love yourself unconditionally also. It is impossible to experience peace and joy if you are beating yourself up. judging yourself harshly, or having high expectations for your every thought and action. Love yourself. Accept yourself. Treat yourself the way you would treat a child, a friend, or your sister or brother. We will continue to discover self-love as we work through the remaining lessons in this book. For now, begin accepting yourself without conditions.

Love yourself no matter what your past, present, or future holds. Accept yourself no matter what you have done or not done. Love yourself no matter how thin or beautifully full figured you are; no matter how large or small your eyes, nose, or mouth; no matter how smart you feel or don't feel, or how many mistakes you have made. Life is a journey, not a destination. Self-love brings peace and comfort. It is your key to a happy and healthy future.

Chopra, Deepak (1994), *The Seven Spiritual Laws of Success,* San Rafael, CA: Amber-Allen Publishing and New World Library

Hales, D (2009). *An Invitation to Health*, Belmont, CA: Wadsdworth, Congage Learning.

YOU ARE WORTH IT

Reflections

LIVE WITH EASE

YOU ARE WORTH IT

LIVE WITH EASE

YOU ARE WORTH IT

16

Be Content

The purpose of this lesson is to help you become more content, which simply means learning to "be". It is not as abstract as it may seem. "Being" is really the basic, fundamental state of all humans. Deep down, we all long to be content. We want to be happy and truly satisfied in life. We want to relax and let go. The good news is we can not only find contentment; we can achieve a state of sheer and utter peace. We can begin experiencing freedom and happiness right now.

But before we get started, we will look at some misnomers that have worked against our level of contentment. Then, we will explore some ideas that will help us overcome the obstacles that block us from experiencing the peace and joy that is ours to savor. We are meant to enjoy the lives we live. We are born to be happy and content. Life throws many curve balls, but we can learn not to let anything steal our serenity. We can hold our hearts and spirits away from frustration, discouragement, and anxiety. We can bask in the love and abundance of the universe and trust God for all we want and need.

Quit Postponing Happiness

One of the first things we need to do to become content is quit postponing happiness. It is time to end the vicious cycle of thinking "I will be happy when _____." You can fill in the blank with whatever fits. I will be happy when I get that promotion. I will be happy when my husband quits doing this or that. I will be happy when my kids listen. I will be happy when I finally get to go on that vacation. I will be happy ____ or ____ or ____ or ____. The list goes on. All we are doing is simply postponing our happiness. We are putting joy on a shelf until we achieve x, y, and z. The problem is when we get where we hope to be, we might redefine our goals. Instead of being satisfied, we strive for something more. Social science refers to this as the hedonic treadmill (Broderick, 2009). The more we acquire and achieve, the more we want. We keep striving for the next success, accomplishment, or possession. We can be like hamsters on a wheel. We move rather quickly going round and round trying to get to that place where we will finally be happy. The only problem is the harder we run, the faster the wheel spins. It is not until we jump off and touch ground that we can find true contentment.

This lesson is about finding happiness in the here and now. Not tomorrow, not next week, not when you get that next promotion or finally go on that dream vacation. It's about finding a bit of your dream today and making a small portion of it come true. It's about relaxing in the moment and appreciating where you are and what you are doing. It's about enjoying those around you including yourself. It's about embracing each step along the journey and pausing to delight in your many blessings along the way.

First, let's take a moment to reflect. Have you been on the treadmill of life? Have you felt like a hamster on a wheel? What are the obstacles keeping you from experiencing happiness in the present moment? What are the goals you want to accomplish before you can relax and let go? Let's take some time right now and consider these questions…

Perhaps you discovered that your happiness has been on hold. If this is the case, I want to encourage you to make a decision to quit postponing your happiness. Whatever is meant to happen will happen. It will not make a difference if you wait to be happy until it does; in fact, you can enjoy yourself even while you wait. There is no reason to delay your joy. Find something in the moment that delights your spirit. Turn your attention to the many gifts that surround you in the present. We are constantly blessed with life's many treasures, from the beauty of a deeply colored sunset to the enchanting dance of a fresh breeze. Happiness is meant to be experienced each and every day!

Accept Yourself

Another suggestion is to accept yourself. Self-acceptance is a large part of finding contentment. Some women are hard on themselves. We have discussed this in the previous lessons. We can be our own worst critics. Perfectionism and high expectations can prevent us from accepting ourselves *as we are*. The hamster wheel was a good metaphor for describing this as well. We push ourselves and the harder we run, the faster the wheel turns. It is time to jump off the vicious cycle of trying to do more or be more. When we touch ground, we discover that we are alright just the way we are. We can learn to accept ourselves and just "be" ourselves.

Self-acceptance is a gift that brings peace and joy. Surrender makes it possible. We can surrender our high expectations, our plans, and our goals. Surrender is not the same as giving up. We can still strive toward our dreams. We can work toward our destiny. And yet surrender brings balance to our efforts. We can shift our focus away from outcomes (the finish line), and become conscious of the beauty of the here and now. We are becoming who we want to be one step at a time. We are achieving our dreams in wonderful increments. We are living more of our destiny each and every day!

Self-acceptance is the foundation of joy. We can learn to appreciate who we are and treasure our strengths and weaknesses. Our shortcomings are great teachers. We grow during times of challenge. Even our mistakes have worked to bring us where we are today. We can accept ourselves, the good and bad. We each have a yin and a yang, a light and dark side of our soul (Moore, 1994). We can embrace the fullness of who we are. We can love ourselves completely for the beautiful creations we are becoming. Like flowers, we are each blossoming in our own elegance.

So relax. Be content. Accept yourself as you are in this very moment. Believe me, you're worth it.

Accept your place in life

Continuing along this theme, we can accept our place in life. It is like the old principle of "Accepting your lot in life." To illustrate, let's look at what a lot actually is. From a zoning perspective, a lot is a clearly defined section of property with absolute boundaries. Just thinking about the dimensions of a lot can be enough for you to visualize being boxed in. Some of us feel this way when we consider our current place in life. We might feel boxed in, like we have no control over changing anything. It is a paradox to consider that often it is not until we accept where we are in life that we are able to move forward. Accepting our current "lot" can become the staging ground for a brilliant and spectacular future.

Learning to accept our place in life releases the needed energy to move forward in directions that are fruitful and edifying. Some of us spend so much energy trying to rearrange the boundaries of where we are that we lack the needed energy to make the shifts we need to succeed as we move through our future. Accepting our current lot does not mean we must stay there forever. Rather, it is the art of accepting where we are today that brings beauty and glory to our lives. This does not mean we will stay here indefinitely. People move from lot to lot throughout a lifetime as they buy and sell property. We too will shift to new and better places as we focus our energy forward and accept where we are in the here and now.

Where are you today? What is your current lot in life? Let's take a minute to visualize and define it.

Now, let's work on accepting it. Take some time here. Embrace your current boundaries. Accept the limitations you face right now. Find the freedom of surrendering what is beyond your control. Discover the peace of being content in the here and now. Prepare your heart. Rest in what is. The future will be here before you know it.

BE CONTENT

Quit looking around

Another suggestion to finding contentment is to quit looking around. We become content when we quit looking around and search within. Some of us have an external locus of control. We focus on what others have and what others are achieving. We may be jealous. We might view life as unfair. After all, we may have invested a lot of time and energy pursuing our aspirations. Many have worked hard in hopes of our dreams coming true. Sometimes when we look around, we do not feel as if we have gotten as far as we would have wished by now. We may envy the things others have accomplished. Look at his home, her career, or how "so and so" seems to get what they want with little effort. When we look around and compare ourselves to others, we are setting ourselves up for disappointment.

Instead, we can be assured that everything in the universe happens in perfect time and we are an intricate chord in this perfect rhythm. When we draw our focus within, we can synchronize ourselves with the beautiful harmony of the journey. We have gifts. We have talents. We are as colorful as any flower in the field. We needn't compare ourselves with others, or compare our journey with the journeys of others for that matter. We each have a unique and incredible purpose. We might not know what ours is, or perhaps we have not reached our time. It could be our hearts are being prepared for something more spectacular to come. Or perhaps we have yet to discover how very beautiful and joyous our lives can be in the present moment just as they are.

The next time you find yourself looking around, stop, and search within… Discover your beauty. Find your heart and soul. You too can have what your heart desires. Limitations are often self-imposed. Our journeys are made up of choices and you can decide to pursue your desires. You can muster up the courage to consider a dream, or the perseverance to follow a hope a little bit further. Ask anyone who has achieved something valuable and no one will say it was easy. Believe in yourself. Endure. You are worth it!

Quit wishing for more or that things were different

Wishing for more or that things were different is another obstacle that works against contentment. Instead, we can practice the art of mindfulness acceptance, which is embracing ourselves and our journeys exactly as they are in the moment. We can stop wishing and begin consciously appreciating our lives. We have so much to be grateful for. Let's turn our consciousness to our many blessings in the moment right now. We can be thankful for our good health, a clear mind, our families, friends, and all the opportunities we have in a democratic society. Acceptance is the key to happiness. It is the foundation for contentment.

We have talked much about energy, and here is another good place to highlight the phenomena of energy exchange. Some of us have put a lot of energy into wishing things were different in our lives. Others have wished for more than they have. I believe we can be content in our lives, no matter where we are or how much we have. We discover a new and brilliant energy when we become mindful of the unique inscriptions of our journey and attune ourselves to the many gifts they hold. We can expend our resources in a positive, productive manner. It is by action that we achieve our dreams. We become more effective when we harness our energy and direct it intrinsically. We move forward in this brilliance. The colors of our world become rich and vibrant.

Let go of worry

Worry is another obstacle we need to let go to find contentment. Some of us are "worry warts". We may not know it, but we are. Think about it for a minute. How often do you worry about how something will turn out, or what someone will do, or the outcome of "such and such"? Someone once told me worry is like rocking in a rocking chair. You rock back and forth over and over again and do not get anywhere. And the experience is far less rewarding. Instead of relaxing, we tense up and hold our breath. We anxiously wait for the next ball to drop. We expect the rug will be pulled from underneath us. It is time to let go and trust in the universe. We are held in endless grace.

BE CONTENT

It will not be easy to let go of worry for some of us. Thought patterns and behaviors are deeply ingrained. Take my word for it. I spent many years worrying. It was not until I studied and applied a model of therapy to my problem that I was able to overcome worry and find freedom and enjoyment. I was studying Solution Focused Brief Therapy in my profession and as a learning technique, began to practice it in my personal life. I was encouraged to practice its unique and powerful strategies in an effort to learn how to apply this theory to the treatment of addictions. I decided to apply solution focused techniques in my personal life in order to overcome a habit. It did not take me long to realize my worst habit was worrying.

I include some Solution Focused techniques that I used to overcome worry in this lesson in hope that you too can grow from this model for healing and change. Let me tell you, I tried everything: prayer, meditation, relaxation, and other forms of letting go. Nothing works better for letting go of worry than these solution focused questions and strategies.

I will start with the miracle question. If you have a tendency to worry, and especially if worry interferes with your level of contentment, visualize the following hypothetical scenario and ask yourself the following miracle question:

Pretend while you are sleeping tonight, a miracle happens. You are freed from worry. It magically disappears. But you do not know that the miracle happened because you were sleeping. So when you wake up in the morning, how will you know the miracle happened and your worry is gone? What are some of the things you will notice, even before you open your eyes?

Envision this scenario for a while. It is your miracle morning. What do you notice? How do you feel? What is different? Do you feel different? Are you more confident? Do you feel more peace or serenity? Are you feeling more positive and hopeful? These are some of the things I noticed in picturing my miracle morning. How about you? Let's take some time for you to reflect and answer these questions…

Now, let's move on to envision the rest of your miracle day. Remember, while you were sleeping you are miraculously relieved of worry. It no longer exists in your life. So suppose you are no longer plagued by worry. What is the first thing you would do when you get up in the morning? Where would you go? What are you thinking? How are you feeling? Is this different from usual and if so, how? What would others say is different about you? What do you think is different about your attitude and behavior?

Again, we will take some time to contemplate these questions…

Perhaps you feel more confidence. Maybe others would notice a skip in your step. Or you might notice your thoughts are more positive and hopeful. Maybe you feel more trusting and accepting of what is ahead in your day. These are some of the thoughts I experienced in creating my miracle day. But the most amazing thing was the longer I envisioned my miracle, the lighter and happier I felt. I continued to ask myself these questions and practice solution focused strategies over the course of two weeks. My thoughts actually began ushering in the miracle. I have always believed that our thoughts create our reality, but this reaffirmed my philosophy. My hope is that you can create a miracle in your life by asking yourself the same challenging, yet enlightening questions.

Another solution focused strategy is to look for exceptions. Just think for a moment, has there ever been a time in your life when you didn't worry? If so, what was going on? How did you deal with the obstacles that came up in your life? What did you do to avoid worry? Did you trust? Pray? Meditate? Take a walk or nature hike? Read a book or relax? How were you able to let go? Let's contemplate these questions for a while…

The last step is relating the answers we discover to our present life. What have you discovered? How did you feel the day of your miracle? What were your thoughts and actions on your miracle day? And how can you apply these discoveries to your life? What did you do

BE CONTENT

before, during those times in the past when worry was not a problem? How can you reincorporate these things today?

I suggest you envision this miracle and ask yourself these Solution Focused questions for at least two weeks if not a month. It has been empirically proven that it takes 28 days to change a habit. Take some time each day to picture your miracle. Pretend your worry is magically removed; and challenge yourself to imagine how you think, feel, and act after the miracle has happened. You will be amazed to discover that it will soon begin to happen in reality.

Enjoy the moment

One of the best suggestions to help you be content is enjoy the moment. I have mentioned already the infinite gifts that are available in the moment. When we set aside the past and the future, all of our hopes and burdens, we are able to enjoy the illuminant peace found in the present. We can rest and replenish here. We can surrender our fears, anxiety, insecurity, and troubles. We can bask in the reality that we have all that we *really* need, right here, right now. It is amazing to become fully conscious of how well we are cared for. The universe holds us in loving arms.

We can enjoy the journey. We can enjoy each moment it brings. What an incredible personal politic! What an amazing way to live. Some of us have spent much of our lives searching, reaching, stretching, trying, and hoping. It is time to rest in the moment and be satisfied. It is our time to relax and be content. I repeat it's the journey not the destination. Let us discover the meaning of this for ourselves.

Find Inner Peace

Learning to be content in the moment leads to deep inner peace. It takes some practice, but the more you let go and relax, the easier it becomes to find a peace so spectacular that it surpasses all understanding. You will find the peace of the universe that a mighty God can provide. It is soothing and electrifying. It is the quantum expression of love. You will understand as soon as you experience the magnitude of its comfort and force for yourself. You will be remade. You will be recreated. You will be renewed.

Once you find inner peace, contentment is yours whenever you seek it. You will be able to pause during a busy day and take some time out to find a place of sacred solitude. It will not take you long to re-experience the state of inner peace once you have discovered it. It is like riding a bike. Once you learn, you just hop on and go. It works each and every time. Before you know it, peace will be a large part of your daily life.

Inner peace is the greatest treasure you can find along the journey. It will transform your world. Begin seeking it today. Look for it. Feel it. Embrace it.

Express your love and show affection

Expressing your love and showing affection is another way of becoming content in life. The more we show our love, the more love we experience. It is the great magic of the universe. Through reaching out we are caring for ourselves. We can all express our unique and precious love. We each have a brilliant spectrum of gifts and talents to offer this world.

The world is so hungry. It is ripe for change. We can potentiate a transformation of the universe; we can be part of the spiritual movement that is growing and evolving. I believe the world is changing. Hearts are being enlightened. Imagine the world entering a new age of peace and love. I write about this in a book *Sacred Peace, a Journey to Inner Freedom.* (Lynn, 2012) Its main point is love is transforming the universe. We can be part of this change as we reach out and share our love with others. It is our highest calling.

The beauty of sharing our love is that it brings lasting and fulfilling contentment. I will say it again. There is no better way to live than in the heart of our destiny. We can express our love to everyone we meet, even strangers. We can show our affection to our friends and family. We do not have to live so firmly within our boundaries. We can trust in the great Love of the universe, the One who holds our hearts with great care. After all, He showed us ultimate love. We can give it as freely as He did.

Live in Gratitude

Another sure way to find contentment is to live in gratitude. It is impossible to be discontent and grateful at the same time. I will keep repeating this oxymoron. If you catch yourself feeling anxious or discontent, make a gratitude list. Write them down, say them out loud, or simply count your blessings in your mind. I guarantee this exercise leads to contentment. You will feel your troubles disappear one by one as you recall one miracle or gift in your life after another. Many of us can count our good health. We have plenty of food, clothing, and shelter. We have friends and loved ones to brighten our lives. Whatever you have, count it: pets, neighbors, jobs, even your spirituality and emotional health. We are gifted beyond imagination. We can simply recognize and affirm this great reality.

Loving Kindness Meditation

We will end this lesson with a powerful strategy to help you be content. It is called loving kindness meditation (Kornfield, 2008), and it is a simple meditative ritual that you can practice to find fulfillment and love. It is rooted in Buddhist meditation, and is designed to help you develop a loving acceptance of yourself. If resistance is experienced then it indicates that feelings of unworthiness are present. Increasing your awareness of self-compassion will help alleviate these negative feelings. In any case, this simply means there is work to be done, as the practice itself is designed to overcome any feelings of self-doubt or negativity. Then you are ready to systematically develop loving-kindness towards others. (Kornfield, 2008)

Lay in a quiet place, somewhere peaceful and comfortable. Gently place your arms by your side, hands open and touching the ground (or bed). Breathe deeply, in and out, until you are consumed by your breath. Relax deeper and deeper into the sensations of peace and tranquility. Let your mind clear of everything. Hold nothing. Let it all go.

YOU ARE WORTH IT

Take ten deep breaths and with each one, fall deeper into this meditation. You will begin to feel as light as a feather or heavy and relaxed, depending on your own personal experience.

When you feel completely relaxed and your mind is clear, you are ready to begin the loving kindness meditation. Entertain affirming mantras, positive words you can tell yourself, as if you are singing a song of love. You might tell yourself you're worth it, you're beautiful, you're precious, and compassionate. You might thank yourself for your journey, your life, and your dedication. It's up to you. You can say whatever comes to mind as long as it is positive, affirming, loving, and kind (hence the term loving kindness meditation.) It is truly beautiful. Try it out. You will love it!

The main point of all the ideas in this lesson is learning the art of contentment. Just "be". We have spent too much of our lives letting peace evade us. It is our time to relax and enjoy. We do not have to postpone happiness. Joy is knocking on the door and we can answer. It has waited long enough for us to surrender. It is here and now. Be content.

BE CONTENT

Broderick, Patricia C. & Blewitt, Pamela, (2009). The Life Span: Human Development for Helping Professionals (3rd Edition)

Kornfield, J. (2008). *The wise heart A guide to the universal teachings of Buddhist psychology.* New York: Bantum

Moore, Thomas (1994). *Care of the Soul: A Guide to Cultivating Sacredness in Everyday Life*

YOU ARE WORTH IT

Reflections

BE CONTENT

YOU ARE WORTH IT

BE CONTENT

YOU ARE WORTH IT

17

Be Yourself

Have you ever felt trapped? Have you ever wondered what you are really doing or why you are doing it? Do you feel stuck, misplaced, or discontent with the way things are? These are all signs that something might need to change in your life. Perhaps you have been living according to the expectations of others. Maybe you are fulfilling a role that was handed down to you through the generations, or prescribed to you by your parents. Maybe you feel the constant pull of the rigid cultural and socioeconomic norms that permeate our society. Whatever your dilemma, no matter what is standing in the way of your freedom and happiness, this lesson will help you find the power to be yourself. It is your way out and your way in. You can escape the trap of discontentment and enter the realms of destiny. When you dare to be yourself, your life becomes spectacular. It is truly amazing!

The world becomes brighter and more beautiful when we dare to be ourselves. I use the word "dare" because it often takes courage to be authentically "you". We live in a society that is highly conforming. Many walk the beaten path and few take the road less traveled. It takes faith and trust in the creative energy of the universe to step off the familiar path and enter the enchanted realms of the unknown. You can develop the confidence to be yourself and begin a journey more incredible than you can dream or imagine. You can discover the beauty of self-expression.

At this point, you may be wondering where to start. The thought of beginning to express the real you more authentically might sound intriguing, but the challenge remains ambiguous. This lesson looks at various strategies that help you learn how to be yourself. My hope is that you not only discover how beautiful and wonderful you are, but that you will also develop the courage to express the depths of your beauty, grace, and love. So let's get started.

Let your guard down

The first step is to let your guard down. Let go of your defenses. Let's look at what this means:

Many of us are defensive. We build walls around us. We are careful and guarded. Many of us grew up this way. We may come from broken homes, broken marriages, broken relations, and/or pasts filled with heartache and tragedy. The world is full of hurt. Many of our journeys have been tainted with the jagged colors of challenge and turmoil. As a result, we slowly erect walls. We build stone upon stone unwittingly, in a desperate attempt to protect ourselves. It was our means of survival. It might continue to this day, except we no longer have to merely survive. The time has come for us to truly live. We can let our guard down now.

When we let down our guard, we begin to see the illuminant rays of a more beautiful world. The once jagged colors of slated gray become a magnificent rainbow array of illumination. Our lives gain beauty and depth as we discover the brilliant colors of who we are. We do not have to be scared. We needn't fear judgment or criticism. We no longer need our walls for protection. We are grown now. We are adults. We are capable, intelligent, creative, talented, and resourceful women with good judgment. We can stand on our own two feet without any need to hide who we really are. It is time. We can spread our wings and fly.

Letting down your guard is a tender process. Be patient with yourself. Baby steps are the key. Becoming more vulnerable is definitely a process that cannot be rushed. Some do not like the word vulnerable.

You might associate it with weakness or hurt. And yet there is another side to vulnerability, a beautiful side, like the dawn of a bright horizon after a long, black night. Vulnerability allows us to become who we truly are, who we are created to be. It allows us to become our finest selves.

Vulnerability allows us to connect with God, ourselves, and the world around. It helps us become authentic. We can let down our walls and open our hearts to experience life and all it has to offer. We miss some of the most precious treasures when we are hiding behind stone walls. We can soften our spirit and experience the joy of wholeness. We are able to fully be who we are.

And so we begin gradually. Small choices and decisions are enough to embark on the journey. Simply consider making a decision today to begin letting your guard down slowly. You can gently dismantle your wall, one stone at a time. Call an old friend. Tell the one you love something he doesn't know about you yet. Share a secret with a trusted mentor or friend. Dance. Sing. Write a poem, a short story, or a book for that matter. We all have a story to tell. Try not to let anything stand in your way. Remember, you are not stuck anymore. You can move freely within your new life.

Accept your imperfections

We talked about perfectionism in lesson fifteen. Some of us hold the bar very high for ourselves. We hate our mistakes. We would rather not have limitations or weaknesses. If only we could make the right move, never struggle, and by all means, not have the problems we do. Sound familiar? It is sometimes hard to look at our imperfections. Perhaps we still do not realize that it is our imperfections that distinguish our complete beauty. Our strengths and weaknesses both comprise our identity. Together, they sculpt us in the direction we need to go. Our accomplishments and limitations lead us along our destiny in balance and harmony with one another.

What are some of your imperfections? Do you struggle with finances? Perhaps it is hard for you to socialize or make friends. Maybe you are overweight, smoke, or love junk food. No one is perfect.

YOU ARE WORTH IT

Everyone has their demons. The important point is that you recognize and acknowledge your imperfections, don't just hide them behind the wall of stone. You do not necessarily have to share them with others, but at least be honest with yourself. Openness and honesty lead to healing. When we admit and accept our imperfections they lose their stronghold in our lives. We are empowered.

We can change many of our imperfections, but some we may need to accept. In all cases, we can learn to let them go. Most importantly, we can love ourselves, the good and the bad, the perfect and the "not so perfect". We are a package deal. I am sure that for each imperfection you have, you could list at least three things you like about yourself (if you think about it for a while). It might not come naturally at first, but as you move through your future, begin embracing your limitations. Not everything is within our power to change. Sometimes we fall victim to circumstances that are outside of our control. And yet many things are within our reach to change. We have freedom and responsibility.

But if you have tried numerous times to change certain aspects of yourself, and after weeks, months, or even years of trying, you discover that you cannot change whatever it is you have been trying to change; then it may be time to embrace the healing realms of self-acceptance. Some of our imperfections are part of our makeup. They are woven in our fiber. We cannot change them. We might not understand or appreciate a particular limitation, and yet when we learn to accept its presence, we can find self-approval and peace. It feels so much better to accept ourselves as we are than to struggle against our grain. It is refreshing to embrace all of who we are, even our weaknesses. We can surrender, which fills our journey with sweet serenity.

So begin accepting your imperfections. Cherish who you are, the good and not so good parts of you. If there is something that bothers you that you can change, by all means try, but if you are at a point where it feels like you are not getting anywhere…Stop.

    Breathe.

        Surrender.

            Accept.

BE YOURSELF

You are beautiful just the way you are. Feel your beauty. Acknowledge your strength. You're worth it.

You're enough

Many women struggle deep down with an empty fear that they are not enough. I believe this is the foundation of many of our struggles and troubles including anxiety, depression, personality disorders, poor relationships (even abuse), low self-esteem, boundary issues, lack of self-confidence, and low self-worth. If only each and every woman could know how special she is! My hope is you will begin realizing how incredible you are in reading this book. You are not only enough; you are "more" than enough. You have value beyond your understanding. If you do not believe this, just trust me for now. I know for a fact that each and every one of us is created with a special purpose and an incredible journey. We are each worth our weight in gold. We are God's angels on earth.

Hopefully you are still practicing loving kindness meditation each day. This is a simple and powerful tool to help you begin feeling your true intrinsic value. I can tell you you're worth it over and over again, and yet until you experience the utter brilliance of your inner beauty, you will not truly understand how valuable you are. It took me years to discover my value. I spent many years feeling as if I was not good enough, like something was wrong with me. My hope is that if you share the same journey, your pain can end now. Life is too short not to appreciate ourselves. It is our season to discover self-love.

You are worth every ounce of water in the oceans and all the stars in the sky. You are worth a million rainbows and the pot of gold at the end of each one. You are worth all the flowers in the field and the variegated colors painted in the sunset. God's love for you is as high as the highest mountain and as deep as the deepest sea. You are royalty in His eyes. We are all precious and incredible. We can discover the greatest reality of our value lies in the reality of love. We were born to love, especially to love ourselves. We are so much more than enough!!!

Express yourself

Expressing yourself is one of the most important aspects of being authentic. We each have so much to offer this world. We live in a world in need. The earth is hungry for our gifts, talents, our sharing, and most critically, our love. The heart of this world is ripe for the many treasures we have to offer. That is why it is imperative we learn to express ourselves. We cannot share our many gifts if we are unable to express who we are. It is time to test our luck, dream, discover, and grow.

Expression may call us outside of the box, beyond the usual comfort zone. We may be asked to travel down roads we have never been, or even go places we have never imagined, and do things we have never done. Some of you may have already received opportunities such as this, but the risk seemed too great. Perhaps you feel safer and more secure inside of the box, within your usual space. Self-expression can help you break outside of this box. Dare to believe in yourself and your abilities. Follow your calling. It is worth it!

Self-expression leads to the richness and fullness of freedom. We can harness the strengths, gifts, and talents we have found in ourselves and utilize our resources to make an amazing difference to a world in need. Some women are musical. They play instruments and sing like nightingales. Others are gifted in the art of healing: doctors, nurses, therapists, shamans, and other spiritual healers. One of the best ways to express yourself is through a hobby such as writing, dancing, photography, painting, crafts, or scrapbooking. It is guaranteed that each moment of the journey dedicated to self-expression becomes a golden nugget in your life. You are helping the world become a better place and brightening your own journey along the way.

Do not worry about what others think

Another part of being yourself is not being afraid to say what is on your mind. Do not worry about what others might think. Many women squelch themselves (if they are not squelched enough by others). We have great ideas. Our opinions are good as well. We needn't shy away from letting others know what we think, feel, desire, and even dream. We do not have to be embarrassed or hide the most precious parts of who we are. In the final analysis, all that matters is what we think about ourselves. Most importantly, can we live with our choices? Are we living our best journey?

As many opinions exist as there are people in the world. We will never please everyone. It is impossible for others to always agree with us. We will face conflict and misunderstanding, perhaps even criticism and ridicule as we continue to express ourselves freely. After all, we are unique. Our ideas are nuanced. Our most authentic selves will differ from the crowd and that's a good thing. That is why it is important to become secure in our thoughts, feelings, and actions. We can be ourselves. It's alright!

So what has been on your mind? Let's spend some time soul searching here. Is there anything you have wanted to say that you haven't said? If so, what is it? Think about it for a while. If you discover an idea, opinion, thought, or feeling that you have not expressed, write it down. Now comes the fun part. Make a poster. You do not have to show it to anyone, don't worry; just begin by writing down what you have been holding back. Write it in big and bold letters. Use bright colors. Make your statement loud and flashy. Hopefully, this will help you prepare to express it out loud the next time you have the right opportunity. We are preparing to break the silence.

Don't be afraid to do your own thing

Social norms are powerful. Many of us adhere to the status quo. We claim to live in a country based on self-determination, and yet we often end up following the crowd. We try to fit it. We feel accepted this way. We might even draw comfort and security from going with the flow. But we are unable to express ourselves most fully when we are trying to fit in. Don't be afraid to do your own thing. You are uniquely gifted with your own special intelligence, talent, and an incredible landscape of ideas and dreams. Your abilities can change the world. Do not settle for what everyone else is doing. Be yourself.

A decision to do your own thing can put you on the path of

destiny. We all have an incredible purpose to our journey. It becomes hard to find our unique potential or design when we are limited by social norms. We can develop the courage to step outside the comfort zone. We can give up our need to have friends, family, coworkers, and/or society affirm and reward us. We can bravely enter the adventurous realms of self-discovery and pursue our deepest and most exciting heart's desires. Our journey may take on a new direction. It might not look like the typical Euro-Western life. And yet our journey will be completely our own. We will not have to compromise our dreams and desires, our hopes and expectations, or any other beautiful part of who we are. We can do our own thing confidently, with faith. This *is* our destiny.

Pursue your interests

Along similar lines, having the confidence and energy to pursue your interests will also help you be yourself. We all have concerns and desires, hopes and dreams, even longings. Some take interest in many endeavors. Others are focused on one or two special interests. Whatever the case, our interests are important to our well-being. We can learn to honor them.

What are you interested in? Some of you might say friends and family, perhaps career, home, and other stabilities, but what about beyond your routine interests? Challenge yourself. Is there anything that interests you that you have not pursued for one reason or another? Perhaps self-doubt stepped in the way and blocked your path. Maybe you question your talents and abilities. What are some of the things you have considered trying but never tried? Maybe you have thought about skydiving, snow skiing, traveling Europe or Malaysia, Australia or Africa? Or perhaps there is a certain sport or style of dancing you would like to learn. It is never too late to begin pursing your interests. Remember this the first day of the rest of your life.

Pursuing your interests brings happiness and joy. It will also lead to more self-confidence. You would be amazed if you knew your full potential. Women are incredible. We are strong, energetic, flexible,

BE YOURSELF

talented, and highly intelligent. Give yourself permission and encouragement to try new things. Don't be afraid. Don't shy away. The journey is enriched when we step outside of the comfort zone to explore new ideas and chase our hopes and dreams. Have fun with it. You will never know for sure unless you try.

Enjoy what you love

One of the most beautiful ways to be yourself is to take the time to enjoy what you love (including those you love). This might sound overly simplistic, but consider for a moment how much time each day you devote to enjoying what and who you love in life. Remember, there are twenty-four hours in a day. Consider we sleep anywhere between seven to nine hours per night and spend at least eight hours per day working (you may not even enjoy your job.) That leaves approximately six hours to enjoy what you love. Where are you spending these precious hours? Are you spending time with your lover? Have you even found a lover? If the answer is yes, have you invested precious energy on nourishing and developing your love? Perhaps you do not even consider your significant other your lover. Consider this for a moment. Wouldn't it be nice?

How about hobbies? Do you have any and if so, what are they? Do you spend time enjoying your leisure and play time? Do you spend enough time with family and friends? How much time do you spend with yourself: relaxing, reflecting, replenishing, or just plain kicking your shoes off and enjoying some quiet time alone? Hopefully you are beginning to love yourself enough to want to spend time with yourself. You can be one of your own best friends.

Reflect for a moment longer on how much time you spend doing what you love, spending time with the people you love. We are considering the average, so just picture a typical week and recall how much time you are engaged in enjoyment. Hopefully, you discover that you are able to spend at least half of your free time on the activities and persons you enjoy (a minimum of 3 hours per day). If not, perhaps you can make some adjustments. The closer you get to six full hours of enjoyment per day the better (and if you are lucky enough to enjoy your career then you are further blessed.) And don't forget to include your precious time alone. Intimate, personal moments can be some of your most enjoyable time in a day.

The point here is the journey is so short that before we know it, it is over. We do not want to miss out on life. Do not fall into the trap of doing too much or working too hard, or even avoiding or putting up walls that hold people at a distance. It is time to let love shine into your life brilliantly and gloriously. We can embrace the beauty and harmony of living an enjoyable, fulfilling life. It is why we are created. We are born to discover the miraculous powers of joy and love.

So what are you waiting for? You can begin living in enjoyment now. We can develop a conscious awareness that assures joy will be an ever present part of our future. Pay attention to your thoughts, feelings, and actions. Discontinue unpleasant routines. Expand precious time spent with the people you love doing the things you love. Go for coffee. Enjoy the brilliant colors of a sunset. Take a nice, long walk or even just sit in nature and relax. Spend quality time enjoying yourself. You are worth it.

You're amazing

The most important reason to be yourself is because you are amazing. You might not realize it, but you are. We are all amazing. Women are gifted in miraculous ways. We possess a wellspring of ideas, talents, abilities, and intelligences. We are creative and loving, supportive and self-sustaining. We have all we need to succeed.

So get in touch with your amazing side. Spend time with yourself and those you love. Let down your guard, there is nothing to fear about who you are. Enjoy yourself. Enjoy your life. The journey is meant for you to be happy, joyous, and free spirited. Life is too short to squander. It is time to be vivacious, delighted, ecstatic, and enchanted. You deserve the best. You are the best. Be your most amazing self! Show others what you are all about. You will be affecting the world in an awesome way. You can help make it a more exciting place.

BE YOURSELF

Reflections

YOU ARE WORTH IT

BE YOURSELF

YOU ARE WORTH IT

BE YOURSELF

18

Be True to Yourself

Women have an interesting history. Finding our true identity in a male dominated society and gaining the rights to fully express ourselves has been a process. For many, the process continues. In a variety of ways the liberation movement is still unfolding. We are discovering new ways to most fully be who we are. One of the greatest gifts we can learn in the process is to be true to ourselves. We have rich and vibrant spirits. We have so much to offer the world, others, and ourselves. We can believe in ourselves and be true to our soul.

In this lesson, we will look at some ideas that can help you be true to yourself. Hopefully you will find some that work well for you personally. The journey becomes easier- and especially more beautiful- as we learn to honor who we are and what we value in life. It might take some practice, but we can all get to a place where we treasure who we are and make choices and decisions based on this inner landscape. So let's get started. This lesson is designed to give you the faith to live a life you believe in.

Don't sell yourself short

The first suggestion is short and sweet. Don't sell yourself short. Do not settle for less than you are or less than you can be. Sometimes it is easier to settle, or at least it may seem that way for a time. The problem

BE TRUE TO YOURSELF

with settling is it prevents you from reaching your full potential. It robs you of your destiny and with that; you give up joy.

One of the most common ways we settle is by selling ourselves short. Perhaps you work at a job that you don't like at all. Maybe you have friends or family members who try to make decisions for you or who are controlling. Perhaps you don't pay enough attention to enjoyment or self-care: nourishing your body, exercise, meditation, relaxation, and leisure. We sell ourselves short in so many ways. It is time to claim our best lives. We deserve the best.

Create your own roles

The next suggestion concerns the roles we choose (or assume) in life. We create our own roles when we are being true to ourselves. We make our own choices and decisions and hopefully, eventually find a path that is rewarding and fulfilling. We began discussing roles in lesson one. Roles can help us follow our heart or move us away from our deepest desires. That is why it is so important to create our own. Roles can help us live the life we desire.

Throughout history, some have had roles handed down through family generations. Perhaps you come from a family of doctors or lawyers, or your parents owned a restaurant or a farm? They might expect you to carry on the family legacy. Maybe a specific education or a particular trade feels like a family requirement. Or, perhaps you have been influenced by the subtle patterns of expectations that are handed down from generation to generation. Many families have them. We know what they are. Think about your own generational patterns for a moment. What messages have you received?

Epidemiologist Erik Erickson referred to the dilemma of not being able to choose your own roles as role foreclosure. Some people are given roles early in life, before they are able to explore and commit themselves to a role (or roles) they truly want. It is best when we are given the freedom of self-exploration, so we can try different things and decide for ourselves what we like and dislike. The good news is it is never too late for the process of self-discovery to begin.

Now let's take a moment and turn to the reflection pages. List your various roles in life. Next beside each one, mark whether or not you chose this particular role in your life or if it was handed down through the generations, or given to you by someone else. (Maybe you have friends, family, or even community connections that try to push you in a particular way). When you consider your different roles, look at all aspects of your life: home, family, career, recreation, friends, community, spirituality and religion, etc…Then, ask yourself if each role is helping you be true to yourself.

Another former psychologist by the name of Donald Super illustrated our roles through the illustration of a rainbow. Our life roles interact with one another like the colors of a rainbow to determine our level of happiness and satisfaction in life. The integration and tapestry of our life roles affect our level of contentment and fulfillment in life. We can carefully create and evaluate each one, and also look at how they are working together (or not working together) as a whole. My hope is that by listing and evaluating your roles you are gaining self-awareness and if necessary, becoming willing to consider some changes to increase your level of happiness. In creating edifying roles, you can find wholeness and harmony in your life.

Our Decisions Become Us

We have mentioned that determining roles involves making our own decisions. This is an important concept because our decisions become us. Everything we do affects who we are. We also affect others. We are interpersonal and interconnected. What we do is not only a reflection of who we are; it influences our future trajectory. Nothing we do is isolated. Not only do we affect others, our actions affect our inner psyches and the world. Our deeds are powerful. Our choices and decisions help us be true to ourselves.

We can learn to move carefully as we journey along life's paths. We can pay attention to our choices, being mindful that we *do* have choices and that our choices are ours. Our choices are like symbols; they symbolize what we honor and value in life. Learn to proceed with

BE TRUE TO YOURSELF

care. Pause if you are uncertain or feel stress. Postpone larger decisions until you are sure you are prepared. Our decisions form our lives. They mold and shape who we are and where we are going. They enhance or purloin our destiny.

Remember your Heritage

Another aspect of being true to ourselves is to remember our heritage. We spoke briefly of how roles are perpetuated throughout our heritage. Our ancestors also pass down valuable traits, rituals, beliefs, and values from generation to generation. Our family history gives us rich and meaningful customs and traditions. We can embrace, remember, and practice these precious gifts in our daily lives.

Generations have changed over the years. We continue to evolve and drift further from our foundations. Individuation can enhance autonomy and diversity, adding to the beauty and dimension of our cultural climate, but it can also take away meaning and depth. An important part of being true to yourself and your family is remembering your heritage, especially special beliefs and traditions. It can thread a rich and vibrant tapestry through our lives and our journey.

Remembering your heritage keeps it alive. Future generations are able to learn the unique ideology of their ancestors and experience the majestic dreams of their forefathers and mothers. You are part of a spiritual connectedness not only of family lineage, but also of love. Your genealogy is such an important part of who you are. It is important to share it with others, especially the next generation of your family. Take the time. Teach the traditions. Practice the rituals. Share the sacred memories. Be true to yourself and your family. It is worth it.

Practice traditions that are meaningful to you

Our discussion on family traditions leads nicely into a look at another way you can be true to yourself. Practice traditions that are meaningful to you. A tradition is a ritual, regular practice, scheduled event or pattern of events; it could be spiritual, religious, celebratory, or even a routine or daily habit. The key is that it is meaningful to you.

Traditions help us remain true to ourselves. They remind us of our hopes and values. Holidays are a good example, like Christmas and Easter. For some, there are spiritual meanings attached to these occasions. For others, there are meaningful traditions such as the Easter Bunny and Santa Clause. Whatever the traditions, these rituals and celebrations bring special meaning to our lives. They can bring gifts like faith, peace, joy, and happiness.

What traditions and rituals do you hold dear? Think about when you were little. Think about your grandparents and relatives; think about your own parents and the special meanings they created around your home. You may discover that you practice some of these rituals already. How do you enjoy traditions? Ponder this question for a moment... Do you miss tradition? If so, what would it look like if you bring it back? How would it change your life, yourself? How could it enrich your journey?

Practicing traditions and rituals are two of the most enriching ways you can be true to your spirit. Try it for a week. Take one of your most precious memories and bring it back into your life in some way. If you grew up in a Christian home, maybe prayer and church are important to you. If you grew up in a Buddhist home, remember your meditations and mantras. Perhaps everyone in the family sat at the table during mealtime. Try it over the course of the week. Prepare an old family recipe. Play an old video or piece of music. Sing an old family song. Have fun with this experiment. You're worth it.

Treasure your life

The deeper you journey toward being true to yourself the more you will begin treasuring your life. You will encounter gifts that are truly amazing. Picture a treasure chest, filled with gold and silver, sparkling coins and jewels. This picture provides a visual of richness and wealth. Now picture the many treasures you can store up in your own personal treasure chest by being true to yourself and acting upon your deepest and most tender dreams and desires. Write some of these treasures down on the reflection pages. The richness and wealth brought about by living in your treasures is infinitely abundant and has irreplaceable value. In fact, it is the richest treasure chest you will ever find.

Treasure your life. It is the only one you have. Your life can be as joyous and spectacular as you make it. The universe longs to show us the best. God longs to show us the brilliance of love. We ourselves are great treasures and we are designed to experience all of the treasures of a heavenly earth. When you are treasuring your life, experiencing love and basking in its sunshine, heaven and earth do not seem that far apart. We can discover bits of heaven here. It is our joy and honor.

Appreciate your experience

Another way we can be true to ourselves is to appreciate our experience. Experience is an important part of who we are. It completes us. We cannot fully appreciate ourselves unless we appreciate our experience as well. Everything happens for a reason, the good and bad. Honoring our experience is another way we can be true to ourselves. It belongs to us. It becomes the fabric of our soul.

What are some of the experiences and challenges that have helped to sculpt and shape you? What lessons have you learned along the way? Some might have been hard. You may have preferred to do without some experiences all together. But let's not forget our wonderful experiences, the beautiful memories and opportunities that came our way just in the nick of time, or the grace and favor we received just when we needed it most. How about the lucky breaks? We appreciate them all.

We know we are being true to ourselves when we come to peace with our experience. We can rest. Relax in the ripples of all you have been through.

Feel... Enjoy....

Accept ... Appreciate ...

Honor and treasure your experience... Discover peace and lasting self-acceptance. Find serenity and happiness.

Honor the Journey

Another important way to be true to your spirit is by honoring the journey. We each have a unique and incredible journey. We may or may not realize it. Some take life for granted. We might not appreciate our many gifts and blessings, especially the smaller ones; but they are always with us, surrounding our every move. We can attune our heart and spirit to them. We can appreciate the moments we are gifted in. We can honor the beautiful segments and even the more challenging times that make up our journey.

Honoring the journey is a byproduct of developing a grateful heart. Gratitude is the solution to so many problems, dilemmas, and challenges. When we are utterly grateful, honor and praise come naturally. We are surely amazed at the mighty energy of grace and love that continuously circle the universe and touch each one of us personally and intimately. It is as if we are held by a loving force so mighty and caring, the energy that holds the clouds in the sky, pours the water in the seas, cares for each flower in the field, lights every star in the night, and loves each of us incessantly. We can honor these gifts that sustain us.

Being true to yourself involves honoring your own personal journey, no matter how many twists and turns it has taken or how many bumps and bruises you have acquired. No one said the path is easy. Yet no matter what our challenges have been we can honor where we are going and who we are becoming. Love and creativity take time. We are becoming masterpieces, spectacular works of art with every step we take. We cannot see the full picture. We haven't seen the magnificent tapestry that lies at the end of our struggles and endeavors. We can honor our journey for bringing us this far. We can trust it to show us better things for our future. We are surely becoming.

Honor your values

Being true to yourself involves honoring your values. We can uphold the ideas, dreams, goals, ambitions, commitments, and responsibilities that are most dear to us. Our values define us. They symbolize who we are and what we believe in. The degree to which we recognize and adhere to our values affects our self-esteem. Values are a foundational part of our self-concept.

Let's consider this further by exploring the answers to some questions. Use the reflection pages. What do you value? Perhaps you have not been in a position to explore your goals, aspirations, or interests. Or, maybe it has been a while since you have taken inventory of your hopes and desires. For some, the idea of considering values might be a new experience. A good way to begin is to consider what is most important in your life? What do you like to do? Who do you enjoy spending time with? Are there certain things you cannot live without? Search your soul as you write things down. Your values are the fiber of who you are.

We can honor our values as a crucial part of honoring ourselves. We do not need to hide them or minimize their importance. It is sure that they help us become who we are meant to be. Honoring our life goals helps us achieve our dreams and desires. It is a huge way we can let ourselves know that we are worth all the happiness and success life has to offer.

Honor your relationships

We have discussed the importance of self-care in many of the lessons in this book. Hopefully you are beginning to love yourself more deeply and intimately with each chapter. We now turn briefly to our connections with others. Relationships are also an important part of being true to ourselves. They enhance our well-being. Women are relational. We are highly compassionate, caring, encouraging, and supportive individuals who need others. Relationships are an inevitable part of our level of happiness and satisfaction. We need to nurture and care for our relationships, giving them the time and attention they require. We can even learn to honor our relationships. Each one is a treasure to our heart.

We need people. We need love. Love flourishes in interconnectedness. Some of us isolate. Reflect on your life for a moment. You might not have many friends. Perhaps you even hold your partner and family members at a distance. Consider becoming more vulnerable and receptive. Move closer to your friends and family. Open your heart to the ones you love. Treasure the time you spend with them. Tender moments with the people who are dear in your life create richness and joy in the journey…

Honoring our relationships is another way we can be true to ourselves. We deserve love and friendship. We need support and encouragement, fellowship and compassion. We are not meant to journey alone. People are placed in our life for important reasons. We are gifted by their presence. We can learn and grow through them; in fact, we learn at the highest frequency when we are engaged in relationships. Learning to enjoy, appreciate, and honor others contributes to an environment in which we can enjoy ourselves more as well. Do not take your loved ones for granted. Honor them always.

Honor the Divinity within you

Honoring our divinity is the most important way we can be true to ourselves. My favorite mantra is "Om Namah Shivaya". It is an old Sanskrit saying that means honor the divinity within you. We all have a beautiful spirit. We each have a miraculous soul. Our lives become spectacular when we learn to appreciate and honor the divinity that lies within us. We can connect with our soul, the most beautiful part of who we are. We can do this anytime, anywhere. Continuously seeking the presence of our own innate divine spirit leads to a life of beauty and grace. It guides us to the sacred and profound.

Spirituality is a gift that develops over time. We can awaken our spirit through simple practices and rituals, precious moments spent in prayer, meditation, relaxation, and enjoyment. We can take a peaceful stroll in nature, visit a synagogue or temple, light a candle… sing a mantra. There are many ways to awaken the spirit. We can feel the divinity within us when we spend time nurturing and exercising our spirituality. We can honor our experience in the divine. It is our greatest joy. It is our lifeline.

This is the perfect place to return to our ongoing reflection on energy. Native American healers believe energy and spirit are one in the same. When we nurture our spirit we are increasing our energy. Similarly, when we focus our energy in the present and expand our awareness with techniques such as prayer, mantras, and mindfulness meditation; we are strengthening our spirit. I agree with this analogy having spent many years practicing the art of meditation. Our spirit and energy are one. Our spirit exchanges energy with the universe and the universe can heal our spirit. We are an intricate part of Mother Nature. It is our home.

Honor the divinity within you. Be true to your spirit. Do not let anything pull you away. Remain focused. Stay centered. Your divinity is the very essence of who you are. It is what you have to offer this world, how you affect the world, and change the lives of others and yourself for the better. Your divinity inspires, encourages, replenishes, and renews. Embrace your spirit. Nurture your divine connection. Care for your soul. Honor your sacredness. Bow in your beauty. Surrender all personality pain. Enter the light. Relax in love.

Find your destiny

We have touched upon the concept of destiny numerous times already, especially in lessons twelve and fourteen. Here, we move a bit further. In order to be most fully true to yourself, explore your destiny. It is your purpose for being, your reason for living, your greatest thrill and joy. You owe it to yourself to discover your calling. Finding your purpose and following your heart provides the best journey imaginable. It is the way to happiness and pure and lasting fulfillment. It is the way to love. Here are some questions that can help you get started…

What are you called to do? What inspires you? What are you passionate about? Have you felt inner nudges, messages of the heart like small whispers of guidance? Let's reflect for a moment… What has your heart been telling you?

Before we end this lesson, let's make a commitment to continue exploring our destiny. The process of discovering our purpose is wondrously edifying. We can help make the world a better place by pursuing our destiny. Many are embarking on a great spiritual revolution. Imagine evolving toward a new and brighter place of peace and happiness. We can discover a journey of light and love. Our destiny will lead us to a brighter future.

Find your place. It is yours. It is calling you. Be true to yourself. Your destiny will bring you to love.

BE TRUE TO YOURSELF

Reflections

YOU ARE WORTH IT

BE TRUE TO YOURSELF

YOU ARE WORTH IT

BE TRUE TO YOURSELF

19

Boundaries

We now turn our attention to boundaries. With them, we have the power to make our lives easier. A life without boundaries can be arduous. Life contains numerous opportunities and challenges. Boundaries help us choose the varying avenues we would like to travel. We have a multitude of choices that can lead to competing interests. Life is not always as simple as we would like it to be, nor is it easy at times. Boundaries help us navigate in ways that help us be happy, satisfied, and effective along life's journey. Personal boundaries are a big part of well-being and success.

Consider the following questions. Do you ever find yourself distracted or off course? Do you find yourself struggling throughout the day to accomplish your plans and goals? Do you seem to get pulled in different directions, making it hard for you to accomplish what you want to get done? If you answered yes to any of these questions, this lesson is designed especially for you. We waver and wane without boundaries. We can end up clear out in left field before we know it. It may be too late before we realize we have ended up in a place we would rather not be. We might have to backtrack entirely and start over.

The first part of this lesson will look at what it means to have boundaries in your personal life. We will explore the characteristics of boundaries and look at the ways in which they affect and improve our lives. Boundaries are protective, nurturing, and empowering. They help us stay on the path we select for our future. Hopefully you are beginning to discover what you would like your life to look like. We have done a lot of soul searching and self-discovery throughout this book. If you are still unsure, that's alright. We will complete some more assignments in this lesson that will help you further establish what you want and need for yourself and your life.

Boundaries can be compared to a rudder on a sailboat. Without the rudder, the wind blows the sailboat in unpredictable directions. The sailor has no control of the ship. The rudder serves to help the sailor stay on his or her course. It provides the boat direction and gives the sailor control. The rudder brings the boat to its desired location or destination. Without a rudder, a sailor winds up off course. It is the same with boundaries. Without personal boundaries, we are disempowered. We lack direction and control. So let's begin looking at the many features of boundaries. They are as crucial to our journeys as a rudder is to a ship.

Self-Definition

Boundaries define us. They show us where we end and other persons begin. They show others who we are, what we care about, and what we want and need. We discussed the fact that women are highly relational. Our lives are affected by our connections with others. It is important to maintain our own identity in relationships. We might unconsciously enmesh with those around us. Some women lose themselves in relationships, friendships, even in their environments. We can strive to consciously maintain our own identities, standards, plans, ideas, thoughts, desires, and attitudes. We can maintain our unique definition. This is crucial to our happiness and survival.

Before we go any further, let's take some time to introspect. How would you define yourself? This question can serve as a means to help you decide what you want and need along your journey. We can keep in mind the fundamental idea that we are valuable and worthy as we move through the process of self-definition. Without this basic assumption, it is unlikely we will be willing or able to uphold any boundaries we create for ourselves. It is healing and empowering to develop belief in our self-worth.

Hopefully, you are gaining a strong sense of value. We have completed many lessons that are designed to help you discover your worth. You are worth the world, worth your time and attention, worth the love and affection of others, and worth a journey you want and believe in. Grounded in self-worth, how do you define yourself? What qualities and characteristics, dreams and aspirations do you prize? How would you describe the most important parts of who you are to someone else?

It might take some time for you to answer these questions. Dig deep. Reflect. Write your ideas down. What aspects of your life and yourself do you want to grow and flourish? What is not working? What are you tired of? Some women never take the time to focus conscious energy on exploring and discovering answers. Let's take the time now. Meditate. Challenge yourself. Be honest. Be open. Discover and define the best parts of who you are. Self-definition is the foundation for boundaries.

Internal versus external boundaries

Now, let's explore the basic characteristics of boundaries as we prepare to apply them to our lives. Boundaries can be internal or external in nature. We can develop internal boundaries for ourselves and external boundaries that apply to our relationship with others. Internal boundaries help us follow our desired course, making good decisions and choices for ourselves including self-care, motivation, behavior, planning, interacting, becoming involved, self-discipline, self-control, and managing our inner landscape. These are personal boundaries that allow us to become all we are designed to be. Internal boundaries help us live our most rewarding lives. They are the personal standards we try to uphold in order to achieve our goals and dreams. They help us live our journey with peace, happiness, well-being, wholeness, and harmony.

External boundaries on the other hand are the guidelines we establish concerning our relationships with others including how we would like to be treated, our time commitments, our expectations for friendship and partnership, patterns of communication, and other social and interactive standards we would like to maintain. These are external because we draw a line between us and other persons. We need this protection and security. We are finding our value and discovering just how special we are. It is easy to get pulled away from who we are or at least who we are striving to become. Again, boundaries help us stay on course.

Boundaries are affirming

Internal and external boundaries are affirming. Discovering, establishing, and maintaining guidelines to support our inner needs, relational life, and desires opens up a whole new world for us to appreciate and enjoy. We are sure to find happiness and satisfaction. We will know peace and contentment. Boundaries affirm our hopes and desires. They reinforce self-love. We can construct a beautiful framework within and around that will help us journey on the road of happiness and destiny.

We are affirming who we are and what we believe in when we establish and maintain boundaries for ourselves and with others. These are concrete statements and actions that help us express our thoughts, feelings, behaviors, and emotions. They not only affirm our commitments, they reinforce our resolve. A set of internal and external guidelines for living encourage us to journey in a way we truly believe in, deep down in our heart and soul. They leave little room for getting sidetracked or drifting astray. They help us reach the destination we choose all the while helping us enjoy the journey along the way.

Boundaries affirm the most precious parts of our psyche, inner landscape, and personhood. They encourage us to express our strengths, ideas, desires, hopes, and dreams in ways that are practical and edifying. We all need affirmation. We could all use a roadmap to make life easier and more rewarding. We all need boundaries. So, before we go any further, let's look at how they can be created.

A Boundary Matrix

Turn to the reflection pages and create the following matrix: On the first page list your strengths and weaknesses on each side. On the next page list your hopes and dreams. It might be helpful to go back to the inventory of strengths you created in lesson twelve to help you get started. Spend some time pondering and completing this matrix. Stay with the reflection pages for a while after you have made your initial lists and add to it later as more items come to mind. The goal is to make your matrix as extensive as possible. You can use all four lists as a basis to develop boundaries for yourself.

When your matrix is complete, begin with the section on weaknesses and list boundaries on another reflection page that will help protect you from your weak spots. An example might be if you lack self-confidence. A personal boundary to consider would be to assert your opinions in your interactions with others. Go through each weakness and try to establish a boundary that can help you protect yourself or overcome your weak spots.

Next, go to your list of strengths. In this category, think about preservation. Boundaries help us preserve our strength also. An example here might be you pursuing a career or life interest that takes a lot of self-discipline. You might decide that increasing your level of self-motivation might be a good internal boundary that can help you stay on track. Or perhaps you have strong family relationships and you decide to commit to spending more time each week with family members.

On another page, we listed our hopes and dreams. Boundaries are especially important here. It is not easy to follow our heart. It takes courage to live out our hopes and dreams. Boundaries can help us continue to pursue our greatest desires. You may have listed something like you hope your family is healthy and happy. In this case, a good boundary might be for you to make a commitment to contributing to the well-being of your family. You might have listed a dream such as pursuing a talent or hobby that interests you. An appropriate boundary in this case might be to dedicate a certain block of time each day to practicing and enjoying your hobby or talent.

Personalize your matrix. Make it your own. These examples are simply to help you get started listing some boundaries for yourself. Do some soul searching. Brain storm and dig deep. Try to fill up all of the reflection pages. Hopefully, you will establish many good boundaries for yourself through this process. You are building a bridge that can fortify your future. You are working to assure the future success of your journey.

Navigating the journey

Returning to the analogy of the sailboat, boundaries help us stay on course and navigate along the journey. Now that you have developed your own inner and external guidelines for yourself, it will not take long before you feel the added stability and direction in your life. Like the rudder helps the sailor control the ship, your boundaries will help you control the course of your life and your destiny. You will not get blown astray (or at least not as often or as far). You will be able to implement choices and decisions proactively, in ways that are supportive and fulfilling. Get ready. Your whole life will change for the better.

The journey is like a wide open sea. There are an endless amount of opportunities and challenges that will be encountered, perceived, evaluated, and acted upon. Learning to navigate proactively, consciously choosing our direction and path, allows us to enjoy the most beautiful journey possible. Opportunities are maximized and challenges become inlets to replenish and grow. Our ability to navigate is our lifeline. It is how we reach a destination we want and believe in. It is how we live a life that is filled with enjoyment and passion.

Boundaries are the framework of self-truth

Boundaries provide a framework for self-truth. They protect our values and preserve what we believe in. They help us be true to ourselves, our inner spirit, and our inner voice; and follow our inner compass. We all have a deep intuition regarding what is best for us. Boundaries help us remain true to our inner nudges. We can compare them to the framework of a house. The walls, siding, and roof protect the home from damage from the elements. When it rains and snows, everything on the inside stays warm and comfortable. When the winds blow, the contents of the home remain stable and secure. Boundaries provide similar benefits to us. They protect our emotions from the elements of storms and challenge. They protect our spirits from the tempest of life.

Boundaries fortify us to live a successful and joyful life. They help us live the truth we find deep within our hearts. It is not easy to stay on course, especially for those who buck the crowd. Some of us are non-conformists, in which case boundaries become even more important. And yet boundaries are designed to help everyone, from the opinionated to the passive, from the extravert to the introvert, and from the creative to the conservative. They have one thing in common for everyone. Boundaries help us live more satisfying and fulfilling lives.

Boundaries lead the way to self-respect

Boundaries lead the way to self-respect. Self-worth is a recurring topic throughout these lessons. Self-respect is a similar concept. When we respect ourselves we care about our ideas, goals, hopes, dreams, plans, strengths, limitations, gifts, talents, and destiny. The more often we practice the guidelines we set for ourselves, the further we grow in self-respect. And the more self-respect we have, the more willing and able we will be to live within our boundaries. These are perpetual ideas. If you wonder what came first the chicken or the egg, the answer is it doesn't matter. Both self-respect and boundaries are important to possess. You can also use these ideas as indicators. If you are having boundary issues, perhaps it is time to reflect upon and evaluate your level of self- worth. Or maybe you have a high degree of self-respect, but lack self-discipline and have therefore never given yourself any guidelines for living.

Boundaries pave the way to self-worth. They will help you realize how valuable you are so you can practice taking care of yourself. Many women are well accustomed to taking care of others. It is our innate tendency, our very nature. We are care-givers. We are compassionate and helpful. Now, we can turn our attention inward and treat ourselves with compassion, kindness, and unconditional positive regard. It is time for us to pay attention to who we are and what we need. Life passes by very quickly and before we know it, the journey is over. Let's make it as beautiful as we can imagine.

Boundaries give us room for ourselves

We all need space. Boundaries give us room for ourselves. Remember the circle in the sand at the beginning of this book. The Native Mayan teacher drew a circle in the sand to demonstrate how small my piece of the pie in my life was back then. He sliced the circle with lines representing my career, responsibilities, children, and love interest; and then he drew my own individual slice as very narrow and thin. He was "right on' at the time. Thankfully over the past few years, I have made changes to make more room for myself in my life. If I were to redraw the circle and divide it into pieces now, it would be much more balanced. My slice is much larger today than it was back then.

Boundaries give each of us more room for ourselves. Space to enjoy ourselves, opportunities to do what we like to do, the time to engage in rewarding activities, and even space for peace and quiet, rest and replenishment. So often, people and obligations crowd in on us. They push against our walls until our piece of the pie shrinks. We usually don't realize it until it's too late. We are able to maintain precious personal space when we maintain boundaries around the section of our lives that is solely ours. Our slice of the pie is dear. When it is balanced well with the rest of our life, we feel comfortable and secure. We are happy and satisfied.

Boundaries can help us realize our hopes and dreams

We can realize our hopes and dreams by adhering to our inner guidelines. We all have aspirations. We each have an important life purpose. We are born with a unique and incredible destiny. You might hope to have an exciting career someday. Perhaps you dream of the day you can retire and travel the world. You may hope to send your children to a good college, find that perfect someone, or be healed of an ailment or problem in your life. You might dream of the day you no longer have to worry or struggle. It is exciting to know that boundaries assist in making our dreams come true. They give us the structure we need to move toward what we want in life.

Hopes and dreams require attention and care. They do not happen on their own. We can consciously and intentionally move toward what we want rather than sitting back and waiting for solutions and outcomes to come to us. Go after what you want! Develop boundaries to help you get where you want to be, whether that is becoming more content where you are or going somewhere else; somewhere better, brighter, or more rewarding. The sky is the limit when you consider what your future can hold. Determine who you are and what you need; and then shoot for the stars. Consider your purpose. Know what makes you happy. Follow the desires of your heart. Honor your boundaries. Honor yourself.

Boundaries help us achieve our destiny

Probably the most important aspect of personal boundaries is they help us achieve our destiny. We have explored the concept of destiny several times already. We can all experience the beauty of discovering and following a destiny designed for us. We are meant to feel the sheer joy and ecstasy of finding our path. Life does not have to be a veil of tears or an arduous journey to be endured. We can utilize our inner guidelines to reshape our lives, filling our mind, body, and spirit with wholeness, peace, and harmony. We are blessed each day we work toward achieving our destiny.

Destiny is available to everyone who seeks it. It comes to all who live in love. Boundaries help us enhance our love for ourselves, which is one of the greatest treasures of all. In fact self-love is an important part of our destiny. You have heard the old adage, Love your neighbors "as" yourself. This implies that one possess a tangible amount of self-love. It takes personal growth in the area of love to be able to realize your destiny. We can establish this boundary for ourselves too if we so desire.

BOUNDARIES

We can strive toward growing in love.

Whatever you do in life, whichever direction you take or choices you make, search your heart and consider your destiny. Your life will be enriched beyond imagination. Your days will be blessed with the brilliant treasures of the universe. Your nights will be peaceful and serene. Destiny will skyrocket you to new dimensions. You will be amazed to see how much you can accomplish and how happy you will be. Discover the boundaries you need to bring you there. Honor yourself and your journey. Make the life you have always wanted happen today! You are worth it.

YOU ARE WORTH IT

Reflections

BOUNDARIES

YOU ARE WORTH IT

BOUNDARIES

YOU ARE WORTH IT

20

Nourish your Spirit

We have emphasized the importance of nourishment throughout this book including nourishing your mind and body. Now, we turn our attention to nourishing the spirit, which is another needed form of nourishment. Our spirits are precious. They store a great reservoir of beauty, awareness, guidance, and power. Our spirit is the essence of our energy. Our connection to our spirit becomes stronger when we nurture our relationship with our inner-being, our soul. We develop deeper, more enduring qualities when we seek to journey with our spirit.

Nourishing your spirit is a critical component of living your best journey. You can strengthen your spiritual connection in several ways. This lesson will look at various ideas to help you develop an intimate, beautiful, sustaining connection with your spiritual essence. Spiritual growth takes time and practice. It is not something that happens overnight. Although miraculous exceptions do occur where people have sudden, abrupt, and powerful spiritual awakenings, most of our spiritual growth happens incrementally and is of a practical variety. Many people grow in spirit by diligently, patiently, and earnestly seeking a spiritual connection each and every day. But no matter your experience, it is certain that your spirit needs nourishment, just as your body does. So let's get started.

YOU ARE WORTH IT

Discover your inner light

We will begin by exploring our spiritual essence. Becoming familiar with your spirit requires consciousness and awareness, spending time in peaceful, quiet meditation and attuning yourself to your inner psyche. If you are one who has not spent much time searching for the spiritual connection, rest assured; it is never too late to begin. You can begin by discovering your inner light. Close your eyes and picture a golden glow surrounding you. Feel its warmth and tenderness. Let it surround you and hold you. Embrace it. Open your heart and let it in.

Your spirit is pure light. It is the love and light within you. It is your divinity. Discovering your inner light opens the door to your spirit. It releases all fear, worry, insecurity, consternation, guilt, shame, remorse, and other illusions. Grace, mercy, and love enter our lives when we enter the inner realms of our spirituality. The light of love fills us. We are transcended. Our lives are changed.

Remain conscious of your inner light a while longer. Bask in the warm, golden glow. Feel the joy of your spiritual core. Experience the fullness of your essence. Allow it to consume you. Perhaps you have been thirsty. We all run on empty at times. Let the spirit of light and love fill you now. Relax and replenish in this beautiful sensation until your heart is overflowing. Feel the peace…tender release…sweet surrender. Let it flow through you. Let it sweep you away.

Take time to worship

Another way to nurture your spirit is to take time to worship. You do not have to be at a church, synagogue, temple, sanctuary, monastery, or mosque. Instead, you can feel free to worship wherever you are, even outdoors in nature or another quiet and tranquil place. Worship is between you and your higher power, it is a personal communion between you and the love of the universe. The more often you spend time in intimate worship, the stronger your spirit grows. And as your spirituality matures and seasons, your life becomes more meaningful and precious. It is miraculous. It is amazing.

You can view your spirit as an inner sanctuary within where you can go and worship anytime, anywhere. All you need to do is pause and seek the sacred place within, that precious place of pure peace and tranquility that exists deep within your soul. Hopefully you began to feel this special place of inner peace as you visualized the golden light. If not, return to the visualization. Stay with it longer this time, in fact, continue to visualize a warm golden light glowing within you until you feel and experience the light of your spirit. Breathe deeply from the core of your being. Relax. Let go. Let your spirit fill you. Trust in its presence. Embrace the arms of love.

Taking time to worship each and every day will give your life new meaning and purpose. It will also help you experience a joy and harmony that are only possible when living in your spiritual nature. Worship is the gateway to heaven. It allows us to experience peace and happiness. We needn't wait for the afterlife. We can experience the gifts and beauty of eternity in the here and now. Worship paves the way to peace. It is the handmaiden of serenity. It is our lifeline.

Nirvana

Meditation and worship together weave an illuminant pathway toward realizing the most awesome present centered awareness you will ever experience, Nirvana. When we practice meditation regularly, we increase our awareness and consciousness of the spiritual realm, the metaphysical and mysterious yet tangible, most incredible part of this world. Nirvana is a completely open and relaxed state of mind, body, and spirit that you can develop as a byproduct of systematically and intentionally opening yourself to God, the universe, nature, peace, and sheer delight. It is a state of complete and utter wholeness, contentment, enlightenment, harmony, and joy. It is our link to heaven. Nirvana is our experience of the sacred and divine.

You will know when you have achieved this ultimate spiritual state as the world begins to look differently. If you are meditating outdoors, you can appreciate nature as it comes alive. Trees, flowers, even the grass become more rich, vibrant, and illuminant. Where ever you are, you can reach deep within your soul to be filled with the sacred peace of

Nirvana. Be still. Listen to your breath. Feel your heartbeat. Experience your emotions. Become completely aware of every sensation within and around you. Let go. Feel your energy extending toward the energy of the universe. Our energies are one in the same. We interact with everything around us on a metaphysical level. Find your connection. Feel yourself commune with the universe. Be part of it. Embrace it.

Experiencing Nirvana is an ultimate way you can nourish your spirit. Try it. Practice it. Meditate regularly and you will discover this illuminant mindset of peace and enlightenment. You will be replenished, encouraged, inspired, and transformed. You will want to spend as much time in Nirvana as you can each day. Your spirit will become resilient and fibrous. You will begin to shine!

Marvel upon the universe

A simpler way to begin nourishing your spirit is to marvel upon the beauty and wonders of the universe. Take time to enjoy creation. Nature offers so many treasures for us to enjoy, from the endless stars shining like brilliant gems against a black velvet sky to the mighty waves that roll in the sea. Everywhere we turn, there are wonders to marvel upon. Slow down. Become aware of your surroundings. Attune yourself to the presence of the miraculous world we live in. Do not miss anything. Life is too short to live without enjoying its many gifts.

My son took me to a moon viewing festival when I was visiting him in Seattle. We watched dramatic ceremonies and eloquent dances; and listened to beautiful, ornate instrumentals leading up to the magnificent appearance of a huge, full moon as it rose slowly in the nighttime sky. I had never before appreciated the moon as I did that night. After meaningful rituals and sacred rites of passage, the moon arose in a golden glow that danced in wonderment and fullness. I was reminded of how special it is to appreciate nature's finest gifts, especially with loved ones. It was a ceremony of praise for the earth as it is one of God's greatest gifts to us. The night was truly amazing!

Another way to marvel upon the universe is to watch clouds floating by on a brisk windy day. Relax and let your mind drift in the puffy, cotton candy clouds floating by, one by one, like an endless parade. Lie on your back or sit out on your deck. You can even just look out the window for a while (it can be a nice break when you are at work.) You can feel the magnificent energy of the universe and appreciate how we are perfectly held and protected within the earth's atmosphere. Everything is cared for in impeccable rhythm and harmony, including us. We can nourish our spirits in the reality of nature's love and care.

Marveling upon the beauty and grace of the universe is a gift that firmly connects you to your spirit. We are pure energy. The cells of our body vibrate at such a high frequency; we appear to be solid mass. We are really billions of cells, potential energy generated, distributed, and transformed through our neurobiological systems. The world we live in is also comprised of pure energy. Sunlight, nature, and all of our surroundings appear to be made of mass, but from a metaphysical perspective, they are truly billions of neurons. Marveling upon the wonders and beauty of the universe helps us connect with our energy and essence. It invigorates the spirit. It gives our system a jumpstart, like recharging a battery. We are renewed in nature. We are made whole.

Enjoy Nature

Enjoying nature is undoubtedly one of the best ways to nourish your spirit. The mind, body, and spirit are all intimately linked. Our bodies (specifically our brains) are made up of cells that contain neurotransmitters. Wellness provides balance to our neurochemical system. Numerous receptors are responsible for receiving signals that promote feelings of pleasure, reward, satisfaction, and happiness. These receptors are stimulated when we spend time in nature. The positive energy in nature's atmosphere literally affects our psyche, our inner emotional landscape. Our spirits are lifted as a result of our neurobiological exchange with nature's energy. We are created to enjoy nature. It is energizing and healing.

Hiking is one great way to enjoy nature. I am reminded again of the trip I took to visit my son. He planned the most spectacular hike anyone could possibly take. We hiked up the nearest foothill to Mount

Rainier in northern Washington. The eight mile trail climbed fifteen hundred feet of breathtaking altitude. The trail was thick with blue spruce pine trees, stacks of granite, and fields of fresh lavender flowers. We were so amazed by the scenery when we reached the top that we sat quietly together soaking in the beauty, serenity, and majesty of the mountain peak. The magical aura of this spectacular scene created the illusion that one could reach out and touch the nearby mountain. Nature appeared animated in an illuminant depth that I have never seen before. We were captivated in awe.

You can find beautiful hiking trails such as this almost anywhere. It is remarkable just how many hiking and biking trails there are in any given city or travel to the countryside. Even if there is no official trail, you can create a path. Find a hideaway deep within the woods, somewhere secluded, tranquil, and serene. Simply start walking. Try to find openings in the woods with markings you will remember so you can find your way back. It will be an adventure. You will feel free and boundless. Explore. Discover. Relax and enjoy. There is nothing like a good old fashioned nature hike… unmarked, uninhabited, and untraveled. Try it sometime. Just remember the bug spray!

You can enjoy nature in many ways. You do not even have to be active. Just sit beside a pool or pond. Notice the illuminant reflections that sparkle all around. See the colors of the sky dance in the water. Lie in a hammock or swing at a park Nature revives. It illuminates. Nature nourishes.

Have meaningful ceremonies and rituals

Rituals are an important part of our spirituality. They represent who we are and what we believe in. They can be as formal as wedding ceremonies, funerals, birthday parties, and holiday celebrations; or private ceremonies like burning candles, incense, chanting mantras, or walking a labyrinth trail. Rituals do not have to be formal to be meaningful and special. Sometimes the tiniest actions and the quaintest expressions can provide the most beautiful, spiritual experiences. We can practice a simple, precious spiritual routine. We can embrace

NOURISH YOUR SPIRIT

little gifts to encourage and renew us each and every day.

Candles are an example. They enchant the spirit. We are uplifted and soothed when we relax by candlelight. You can also add various scents to tantalize your emotions. Have you ever been candle shopping? If not, give it a try sometime in the near future. Spend an afternoon shopping for candles. Search the internet for specialty shops in your area that offer a wide assortment. It is fun to explore the little local shops (especially when they carry homemade goods). Take the time to smell the various scents. Attune your spirit to each one. Which scents lift your spirits? Which ones bring you feelings of serenity and peace? Are there any that make you feel happy and energized? Pay attention to your emotional responses as you sample the scents. Then, choose your favorites. And don't forget to burn them when you get home. Candles are meant to be enjoyed, not just set on a shelf.

Another private ritual is burning incense. Many of the candle stores also carry incense. Notice your spirit's response as you smell the various scents. Incense is powerful. It smells heavenly. Sit in a quiet room and watch it rise and float in the air. Breathe the aroma. Feel the deep serenity and tranquility it brings to the spirit. It is nourishing to the mind, body, and soul.

Another precious ritual we can practice is chanting mantras. Chanting is very powerful. The ancient Egyptians chanted to help them defy gravity and lift the huge boulders to make the pyramids. It is speculated they began chanting as they attempted to lift each one; and the power of their communion of songs helped them lift tons of rock, defying all odds. You can discover the power of mantras for your spirit. If you are not familiar with any, many Sanskrit mantras and poems can be found on the internet. You can also make up your own. The key is to keep them short and write your mantra in a way that flows when it is chanted.

Then, practice chanting. Find a quiet time of the day, one without scheduled events or interruptions. Next, find a quiet room or peaceful place outdoors. You can hum, sing, or simply chant. Focus on peace and harmony. Sing or chant as smooth and effortlessly as you can. You may get louder, yet be sure to maintain a stance of effortlessness. Feel the flow of your words. Let them be smooth on your tongue. Chanting rings in an even tone. It is seamless. It is beautiful.

Surround yourself with meaningful things

Another great way to nourish the spirit is to surround your life with meaningful things: memories, pictures, wind chimes, statues, fresh flowers or antique floral arrangements, porcelain figurines, china, or crystal. These are all examples of small, yet meaningful things you can place around your home and office in order to connect with your inner spiritual self.

These can serve as ornaments or symbols of the most precious parts of your life. Perhaps you travel and collect souvenirs from various destinations. Maybe your kids are grown, but you have pictures and photos on display. Perhaps you like soothing items such as wind chimes, free flowing sculptures, and paintings. Whatever adds meaning to your life, make sure to include these items in your décor. We are affected by our surroundings. We are influenced by our external environment. Decorate your life with meaning. Treat yourself to a journey filled with treasures.

Dance and Sing

Dancing and singing also nourish the spirit. Movement and sound help the spirit flow. As we flow with the music, our bodies relax and become more vibrant and beautiful. Dancing can make you feel more sexy, voluptuous, and free. Singing brings us happiness and a feeling of lightness; it helps us be more carefree. The more often we sing and dance, the happier and more free spirited we are. It lightens the journey. It provides a simple way to enjoy and appreciate life.

It does not need to be formal, in fact impromptu is better. It is most fun to dance and sing when no one is watching. Sing in the car or at home with the radio, your favorite music album, or stream an assortment of songs from Pandora. You can dance all by yourself. Dance in the mirror, in the kitchen, in the middle of the living room…wherever you want. Sing and dance while you are making dinner or folding laundry. Let down your guard. Release your reservations. Let your body do the talking. Let it move the way it wants to. Do not worry. It's OK if you're off rhythm. The more you let go, the more beautiful your movements and song can become.

Song and dance will brighten your life. They open up a whole new world. No matter what your circumstances, no matter the weight of your burdens or the depth of your challenges, the simple acts of dancing and singing will improve your mood and lighten your spirit. Give it a try. After all, no one will know (except perhaps your family if they are at home with you). Who knows, maybe they will join in the fun? Start dancing. Sing. You'll love it!

Spend time with females

Friendship is another way to nourish the spirit. Gals need friends. It is important to have close female friends who we can talk to about anything and everything. You cannot have enough or too many friends for that matter. Friends enrich the journey. We can share secrets and joys with one another, have fun together, or just enjoy the quiet company of each other. We can talk, laugh, play, exercise, or sit quietly together. No matter what you do with friends, it is time well spent. Friends pick us up when we are feeling down. They encourage and support us. They inspire and affirm us.

Some women find it difficult to make friends. Perhaps you have been hurt in the past and you remain defensive. Some of us erect walls of protection and will not let anyone in. It takes courage to reach beyond the familiar zone where we meet new people. It takes faith to let others in. We can take baby steps toward becoming open to new friendships. A simple greeting can go a long way when you encounter someone new. Perhaps this will lead to conversation. You will be surprised to discover how similar women are. We have so much in common. We share many of the same strengths and weaknesses. We enjoy a special bond.

On the other side of matters, perhaps you have many friends, but rarely socialize. Some of us have the tendency to isolate. We might be too tired after a long week at work to get out and mingle. We might make excuses to just stay home, relax, or be lazy. Although there are times when relaxation and solitude are healing and replenishing, it is unhealthy to isolate. Try getting out once in a while. Call an old friend. Ask a group of friends to go to dinner or coffee. Take a friend to a movie or ice cream. See a play. It does not have to be a big event. We are often most pleased with the simple and small in life. Rekindle your female relationships. You are *so* worth it!

Seep into the treasures of the moment

Seeping into the treasures of the moment is probably the best way to nourish your spirit. We have already discussed the infinite blessings that continuously surround us. Now, let's focus on literally "seeping" into these treasures. Other descriptive verbs that can be used are basking, absorbing, enjoying, consciously appreciating, or meditating. We let go and relax. We can absorb the treasures around us into our heart and soul. We can enjoy the tiny gifts that grace our path. Our spirits become fully conscious. We awaken!

We are remade when we seep into the treasures of the moment. We are restored here. We have already talked about "thought stopping". If we find our thoughts drifting away from present awareness, away from the moment we are here to enjoy; we can gently, kindly, and with self-compassion…stop our thoughts and redirect our attention to the treasures we find in the here and now. Our spirits not only awaken, they come alive! We are nourished beyond belief. We are renewed.

The treasures of the moment heal our spirit. They soothe the soul. Women deserve the very best. We need to nourish ourselves, not only our mind and bodies, but especially our spirits. Do me a favor. Make a decision today to begin nourishing yourself, inside and out. Self-care is the most important commitment you can make to enrich and brighten the journey. It is the foundation of wellness. It is the bridge to a wondrous and joyful tomorrow.

NOURISH YOUR SPIRIT

Reflections

YOU ARE WORTH IT

NOURISH YOUR SPIRIT

YOU ARE WORTH IT

NOURISH YOUR SPIRIT

21

Old Me, New Me

My hope is through reading this book, you have felt yourself changing and transforming, releasing old patterns and worn out habits and discovering a more joyful you. The last section of this book is devoted completely to joy. We have been preparing our hearts. In this final lesson on wellness, we will become ready, willing, and able to let go of the "old me" in final preparation for embracing a "new me". We have reached the point of no return. Like slowly climbing the first and most thrilling hill of a roller coaster ride, our anticipation has been building. We want to experience the exhilaration and happiness available when we ride the hills and valleys of life. We want our ride to be spectacular. We are preparing to cross the point of no return now, and take the plunge into a journey of joy!

We have made many positive changes. Hopefully, you are beginning to experience a "new self". We are learning to take better care of ourselves each and every day. We are making healthier, wiser choices. No doubt we want to continue this new way of life. The first step is to make a firm, yet loving inner commitment to ourselves to stay on the path of self-love. But beyond this substantial resolve, there are some additional pointers to keep in mind that will help you journey in the arms of love and self-compassion. Let's look at them before moving on to the final section of this book.

Remember what you have learned

As you move forward through life, remember what you have learned about yourself. It is easy to slip back into old patterns when life gets stressful. Instead when you are challenged, try to recall the lessons you have learned and especially, remember where your old behaviors got you. Perhaps memories of consequences lurk in the back of your mind as a reminder of who you do not want to be anymore. These are gifts of endearment. They represent the "old you". Just remember, she is gone now. She no longer exists. We can look upon our old selves with kindness and compassion, forgiveness and love. When we change our lives, it is like we are reborn. We are re-created. We are new beings. We can think, feel, and act in new ways now.

Life's lessons mold and shape us into who we are created to be. The lessons we learn, even the hard knocks sculpt us into our best selves. Hold each lesson dear to your heart. Do not forget the knowledge and experience you acquire along the journey. We no longer have to repeat our mistakes when we remember what we have learned. We can travel securely. We are led to happiness and satisfaction.

And yet no one is perfect. We are sure to encounter challenging times in our future, and there may be times we slip back into old habits no matter how diligent we are. The good news is we can start over again anytime. It is never too late to begin anew, and there is no limit to the number of times we can start over. If you find yourself slipping back into old patterns of thought, feeling, and behavior; you will know it fairly quickly. The longer you live in self-devotion, the better you feel. Clear signs will indicate you are falling away from your new self: feelings of depression, anxiety, boredom, despondency, irritability, disappointment, and frustration. These are all indicators that it is time to reflect upon what has changed. Remember what you learned and return to the basics. You're worth it.

Does this fit anymore?

Another way to maintain the new you is to periodically ask yourself, "Does this fit anymore." The word 'this' can stand for about anything.

Does your job fit with what you want anymore? How about your circle of friends, your community engagements, your political endeavors, even your hobbies and choices of recreation? Consider everything. Many of us live with our eyes closed. We ignore what we really need in life. Instead, we can strive toward living in conscious awareness. Self-awareness is the key to staying on track, continuing to live the life we want and need. Engaging in the regular practice of self-evaluation is not only curative, it is healing.

You might be amazed at how many things no longer fit with the way you want your life to be. You may need to make changes. Relationships might end. New ones begin. You may be inspired to change careers, go back to school, take time off and travel, mend broken friendships, and/or pursue a dream or desire. In any case, do not be surprised if you find yourself discarding many attachments of the old self. Do not panic. You will be alright. You are making room for the new. Sometimes giving up attachments (the things we cling to) can cause feelings of vulnerability and fear. Try not to let this stop you. If you experience anxiety, simply pause and reassure yourself you are heading toward a bright and beautiful future. You are working toward becoming who you have always wanted to be!

The journey is a process of discovery

Another important concept to keep in mind is the journey is a process of discovery; we will continue learning as long as we live. The new you will continue to evolve and change. Our best selves are not stagnant. We continue to assimilate and accommodate with new information and experiences through which we grow and mature. The process of evolving along the journey is filled with self-discovery, personal and spiritual growth, even transcendence and change. We will continue to learn every day of our lives. We grow at an even higher pace when we remain open to life's many lessons. We are enlightened.

We return again to the expression "It is the journey, not the destination." These ancient words of wisdom are especially applicable to human change. You may become frustrated in your future at times.

You might not feel like you are as far along as you would like to be. Relax. Trust the process. You are becoming. The most beautiful works of art have taken years to create. Try to visualize yourself as a beautiful piece of art in progress. Be gentle. Be kind and loving. Treat yourself with compassion. You're almost there!

The Sky is the Limit

So now what? You have passed the point of no return and you are ready for the most thrilling ride imaginable, a life you have always wanted, a time for your hopes, dreams, desires…yourself. The sky is the limit, in fact beneath the entire sky there is no limit to what you can do! What are you feeling? Are you excited, scared, a little of both? It is common to experience a mixture of emotions (some of them conflicting). Think of how you have felt approaching the point of no return on a rollercoaster. Your heart may have been beating hard; you may have been filled with anticipation, anxiety, and thrill. You want to take that first plunge and you don't, both at the same time.

When you cross over to the "new me", it is also like passing the point of no return. Why return? We have learned so much. We have come so far. We have entered our best life and we want to continue making our journey the best it can be. We would like to continue being the best we can be. And there are no limits to our success, no boundaries except those we choose to maintain for our well-being. Open your mind to this new reality. Your life is limitless. The books you open and the future chapters you create through your gifts, talents, and works; no one can close. Strive to be all that you can be. The world needs it. You need it. And, you're worth it.

A New Outlook

You will have a new outlook. Everything will literally appear different. The power of human thought is incredible. We have changed our cognitive patterns. We are no longer as negative. We are enlightened, empowered, confident, and more positive. Our new outlook is a major part of our new self. Situations that used to seem insurmountable are now manageable. Experiences that used to cause us confusion and angst become clearer and comfortable. We are brilliant, precise, relaxed, and ready to be more joyful. We have been transformed.

Our new outlook helps us continue to navigate the unknown waters ahead. Life is a journey in faith. We never know exactly where we are headed or what to do. We form our lives by the choices and decisions we make. Some bring us nearer to our destiny, others push us away. We are not perfect. It is alright. It is the process of coming closer and falling away that adds depth and fiber to the journey. We can keep our eyes on the prize, our destiny or dreams or wishes (whatever resonates with you). Our new outlook will get us there, wherever it is we want to be. Just keep moving forward and do not lose faith. Your journey will be filled with beauty and grace. You will see.

New Behavior

And with a new outlook comes new behavior. We have outlined this formula in previous lessons. Our thoughts lead to feelings and both lead to behavior. Thoughts and feelings become our outlook. They make up our perceptions. So many things in this world are based on our perceptions. Everything we do and say is based on perception. In essence, our perceptions are our reality. Behavior is an extension of this formula. So as our outlook changes, so does our behavior. It follows suit.

What do you hope your behavior will look like some day? What are your ideals for yourself? Consider what you want the "new me" to look like in full fruition. You can even act as if, which means you can behave in the ways you have decided you want to behave, you can act as if you are the person you want to be. The formula also works backward. Your behavior can affect your feelings, which in turn can influence your thought processes. Sometimes we need to do what we know is best for us despite how we are feeling. We may be having an "off day" and simply need to continue putting one foot in front of the other toward our goals and ambitions. Or, it may be we need time out. Everyone needs time to rest and replenish.

You will happily discover positive changes in your behavior as you move through a future you believe in. We have entered a new journey and our lives can be as incredible as we make them. Embrace the new you. Take care of her. She needs you.

Lead your most incredible life

We are now ready to lead our most incredible life. Are you ready? If not, what's holding you back? Perhaps you need to return to some of the previous lessons and work through some more remnants of your past. Maybe you need to reread lesson fourteen on self-confidence. Or perhaps you need to do some soul searching. What are you afraid of? Fear is what generally holds us back. Search deeply, openly, honestly. Be true to yourself. Honor your soul. What are you feeling? What do you need to do before you can move forward?

The expressive arts provide wonderful tools that can help you soul search. Writing, dancing, music, painting, drawing, and other free forms of art can help you access your subconscious and bring it to consciousness, where you can begin to discover your hidden emotions. Whatever you uncover let it be. Deal with your entire self. Embrace your yin and yang, your light and darkness, your beauty and raw emotion. Prepare to live the most incredible life you can, a world beyond your wildest dreams. We are embarking on the outskirts of a new reality, a journey filled with light, love, and happiness.

Self-love brings us joy. We are going to dedicate the final lessons to this topic for joy is the light of the world; it is what lights our hearts, minds, and spirits with the gifts of love and the feelings of abundance and grace. We deserve these gifts. We have earned our feelings. No one can take them away, not unless we let them. So here we go. It is time. We see the point of no return. Our hearts are beating. We are thrilled and we should be. We are crossing the threshold of the ride of our lives! Our journeys are meant for us to experience joy. We accept this. We embrace it. We love it!

YOU ARE WORTH IT

Reflections

OLD ME, NEW ME

YOU ARE WORTH IT

OLD ME, NEW ME

YOU ARE WORTH IT

Section Four
Joy

22

Fall in Love with yourself

Hopefully, the lessons in this book are helping you discover self-love. You are precious and beautiful. You are worthy and incredible. You are sexy, intelligent, elegant, and creative. Now, it is time to fall in love, not with someone else, but with you. Consider this whole lesson a love letter written just for you. It is filled with suggestions on how to create the love story of your life …with yourself. And believe me, it is worth it! A personal love affair is one of the most effective ways to create sustaining joy in your life.

I had a dream a few years back, shortly after my kids grew up and moved out on their own. When I first awoke, all I could remember was picking up a small child and hugging her. She wore a dress and had blonde hair and pony tails. I continued to vividly feel how good it felt to hug her well into the morning. My vision of the child remained so clear that I did some dream work to analyze its meaning. Dream work is very powerful, informative, and healing. We can learn a lot about ourselves, especially our unconscious thoughts and desires by analyzing and reflecting upon our dreams.

After reflecting for a while, I realized that I was both the adult and the child in my dream. I was picking myself up and embracing my inner child. The child in my dream looked just like I did when I was little. My mom always put me in a dress and fixed my hair in pony tails. My body filled with goose bumps as I began to realize the latent meaning of the dream. I had spent over twenty years caring for my children, raising them, caring for them, supporting them, and nurturing them. It was now time for me to look at caring for my needs. The dream was to help me prepare to embrace myself.

Let's complete an exercise in guided imagery based on this dream. Think of yourself for a moment as a little girl. Picture yourself when you were about two or three. Now visualize picking yourself up, as if you are embracing your inner child. Prepare to love yourself…completely, fully, wholly. If you have children, imagine loving yourself as much as you love your kids. Wow. That's a lot! This image becomes a perfect prelude to discovering the beauty and depths of self-love. Now, let's look at some simple strategies to help this love grow.

Let go of your fear of abandonment

One of the first steps in falling in love with yourself is to let go of fear of abandonment. Some of us are dependent on relationships. We become attached to others mentally, physically, psychologically, or perhaps spiritually. We may be afraid to be alone. Yet we are in danger of losing our precious connection to ourselves when we are insecurely attached to others. When we learn to be content on our own our relationships become beautiful extensions of who we are. We do not need to surrender all of our energy in them or to them.

We are free to fall in love with ourselves when we are not enmeshed with others. We can fall deeper into the arms of beauty and self-love as we dare to stand on our own. We do not have to be afraid. It is alright to be alone, in fact, solitude brings sweet serenity. Instead of feeling abandoned, we can be empowered! We can embrace ourselves like the child in our visualization and offer ourselves comfort, security, support, love, courage, kindness, guidance, and joy. We are in the best place to care for ourselves; after all, we are always right by our side.

FALL IN LOVE WITH YOURSELF

Embrace Intimacy

Embrace self- intimacy. Embrace yourself. Hold yourself with care and compassion. Fill your inner landscape with caring thoughts. Self-love is a frame of mind that will help you be gracious and kind to yourself. It is a psychological position rooted in your heart and soul. Pause and feel the inner sanctuary of love. We all have a sacred place deep within from which love pours freely through our spirit. Harness this energy and feel its presence. Allow it to move within. Let it rapture you.

We can learn to be intimate with ourselves. It may feel unnatural at first. You may be accustomed to caring for others, especially if you are a wife, companion, or mother. But now, it is time to turn our attention and affection inward. Nurture yourself. Love yourself. Be intimate with yourself. Give yourself a massage from head to toe. Take a hot bubble bath. Make love to yourself. It is not shameful, it is liberating. We can please ourselves. It is fulfilling and satisfying. Loving ourselves brings ecstatic joy.

Pamper yourself

Another way to fall deeply into this liberating love affair is to pamper yourself. Treat yourself to personal services that are designed with your beauty, comfort, and healing in mind. Full body massages are wonderful for relieving stress, tension, soreness, and providing deep muscle relaxation. A day at the beauty spa is another great way to pamper yourself. Enjoy a facial, pedicure, get your nails and hair done, or take advantage of the many soothing, replenishing, renewing, and revitalizing treatments available for your hair, skin, nails, muscles, etc. Invest in your health and beauty. Shower yourself with love. You're worth it.

If you are on a limited budget, there are still many ways to pamper yourself at little cost. You can find a soothing liquid soap of luxurious lathering and scent. Take a warm bath and exfoliate your body from head to toe. You can use a loofa or exfoliating towel. Take your time. Appreciate yourself. Nurture your skin. Enjoy. You can also take a steam in your bathroom. Shut the door tight and block the opening beneath the door with a towel. Run the shower as hot as you can with the shower doors open. The room will quickly fill up with steam until it becomes a sauna. Sit down and enjoy your private, little steam room. It is good for your skin, lungs, muscles, and spirit. Native Americans experience the energy of spirituality in sweat lodges. The steam is soothing and healing to the spirit.

Other inexpensive methods for pampering yourself are painting your nails, giving yourself a pedicure, your hair a hot oil treatment, applying a restorative face mask, even going through your jewelry box and restoring and polishing pieces of old jewelry so you can wear them again. Dig through your makeup and experiment with colors you do not wear very often. One last idea is to try different hair styles in the mirror. You can do small things to pamper yourself around your home. Be creative and resourceful. You will be amazed at how many ways you can pamper yourself without spending a dime.

Focus on loving thoughts

We have already talked about the importance of positive thinking and self-affirmation. Hopefully, you have been practicing cognitive re-structuring, changing negative thoughts to more positive and rewarding patterns of thinking. Now, we are ready to change our inner dialogue. We can begin consciously carrying loving thoughts about ourselves throughout the day; being compassionate, kind, and encouraging to ourselves. We can support ourselves as we have supported other people in our past. We have a frame of reference. We know how to be loving and kind. We now turn our compassion inward and focus our regard for ourselves in a way that is gentle, affirming, validating, and edifying.

Consider being in a relationship with someone else. It can hardly be a success if you are being critical, judgmental, or harsh. If you put the other person down, call them names, and deliver insults the result is to push them away. Walls come between you. It can hardly be a love affair. The same applies to your relationship with yourself. To have the love affair you deserve, you can speak to yourself kindly and with encouragement. You can even sing to yourself in love songs. Chant loving mantras. Remember the affirmations you wrote down in lesson thirteen. Turn them into mantras and say them when you are feeling challenged or discouraged. Communicate with yourself in loving ways. Make your inner journey a sweet serenade.

Focusing on loving thoughts keeps you firmly rooted in joy. You can appreciate yourself, your journey, and your life. Life is so much happier, the journey so much brighter, and you can be more fulfilled and joyful when you focus your time and attention on love. Love conquers all hardships. It relieves stress and anxiety. It blesses us with peace and serenity.

A Romantic night alone

Another loving thing you can do for yourself is to have a quiet, peaceful, romantic night alone, just with you. You can listen to soft music, light candles; put out freshly cut flowers, wear a silky robe, and watch your favorite movie classic. You can eat gourmet chocolate, drink fine wine or cappuccino, even order in dinner. Have an intimate, romantic date with yourself. Make it special. Treat yourself like a queen. Engage in affection. Bask in self-love. Consider it your own private evening to enjoy.

You can also take yourself out on a date. Plan your dream date. Think of your favorite restaurant, coffee shop, theatre, or playhouse. Where do you want to go? What do you want to do? It is completely up to you; after all, it is your date! Spend some time making it all that it can be. Pay attention to every detail. Find a quaint table for one in a quiet corner of your favorite, gourmet restaurant. Purchase a balcony ticket to an opera, ballet, or play you have wanted to see. Afterwards, treat yourself to a nightcap. Perhaps a fine desert or a luxurious cup of coco would be the perfect finish to a wonderful evening just with you. Splurge. Remember, you are worth it.

Take a long walk on the beach

Another simple way to express self-love is to take a walk on the beach. It is one of the most invigorating, relaxing, and rewarding activities you can enjoy. I have taken long walks along the beach since I was a young girl. Like sailing, I have always loved the beach. Walking upon the sand, I feel like a tiny, precious grain in God's majestic creation. I look across the sea or ocean and the vastness of this great universe encapsulates my spirit and lifts my soul. My favorite sea is the Caribbean. My heart rushes in and out with every wave that laps the shore before me. My footsteps are laced in the creamy white sand that shelters crystal clear waters, variegated in deep blue, sheer aqua, pinks, and purple. I am swept away.

Another fantastic beach to walk is on the north shore of Oahu, Hawaii. The tide is so high that the waves crash with great strength and beauty against a garden of coral shoreline. The ocean waves tumble fiercely to the shore. The air is filled with the constant sound of crashing waves. The ocean rushes in with no mercy. It is exciting and exhilarating. It feels as if the energy of the universe converges here. It is an awesome experience to walk the beach and enjoy the natural chaos of the earth. It is captivating and thrilling.

Try it sometime. Take a long walk on the beach barefoot and just stroll for a whole morning, afternoon, or evening through the waves and sand. You will fall in love. In love with nature, the universe, and yourself. Be mesmerized by the great beauty and treasures that surround you. You will be enchanted. You will be soothed. You will be renewed.

Balance your love

No matter what you do, balance your love. Women have much love to give. No matter how deeply or madly we fall in love with ourselves, we still need relationships. Most of us want the companionship of a partner in life. We can remember to keep our balance. It is easy to jump into other relationships and forget about self-care. Hopefully, self-love has become the core of your being, your center, the essence of who you are. Give your personal love affair first place in your life and all other relationships you encounter will be enriched. To thy own self be true.

FALL IN LOVE WITH YOURSELF

Balancing your love balances your life. It creates wholeness and harmony for you and those around you. It's contagious. The people you encounter along the journey will want what you have. They will hope to discover your secrets. Joy will radiate from your spirit and into the space surrounding you. People will want your energy. They will want to share your joy. It is the true miracle of beauty. It radiates most fully from within.

Make a commitment today to balance. Choose the journey of wholeness, harmony, and love. Fall in love with yourself. This is the beginning of many miracles for you and your future. Come on. Don't be shy. Do not be embarrassed. Pick yourself up. Embrace yourself. Love yourself like the beautiful, tender, precious child you are. You are a child of God. We are all precious children of a master creator. He loves every part of us, good and bad, weak and strong. We can love ourselves unconditionally as well. It is time. The love affair of a lifetime is before us. The time has come to engage.

YOU ARE WORTH IT

Reflections

FALL IN LOVE WITH YOURSELF

YOU ARE WORTH IT

FALL IN LOVE WITH YOURSELF

YOU ARE WORTH IT

23

Enjoy Yourself

One of the most basic ways to experience joy is to enjoy yourself. Make time to play and have fun. We live in a hard-working society. Our work ethic is admirable, but it can also be exhausting. Women are especially vulnerable to societal pressures. We have multiple responsibilities. Since the liberation movement began, we have been expected to raise families, care for households, and hold successful careers. These pressures make it even more important to take the time to enjoy ourselves. Life is short and at the same time, the journey can seem long and difficult. We need some reprieve. We need joy!

This lesson will look at some simple ways to have fun and enjoy life. Perhaps you already get a sufficient amount of recreation time. That is great. If not, don't worry. It will not take long for you to adapt and create space in your life for pleasure and entertainment. Some simple suggestions may be just enough to get started. Hopefully, you will continue to discover more activities that make you happy as you move forward along the journey. Your life does not have to be dull or boring. The journey is not meant to be arduous. Contrarily, we are meant to experience happiness and joy. Our journeys can be joyous, and free.

Have fun

Let's begin by experimenting with some simple strategies for having fun. Try these ideas in the near future. They are all basic forms of play. Take off your shoes and run barefoot. Or, take a stroll in the grass. Walk in the rain. Leave your umbrella at home and feel the rain on your body and face. Play Frisbee, beach ball, volley ball, hula hoop, or crochet. Do something different. Build a sand tray. Swing, slide, go rock climbing or ice skating. Take a swim. Simple activities can relieve stress. Playing helps you feel young. It will revitalize you.

Plenty of venues exist for entertainment. You cannot help but enjoy yourself when you are having fun. The point is let go and enjoy. Leave worry and reservation behind. Kick up your heels, skip, jump, run…whatever you feel like. Do not hold anything back. The best way to have fun is to just go for it. Dive in! It is worth it.

Vacation

Another great way for enjoyment was mentioned in lesson four. Go somewhere to get away. Take a vacation. Everyone needs a break. Sometimes it is easier to let go and relax when you go somewhere else for a while, if only for a few days. Vacations are replenishing. You can be refreshed and renewed and thereby strengthened. You will be more effective when you return. Most importantly, you can have a whole lot of fun while you are gone.

Try new places and experience different cultures. If you have the funds to travel, visit other countries. Instead of staying at popular resorts, book a room near the town square or at least where the villagers or residents live. Immerse yourself in their lifestyle. Eat their food, listen to their music, and experience their folklore and tradition. This is one of the best ways to enrich your life and your journey. Explore new things. Enjoy unique and authentic experiences. Enjoy diversity. Enjoy yourself.

Spend time with people who make you happy

Another way to enjoy yourself is to spend time with people who make you happy. Family and friends brighten the journey. They appreciate our feelings, ideas, dreams, and goals. Not everyone we run across in life is encouraging; in fact there are even family members who may be critical, judgmental, and discouraging. We need to protect ourselves from negativity. We do not have to spend time with those who bring us down. We have choices in life. Spend time with those who lift your spirits and try to limit your contact with those who weigh you down. Do not let anyone steal your enjoyment.

To help us understand why people influence us so much, let's return to our ongoing analysis of energy. People exchange energy with one another. We have discussed this phenomenon in earlier lessons. Our energies combine when we are near others, especially for extended periods of time. We literally absorb the energy expelled by others, and they absorb our energy. On a metaphysical level, we are all part of the universe and we exchange atoms with everything around us: nature, people, our geography, and environment…every part of the earth. When we invest time with people who radiate positive, loving energy; we become more joyful and encouraged. When we spend our time with those who are negative and discouraging, we become despondent and depressed.

The energy we exchange with others is further perpetuated by our neurochemical design. We each possess mirror neurons, which function to perceive and mimic the feelings, emotions, reactions, and behaviors of others. (Siegel, 2010) We are designed in part to mirror the perceptions and responses of other people. It is powerful. It affects our well-being. We need to be careful in choosing our company. Despite how hard we may try to resist negativity or even abuse, we are hardwired to be affected. Spend time with people who make you happy. Surround yourself with caring, encouraging, loving, kind, and generous people. It is guaranteed to make your journey and life more joyful.

Spend time with the ones you love

By far one of the best ways to enjoy life is to spend time with the ones you love. We do not always take the time to enjoy our friends and family, even our loved ones. We get busy. We may have numerous responsibilities or competing interests. We get wrapped up in our plans and goals and before we know it, we are giving our loved ones what little is left of our time. You might work the late shift and get home after everyone is in bed for the night. Or, you might work a couple of jobs trying to keep the family afloat (especially if you are a single parent). Perhaps you run a small business on the side of your full time career. We can think of many examples of becoming too busy to spend precious time with the ones we love. If you are one in this growing population: stop…or at least slow down. Consider what is most important in your life. Reflect upon who is most important to you.

We need love. Love is the highest form of joy in the universe. Love empowers, it encourages and invigorates. Love heals. Sharing our love with others is the greatest gift we can experience on this earth. Give your time and attention to those you love. Let them each know how much you care. Leave no stone unturned. Show everyone you love just how much they mean to you. Be receptive to what they have to give. Sit with them. Be still with them. Be silent together. Have fun. Laugh. Sing and dance together. Whatever!

Our loved ones need us. We need them. Treasure your time together. You never know how long it will last.

Limit your work week

Another suggestion for enjoying yourself is to limit your work week to forty hours if you can, which includes the work you bring home. We live in a highly motivated society involving work standards and norms. Many Americans are accustomed to working over forty hours per week with only two weeks of vacation per year. Many have only one week of vacation and work fifty to sixty hours per week. It is common for people to work two or more jobs in these hard economic times. While in other countries like Italy, people barely work forty hours per week and take around one month vacation per year.

Experts advise a forty hour work week is a good average. Some situations cannot be changed, but there are solutions to accommodate a comfortable work schedule, which allows sufficient time to enjoy life. Consider your spending. Where can you reduce expenses? Many discover they can cut their spending by at least 30% if they commit to manage the budget. You can work fewer hours and still get by. Give yourself a break. You will be amazed at how little it takes to "really" get by. We think we need a lot more than we actually do in this society, which is one of the biggest reasons we work so hard.

Balancing work and relaxation leads to enjoyment. How much have you been working? Maybe you have not even thought to add up the hours of your schedule. If you discover you are well over forty hours per week ask yourself the following question, "What am I gaining?" Perhaps you have a short-term strategic goal in mind. Or maybe you have simply fallen into a pattern of overworking. These patterns can be dangerous. They become ruts before we know it. Too much work can steal our joy, or at least crowd it out. Take care of yourself. Try not to overwork. It is not worth it.

Explore new hobbies

Another great way to enjoy your life is to explore new hobbies. Let's return to the discussion we began in lesson eight on experimenting with new activities. Try to have fun in fresh and exciting ways. Challenge yourself to do things you have never done before. Sailing is one of my favorite hobbies. If you have never tried it, definitely do. It is a great way to enjoy nature and relax, but it also requires strength, coordination, and strategizing. It is both exhilarating and soothing. It provides the perfect mix of challenge and serenity.

We also mentioned the expressive arts, which are great hobbies. Painting, music, dance, pottery, theatre, drama, poetry, etc… Put up a large easel in a corner of your home, apartment, or office. Experiment with oil, water colors, chalk, and colored pencils. Purchase a second hand instrument from a flea market or pawn shop. Look up the chords to some of your favorite songs on the internet and play them for fun. Speaking of music, remember interpretive dancing. Let your body flow naturally with whatever is playing on the radio. Or, choose a CD that fits your mood and dance in a way that expresses your emotions.

Another wonderful hobby that is both relaxing and challenging is Pilates. It is especially good for middle aged women in that it strengthens and tones the body's core. I include it again here because it is so invigorating. It provides serenity, tranquility, peace, awareness, and enjoyment. It is a hobby that is good for your spirit. The movements encourage you to connect with your mind, body, and soul. It is great for centering in wholeness and harmony.

Hobbies are relaxing and enjoyable. It is so important to enjoy yourself. Enjoyment creates wholeness and harmony in your life. It enriches the journey.

Get lost for a day

Another way to discover enjoyment is to get lost for a day. Turn off the ring tone on your mobile and leave all your worries and cares behind. Take a friend or go alone. Have fun by disappearing in something you love. Not sure what you can do for a day? Here are some ideas to brainstorm some simple things you can do.

If you like antiques go antiquing for the day. Many towns have antique shops and each one is packed with unique pieces of history, beauty, and art. You can spend hours sorting through treasures like ornate statues, finely embroidered linens, elegant dishes, tea sets, and beautiful porcelain dolls. You will be lost in enjoyment before you know it. Antique stores are full of interesting treasures. Travel from one to another and before you know it, you will have completed a full day of pure fun and delight.

Another way to get lost is to frequent quaint old book stores. Reading is a great way to escape the pressures and concerns of life. It is relaxing and enjoyable. Browsing old book stores is especially exciting because there are a wide variety of books, authors, subjects, and material. You can spend hours in a single store. Find a few books you are interested in and sit down with a latte or chi. Kick back and read. It is tranquil and stimulating. Take your time. There is no hurry. When you finish at one bookstore head to the next one on your list, or search your GPS if you are not sure where to go next. You can easily get lost for an entire day in this simple form of enjoyment.

Another exciting way to get lost involves mini-travel. Many harbors and bays have water taxi services that will take you from shop to shop where you can discover all sorts of trinkets and treasures. An example of this is the Inner Harbor in Baltimore. Numerous specialty shops surround this unique inlet of water. You can taxi around the harbor from place to place. It is fun to see the stark nuances of each shop. They are all uniquely designed and specialize in authentic lines of merchandise. Many of the items are hand crafted. You will be pleased at all there is to discover. Before you know it, the sun will be setting on the harbor!

Another great place to get lost shopping for the day is the old market. Many of the downtown areas in major cities have an old market. You can find items like fine second hand jewelry, gypsy style clothing, antique purses, fancy hats, designer shoes, and beautifully inscribed statues and sculptures. They also have authentic restaurants and gourmet coffee shops with darling street tables for outdoor dining. Many are nestled in the midst of lattices of hanging vines and flower baskets. Take a carriage ride to complete a perfect day. Many of the old markets have horse drawn carriages. Enjoy the ambiance!

But no matter how you choose to get lost for the day, leave all your troubles behind. They will be there when you get back and hopefully, they will no longer seem like such a big deal. Escape, get lost, and enjoy. You deserve it. You need time and space to relax and be unburdened. Try it at least once. Plan a day of pure and simple enjoyment. Run away with yourself. Disappear in fun! You are definitely worth it.

Be Creative

Creative expression is a beautiful way to find enjoyment. Creativity delights the soul. It is the gateway to heaven. The expressive arts are healing, empowering, and transforming. We have discussed many of these already: painting, writing, sculpting, dancing, or playing an instrument. Sand art is another special way to be creative. It is used in therapy to promote self-discovery, healing, and change. Creativity not only leads to enjoyment; it also leads to peace of mind. It is soothing and powerful.

We all have creative ability. We can tap into our natural abilities and discover the joy of expressing our gifts and talents. The best part is we make the world a more beautiful place through our creative energies. Creativity is an expression of love. It is a way for us to share our love with the universe. It helps us grow in self-love. Do not stifle your creative side. Embrace this precious part of who you are. Let your creativity shine. Share your gifts with a world in need: in need of more color, spontaneity, peace, and joy. It is worth the effort. You will enjoy happiness and serenity.

Delight in Nature

Another great way to find enjoyment is to delight in nature. In nature, we are unencumbered and free. Spending time in nature unravels worry, stress, and discouragement. It is like magic. You will notice the abundance of God's tiny miracles when you spend time outdoors. He impeccably cares for the entire universe from the smallest sparrow to the tiniest flower in the field. We are part of this great universe. We are also cared for in perfect rhythm and harmony.

We can enjoy ourselves and have fun in nature. Walk through the forest. Take a run in the rain. Pick flowers and chase butterflies. We can also relax and replenish in the great outdoors. Nature is simple and pure. It brings out the most vulnerable and sacred parts of the inner self. Our energy is renewed as we let our spirit free and absorb our surroundings. Delight in nature regularly. Make it a routine. Get outside and soak in the sun, trees, clouds, birds, open fields, ocean, and mountains. Whatever gifts are around you, by all means enjoy them! It is a simple way to joy.

Giggle and Laugh

No matter what you choose to do for enjoyment, do not forget to giggle and laugh. Laughter is healing and encouraging. It lifts the spirit. The old saying "laughter is good medicine" is true. Even just smiling

ENJOY YOURSELF

will elevate your mood. Try it. The next time you are feeling blue, simply smile. This concept follows from our previous discussion of how behavior can impact feelings, which in turn influences the thought processes. A simple smile, giggle, or laugh can turn our hearts from negative to positive very quickly. It is truly amazing.

So have fun. Enjoy yourself! Laugh, smile, play, explore new hobbies, take a vacation, and spend time with those you love. Or simply get lost for a day shopping or delighting in nature. Whatever you do, try not to work too hard. Make time for you. You can be your own best friend. Learn to appreciate yourself and your free time. Live it up! You are worth it.

Siegel, Daniel J. (2010). *The Mindful Therapist, A Clinician's Guide to Mindsight and Neural Integration*: WW Norton and Company, New York, NY

ENJOY YOURSELF

Reflections

YOU ARE WORTH IT

ENJOY YOURSELF

YOU ARE WORTH IT

ENJOY YOURSELF

24

Self- Satisfaction

This lesson is about learning to be satisfied. It involves peace, contentment, love, satisfaction, wellness, wholeness, and harmony, which are all interconnected. The goal of this book has been to help you find the gift of true satisfaction with yourself; to be comfortable and content with who you are and where your journey is headed. My hope is that you are beginning to enter a new season- a time that is incredible and exciting, rewarding and joyous. Self-satisfaction is a major part of this process for without it, we cannot be truly happy. We are not fully free.

The term self-satisfaction is often misunderstood. Some think this topic is self-gratifying or even selfish. So before we begin, let's look at the difference between selfishness and self-love. It is important especially for women to learn to care for the "self". We need self-love. Offering kindness and compassion to ourselves leads to self-satisfaction. These things are not selfish; rather they are nurturing and necessary. It does not mean we disregard the feelings of others, and yet we are sure to take our own feelings into consideration when making decisions and living our lives. It is living the philosophy "You're worth it".

Learning to be satisfied including making choices that lead to self-satisfaction is a big part of self-love. We feel good when we are satisfied whether it is with life, our relationships, our appetite, our love life, or anything else we need or desire. Loving ourselves involves feeling good.

SELF-SATISFACTION

We have spent enough years in self-sacrifice. Some of us have even hurt ourselves. We have starved, binged, denied ourselves, or overindulged depending on the stressor. We have withheld joy and punished ourselves. We have held ourselves in bondage, away from the gifts of peace and joy. Well a new day is here. It is time to be happy. It is our season to be joyful and satisfied.

Please yourself

One of the best skills you can learn in life is to please yourself. Take a special interest in yourself. Invest in your happiness. Perhaps you may have gone to great lengths in the past to please others. Women are caretakers. We are accustomed to satisfying the needs of others. Now, the time has come to begin considering your own needs. We can please ourselves. It's alright. It is not selfishness; it is self-care. It is self- nourishment. It is the actuation of self-love.

One of the advantages of learning to please ourselves is we do not need to rely on others to make us happy. We can be responsible for our own happiness. We are free in life. We have choices. We are not victims. Some people wait for others to help them be happy, or even expect others to make them happy. This is a formula for failure. It doesn't work. We can take happiness into our own hands. We know what we want and need better than anyone else. How about creating our own happiness? We can call a friend when we are lonely, go places and do things even if no one else wants to, and be happy and joyful even when those around us are disgruntled or angry. Our emotions are independent. We can own our journey including the outcomes.

Pleasing yourself involves not expecting others to satisfy your needs. Some of us are passive. We sit back and expect others to understand us, love us, protect and care for us, and support us. Maybe we have not discovered how liberating and satisfying it is to understand ourselves the way we need to be understood, to love ourselves the way we need to be loved, to protect and care for ourselves the way we need to be protected and cared for, and to support ourselves in ways we need to be supported. We can intentionally live a life that satisfies our deepest needs. We can choose a journey of joy and all that comes with it. We can build our lives around the valuable women we are.

Go after what you want

If you want something, go after it. Don't just wait for it to come to you. Granted there are times when we need to be patient, but that doesn't mean we cannot work toward our goals in the meantime. What are some things you have wanted over the past year? Maybe you have wanted a new car or home or job? Perhaps you have wanted more intrinsic gifts such as serenity, joy, or peace of mind. Maybe you need a miracle? You could be praying for better health, financial stability, or the restoration of a broken relationship. Whatever it is that you want, go for it! Great things do not usually come easy. We can do the footwork to make things happen. Then, we can believe in the best. We can have hope for our future!

Going after what we want eventually leads to self-satisfaction. So many women do not have the courage to pursue their longings and desires. We may not think we deserve to be happy. We might doubt that we can be successful. Or, maybe we are just too busy to consider our needs. Whatever our reasons, we can begin going after what we want. We can work toward all we hope for. We are so precious, caring, intelligent, inspired, resourceful, creative, and equipped to make a difference in this world. We can follow our aspirations. We can journey in our passion. It is our destiny. It is our greatest gift.

Pursue your interests

Pursuing your interests is another suggestion that naturally follows suit. Have you ever found yourself wanting to do something different or try something new, but you could not find the time or motivation? Or, is there somebody you have always wanted to become, but questioned your talent and ability? Doubt and reluctance lead to despondency, discouragement, and dissatisfaction. Instead, we can pursue our interests with faith and vigor. This not only leads to a satisfying journey, it leads to an incredibly amazing life. We can be satisfied beyond belief.

SELF-SATISFACTION

What are some of the things you are interested in? Let's pause and reflect upon this question for a moment. Now, challenge yourself further. What interests are you currently pursuing? Write them down. Hopefully, you discover there are already some interests you are pursuing in your life. Maybe you enjoy your career, your circle of friends, a love affair, your family, or special hobbies. Perhaps you enjoy your weekend activities, community engagements, or other social involvement. But if you look at your notes on the reflection pages and discover that you are not pursuing anything of interest; thoughtfully consider change. You are meant to be happy. You are created to be satisfied and whole.

Search your heart and discover your desires. Pursue your interests. Life is too short to waste time doing things you do not enjoy. Our interests can even lead us to our life purpose. Pursuing our desires is an avenue to destiny. We can reach out it amazing ways. We can share our love with others and affect the world. This leads to the ultimate form of self-satisfaction. We can be satisfied with ourselves, God, the universe, our relationships, and our circumstances. We learn the gift of acceptance. We accept the journey. We accept ourselves.

Chase your dreams

Chasing your dreams is another way to create satisfaction in your life. We all have seeded desires in our hearts. Each one of us has precious hopes and dreams. We listed these in lesson nineteen. Now, it's time to chase our dreams and desires. Literally run after them. No one else will do this for you. It is up to you.

Don't let anything stand in your way. Navigate. You are resourceful. If you want something bad enough, you can make it happen. It may require change or sacrifice, but what are you sacrificing really? According to an inspiring book titled *A Course in Miracles*, sacrifice is often merely an illusion. Take an honest look at what you might be "giving up" to follow your heart. Are you giving up income and stability, continuity, or predictability? How important are these things in your life? Or, are you giving up routine, boredom, and stress? Many times if we search beneath what we think we are sacrificing, we find we are not sacrificing at all; in fact, we may be gaining peace and satisfaction. After all, there is more to life than money.

Chase your dreams and you can be satisfied beyond belief. Lay down your guard. Explore. Discover. Live! You are worth it.

If it is uncomfortable, quit it

It is a misnomer to think we must continue to do things even if they are uncomfortable. If you discover something is a struggle for you, consider quitting it. We do not have to continue doing things that hurt us physically, emotionally, psychologically, or spiritually. The first is probably the most obvious. You might wear high heels to look pretty, but by the end of the day your feet are aching. Quit it. Purchase lower heels or try squared toe shoes. Or maybe your job involves lifting or standing long hours and your body is developing aches and pains. You do not have to suffer. What other opportunities might be available? Explore your options. The world is filled with opportunity.

You may be in a relationship that is causing you pain. Emotional, psychological, and spiritual hurt can be the most detrimental to us. Or, perhaps you are causing yourself grief. You can quit this too. Sometimes we need to seek help, but there are solutions. We just need to reach for them. We have the power to break negative cycles in our lives.

You do not have to live one more day in misery. The time has come to rid your life of pain and sorrow. Leave discomfort behind once and for all. Sure, life is full of challenges. We will continue to encounter difficult situations; that is part of the journey. There are also times when we need to endure to get where we want to be in life. We may choose to make a temporary sacrifice for a greater good. The point is we no longer create difficulty for ourselves by remaining in discomfort. Instead, we can be comfortable. We can live in ways that promote peace and satisfaction, happiness and joy. It is our hope and honor. It can be our journey.

Small ways to create satisfaction

We can create satisfaction in our lives in small ways too. In fact, sometimes the smallest things make us the happiest. Consider the

SELF-SATISFACTION

following ideas as tiny gestures to show yourself how much you care.

Treat yourself to a nice dinner at home. Take the time to prepare and serve your food with love. Make your favorite recipe or try something new that you have wanted to try. Serve yourself attractively arranged, richly flavored, colorful foods. Add creative garnishes to your dinner. One idea is to make a flower out of fruit by cutting a peach or strawberry into slices that look like petals. Simply arrange them in a circle and put the pit of the fruit in the center of the flower. You can also add a vegetable garnish by arranging your favorite vegetable on the side in a creative way. The idea is to prepare a meal with care and kindness. Sit down to a nice table setting. Use your best table cloth. Relax and take the time to enjoy your food.

Another small way to find satisfaction is to create a media library for yourself including all your favorite music. Music soothes the soul. It lifts the spirits and helps us relax. Build a library of your favorite albums on your laptop computer, IPOD, IPAD, or other device. You will be able to listen to your favorite songs whenever you want. Better yet, take your music library to the pool, a quiet room, out on the deck or patio, beside the fireplace- anywhere you will be able to relax and enjoy.

Other small ways to add satisfaction to your life can be found back in lessons twenty and twenty two (and throughout this book.) Hopefully you will begin discovering your own unique ways to become more satisfied in your journey. Keep in mind; we do not need big things to make us happy. Some of the best of life's gifts are the tiniest miracles. So go ahead, seek satisfaction in small and practical ways. It is worth it.

Check in with your feelings

A final suggestion is to periodically check in with your feelings. Ask yourself the questions, "How do I feel?" and "Am I satisfied?" Then, sincerely seek the answers deep within. Feelings can be a gauge to help us take care of ourselves and if necessary, chart a new course for the future. We can regularly "check in" and process our feelings. This helps us stay centered. We can stay in touch with our core. We are connected and congruent in this way. Our journeys are filled with wholeness and harmony when we recognize, claim, and deal with our feelings along the way. Working through emotions can be difficult, but it ultimately leads to joy.

You might not be accustomed to exploring your feelings. You may not even allow your feelings to surface. Perhaps you run from them or bury them. You might escape. Many women share this story. It is not easy at first to "feel" your feelings, especially the painful ones. But like so many other challenges, practice makes it easier. Get more familiar with your inner self. Experience your feelings. Reach deep inside and stay with them as long as you need to. Reflect. Ironically when we avoid our feelings, they do not go away. If we do not work through them, they linger and resonate. Begin checking in with yourself to acknowledge and process your emotions. You will discover it gets easier.

Begin seeking satisfaction in your life. It is intimately linked to joy. Satisfaction brings feelings of wholeness. Many women suffer from compartmentalization. Our inner landscapes are broken and divided. We hold love at arm's length all too often. We separate ourselves from our true feelings, our inner selves. We are finding the courage to change. We want peace and harmony. We need self-love. The only way to get there is to begin the journey. Begin finding satisfaction. Discover the beauty of self-love. You are worth it!!!

SELF-SATISFACTION

Reflections

YOU ARE WORTH IT

SELF-SATISFACTION

YOU ARE WORTH IT

SELF-SATISFACTION

25

Nourish your Soul

We have dedicated three lessons solely to the topic of nourishment. Nourishing your mind, body, and spirit are all critical components of health, wealth, wellness, and joy. And yet, increasing your level of joy also involves nourishing the soul. Some of the ideas in this lesson are similar to those in lesson twenty on the topic of nourishing your spirit. But this lesson will take you to an even deeper level. Your soul is your essence, the very core of who you are. It is where you shine the brightest. It is your connection to love and beauty. It is your passageway to peace.

Learning to nourish your soul takes time and practice. You can be conscious and attentive to its presence. This is done intentionally. We can increase our awareness of our essence, our inner being, the intimate place deep within from which wholeness and harmony flow. The more we consciously connect with our inner core, the stronger the connection becomes. It is similar to exercising with weights. Your muscles become stronger with repetition. Our soul connection also becomes stronger with repetition- quiet…tender moments spent in prayer, self-affirmation, communion, meditation, loving kindness, appreciation, and reflection. We can dedicate time each day to nourishing the soul. This lesson provides practical and effective ideas that can help you get started.

Live in reverence

One of the best ways to nourish the soul is to live in reverence. You might not be familiar with this concept. Living in reverence is simply living in awe. It is appreciating the infinite gifts of the universe, bowing in the arms of unconditional love, recognizing the abundance of mercy and grace, and seeing these gifts unfold within and around you. Living in reverence is having the knowledge that all is well, trusting in the abundance of the universe; and feeling the unconditional love available to each and every one of us in this world. We can stand with open arms before our higher power, the light of the universe, the creator of the heavens, and the healer of our hearts and say thank you- time and time again- for life is good.

Living in reverence not only nourishes the soul, it is our gateway to joy. We discover peace in the here and now. It is the feeling of utter joy we receive when we are living in gratitude. You might feel a mystical wave of relaxation pass over your body. Perhaps you notice the colors of the evening sky light up in vivid passion, or you pause before a busy day begins to appreciate the brilliant dawn. Maybe you catch the tears of a loved one, or hold the hand of someone who is hurting or troubled. These are all heavenly experiences. We can appreciate them in reverence. They nourish the soul.

Quiet Solitude

Another way to nourish your soul is to spend time in quiet solitude. Solitude is healing and replenishing. We all need time alone to ponder, reflect, relax, and recharge our battery. Let's return again to our analysis of energy. Our energy levels are slowly depleted as we work, face the responsibilities of everyday life, and take care of our families, children, homes, and jobs. We can regain our energy by meeting our *own* needs in quiet solitude. We can ask ourselves how we feel and what we need. We can search our souls for the truth within. Be still. Embrace serenity. Discover the peace and comfort of spending time alone.

Some women are afraid to be alone. We fear isolation. We are not unique. The fear of isolation is one of the greatest existential concerns of human nature. (Yalom, 1994). Deep down, we might be scared to rest in quiet solitude. We are accustomed to being busy, and we are usually in the company of others. Many are connected in a web of relationships, which may include a primary partnership, family, friendship, coworkers, and community. The thought of our ultimate aloneness may be frightening. After all, when all is said and done, who do we have? Who can we count on? Who is always by our side through thick and thin? The answers lie within. It is us. We can spend time in quiet solitude and become more comfortable with our ultimate aloneness. Our whole perspective becomes more secure here. Our vision becomes clearer, our hearts softer, and our souls nourished and enlightened. The miracle of change happens.

Solitude brings about the gifts of self-love, peace, serenity, and joy. We can grow in faith and determination. Feelings of wholeness and harmony grow as we create a space between us and the world. It is not a space to divide, but to breathe. We remain connected to the universe and grounded in our personal energy. The positive energy within us expands as we relax in quiet solitude. As we realize comfort in our aloneness -taking care of ourselves- our level of joy increases to overflowing.

Metta Practice

Another great way to nourish the soul is through metta practice. Most simply, metta is the process of affirming ourselves and embracing the world through positive internal dialogue. It includes softening your feelings and emotions and practicing giving others and yourself positive, affirming, loving, kind, and compassionate messages. It can involve meditation as in loving kindness meditation, or simply pausing throughout the day when feeling aggravated, restless, or stressed, and calming your spirit by taking a few deep breaths followed by thinking loving and kind messages. Metta encourages thinking kindly and compassionately about others and ourselves, and loving ourselves unconditionally. Some view metta practice as a form of prayer. In many ways it is like a never ending prayer, one we live out in our daily lives. It is simple, practical, and beautiful. It provides a constant source of nourishment. It is similar to meditation in that metta consists of letting go of stress and anxiety to fully embrace the beauty of the universe and ourselves. After regular metta practice, you will begin living in the gifts that are always surrounding you. Regular metta practice will change your outlook, perceptions, and consequently, your life. Your journey will become more joyful and brilliant than you can imagine.

Prayer and Meditation

I have heard it said that prayer is talking and meditation is listening. Both nourish the soul. We need to talk to our higher power. We can develop an intimate friendship with God, which includes casual conversation. We can pour our heart out. We are heard and understood. It feels good to release our thoughts, feelings, and emotions. Don't hold back. Share everything with your higher power. Disclose your deepest, darkest burdens. This is how we heal. It leads to freedom.

Meditation on the other hand is more like listening. It is clearing the mind so our higher power and the universe can affect us. Many of us are used to doing most of the talking. It might be a rarity for you to be quiet and still. But there is wisdom and power in silence. Try it. Be still and listen. Not to anything in particular and not for anything in particular. Just listen… Be attentive without expectation or judgment… without focus. Your soul will be nourished in the silence of surrender. Meditation energizes. It replenishes. It is the soul's link to peace and joy.

Read spiritual books

We already reviewed a simple way to nourish the soul, which is to read spiritual books. Devotionals and meditation guides provide daily nourishment. Many are designed with inspirational passages for each day of the year. Scripture is also nourishing. The psalms are especially soothing and relaxing. Another inspiring book that is nourishing and enlightening is *A Course in Miracles*. It is based on ancient scripture, and yet it reflects a new age view of love and forgiveness. It is an incredible book to study in increments. These all nourish the soul.

Other spiritual books that have great nourishing power are written by authors such as: Khalil Gibran, Marianne Williamson, Eckhart Tolle, Deepak Chopra, CS Lewis, Emily Dickinson, and Henry David

YOU ARE WORTH IT

Thoreau. Some of the best meditation guides are written by Melanie Beatty such as *The Language of Letting Go* and *Journey to the Heart*. I have written encouraging meditations in the books *A River of Hope, Seeds of the Heart,* and *Bits of Heaven*. Read or write your own meditations. Open yourself to inspiration and healing.

Reading spiritual books is a simple, inexpensive, and easy way to nourish your soul each day. Words have the power to stroke your inner landscape, creating harmony and peace for your inner dialogue. Reading inspirational books can clarify our thoughts and restore the balance of our emotions. Explore Amazon and order a meditation guide, or dig out the ones you stuffed in your closet a while ago. Set them in a place where you will see them every day. Decorate the space around them. Make it special. This can be a gentle and special reminder to read a little each day. After all, you're worth it.

Spend time outdoors

The suggestion to spend time outdoors has come up in many lessons, but it is especially important when it comes to nourishing the soul. We are refreshed and rejuvenated outdoors. Nature is invigorating and healing. Our energy directly exchanges in the incredible vibrations of a mighty universe filled with grace, love, mercy, and joy. Nature changes our molecular structure. It helps balance our neurochemistry. Stress, discouragement, depression, and all other forms of negativity disappear when we soak up the sun and feel the fresh breeze on our face. We are made whole.

Nature provides many beautiful sights to nourish the soul. It is an endless work of art. Colored leaves flow with the autumn winds, creating a rich and vibrant collage against the clear and crisp blue sky. Illuminant rainbows of brilliant colors light up the dark sky after cool spring rains. Summer is filled with the beautiful patchwork of wildflowers and butterflies. Winter is etched in white snowcapped mountains and dark pine trees hanging heavy under thick gnarly woods. We are nourished deep down when we take in these sights and spend time absorbing the beauty of the earth. Our souls are enriched.

Bask in the gifts

One of the surest ways to nourish your soul is to bask in the infinite gifts that are always surrounding you. I will say it again. We are so blessed. We are constantly surrounded by the gifts of divinity and love. Some are invisible like the air we breathe. Others are mightily clear like the glorious peaks of a mountain range reaching toward a white puffy sky, or the precious sounds of a newborn baby. Or, the subtly present like the chirping of birds, the song of evening crickets, and butterflies dancing in the wind. Bask in these gifts. They are ours to enjoy. They nourish the soul.

Bask in the gifts of an evening sky. Enjoy a sunset. Sit somewhere quiet and watch the colors change and turn, twist and paint upon the darkening canvas of a starry night. Continue to watch as the colors slowly seep beneath the horizon, leaving only an illuminant etching of the day's precious memories gone by. Recite a mantra or prayer as the rescinding remnants of color fade into the slated black sky. Feel your soul as it is renewed in these gifts. Basking in our gifts brings great joy. It leads to rebirth.

Live in Abundance

We are continuously surrounded by gifts. The universe is abundant. When we are living in our gifts, we can enjoy abundance. Some of us are limited by the illusion of scarcity. We might think there is a shortage of favor or grace, or at least that luck is rationed. Some of us envy others. We wish we had the same gifts, talent, or opportunity. The truth is the universe contains an infinite number of gifts for each and every one. More for some does not mean less for others. We can awaken to the ultimate reality of abundance and break free of the illusion of scarcity. Clarity helps us appreciate our gifts. Awareness increases joy. We live in a world of abundance. Our journeys are blessed beyond belief.

Where are you at with your feelings of abundance today? Do you feel grateful, or are you disillusioned and dissatisfied? Perhaps you are somewhere in between. In any case, there is a sure way to connect with the abundance of the universe. We talked about meditation and metta practice. You can increase your feelings of abundance by focusing on appreciation and utilizing these spiritual techniques. In fact, challenge yourself.

Spend a whole day living in metta. Go about your activities as usual, yet try to maintain a meditative or metta state of mind as you participate in your day. Hold your heart, mind, and spirit in appreciation of all things and all people, Offer yourself unconditional love. If you catch yourself drifting into worry, doubt, or fear…any negative thoughts, gently stop and turn your attention back to appreciation. You will feel the abundance of the universe pour upon you. It will fill you with pure and utter joy!

Share your gifts with others

The wonderful offspring of being blessed with so many gifts is that we can share our gifts with others. Whether it is our time, our talent, our inspiration or encouragement, our finances, or a simple helping hand; sharing our gifts increases our blessings exponentially. The journey becomes amazing!

Reach out and share your gifts with others. Giving and sharing are like magic to the soul. We are happy and satisfied when we are reaching out and touching the lives of others. There is simply no better way to live. Your journey will be rich, joyful, and fulfilling. The best part is you will be helping others. We each play an important part in making this world a better place.

Most of us are probably more familiar with the concept of nourishing our bodies than we are with nourishing our spirituality. Nourishing the soul might seem like a foreign concept, even after reading this lesson. And yet it is so important. Simply practice some of these ideas and before you know it, you will feel more connected to your body, mind, and soul. Our soul is our lifeline. It is our connection to true beauty, divinity and eternity. It is where we find contentment and joy.

Take care of your soulful nature. Nourish yourself at the deepest level Come up with a daily plan that allows you to nurture your spirituality. You might use some of the ideas in this lesson or perhaps you have developed some of your own practices over the years. We are all at different places along the spiritual journey. Share your experiences and discoveries with others. You will brighten the universe.

Yalom, Irvin D. (1980) *Existential Psychotherapy*, Basic Books: Yalom Family Trust

YOU ARE WORTH IT

Reflections

NOURISH YOUR SOUL

YOU ARE WORTH IT

NOURISH YOUR SOUL

YOU ARE WORTH IT

26

Have Faith

Faith is one of the surest ways to bring joy to your life. It is the feeling of peace and contentment we have deep down when we trust God and the universe to care for our every need. Faith involves trust in the unseen. It is the understanding on a fundamental level that everything works together for good. It is trusting in the larger tapestry, a magnificent work of art that is being painted above our finite vision. Faith assures us we are on the right path. It helps us navigate through uncertainty, challenge, and fear. It is a process of discovery and strength. It is a process that leads to joy.

Faith is intricately linked to our level of spirituality. We have talked much about nourishing our spirit throughout this book, but before moving forward in our discussion; let's look at what we mean when we explore the concept of spirituality. According to Gerald and Marianne Corey, spirituality encompasses our relationship to the universe and is an avenue for finding meaning and purpose in living. It is an experience beyond the merely physical realm that helps us discover unity in the universe. They go on to say it is the practice of letting go of external noise and connecting with your inner self. (Corey, 2010)

I believe faith makes spirituality possible and simultaneously, spirituality leads to deeper levels of faith. When we embrace spirituality, we develop the eyes of faith. Life begins looking differently. Our perceptions and perspectives change. We begin seeing new dimensions: love, abundance, goodness, and joy. We become more positive and grateful. Faith helps us know everything will be alright. It helps us trust in the natural rhythms of the universe.

It is easier to refer to faith idealistically than it is to live in its actuation. Having faith is easier said than done. It is simpler to claim faith when all is well, but how about during times of challenge and trial? After all, this is when faith matters most. In either case, faith does not just happen; rather, it is cultivated. Faith develops over time and usually through facing hardship and challenge. It matures as we grow spiritually.

This lesson will look at some of the ways we can cultivate our faith. We will journey even deeper into new realities that bring about joy. Open you heart. Clear your mind. Attune to your spirit. Faith brings it all together. Let's prepare to embrace it…

Believe in Abundance

We discussed the gifts of abundance in the previous lesson. Faith is a *belief* in abundance. It is the sure knowledge that the universe provides endless love and care to each and every one of us. We will receive exactly what we need, precisely when we need it. No matter what we are going through, no matter how hard times get, or the magnitude of obstacles and challenges we face; we will be cared for in magnificent ways. We can trust in the power of providence.

You may be wondering about the idea of trust. Some of us are not comfortable with this concept. We have spent years as survivors. We pride our independence and self-reliance. Many have been hurt. We have been deeply wounded or at least negatively affected by the actions of others who we had trusted. Perhaps you have been abused, neglected, or otherwise taken advantage of. Thankfully, trust can be rebuilt. Like faith, it is a process. We can learn to trust again.

We can build trust in the assurances that are lasting and sustaining. We can increase faith in our higher power and the infinite abundance of a mighty universe of love, endless grace, and mercy. We needn't struggle alone. We do not have to live by our own strength and will power. Nor do we have to give up our power, hoping others will provide for and care for us. People are fallible. Instead, we can place our trust in the infallible, omnipotent, omniscient, and eternal love of God, the universe, and the energy of love that empowers each of us within. Believe in abundance. Have faith!

Everything happens for a reason

Another idea that helps build faith is to remember that everything happens for a reason. You have probably heard this mentioned time and again, and it is true. The universe balances upon a multitude of dichotomies. It contains light and darkness, good and evil, beauty and challenge, hurt and healing. One could not exist without the other. This reminds me of an old movie where George Burns was playing God and summed up life to a boy questioning him by pulling out a coin. He said, "It's simple. A coin has two sides, heads and tails. Without both, there would be no coin."

Thinking back throughout your past, was there ever a time of challenge when you did not understand the reason for your misfortune, but later on, it made perfect sense? Events work together for good along the journey. They may not make sense in linear form, but more often than not, they are leading you somewhere bigger and better, or at least to a place that is more rewarding. We grow in faith when we keep this in mind. We can learn to accept the unknown. We can believe in the providence of an omniscient love that holds us in perfect grace and harmony. We can trust in the power of love in the universe. Everything happens for a reason and the reasons are good. We can surrender to the divine.

Surrender

It is impossible to talk about faith without discussing surrender. Faith helps us surrender. It lets us know that everything will be alright, even if we let go. Some of us equate surrender to defeat. Ironically, surrender is the wellspring of empowerment. Surrender allows us to let go of all our worries, anxiety, fear, concerns, challenges, and doubt to embrace a power that is infinitely rewarding and satisfying. It is the beginning of change. It is the handmaiden of beauty and freedom.

We have reviewed several tools in the previous lessons that can help us discover the power and energy of surrender - techniques such as relaxation, play, creative arts, meditation, and metta practice. These exercises can help us let go of worry and struggle and trust in the strength and energy of God and the universe. Surrender is the key to joy and happiness. It provides a way for us to move outside of problems and into solutions. We can lay down resistance and embrace the serenity of acceptance.

Christopher Germer offers a simple formula that can be applied to the concept of surrender.

$$\text{Pain} \times \text{Resistance} = \text{Suffering}$$

He states that "pain" refers to the unavoidable discomfort that comes into our lives, such as an accident, an illness, or death of a loved one. "Resistance" refers to any effort to ward off pain, such as tensing the body or ruminating about how to make the pain go away. He says "suffering" results from resisting the pain. (Germer, 2009). Returning to his formula, if our resistance is "0" (when we surrender); then our suffering will also be "0". Our knowledge of simple math reminds us that anything times "0" equals "0". Surrender frees us completely from suffering. It gives us peace.

Another great method we have utilized in other lessons that can help you surrender is loving, kindness meditation. Sit in a quiet room and place your mind on love, trust, and compassion. Feel your resistance dissolve as you relax your muscles…your face, your limbs, even your organs. Breathe deeply. Surrender your troubles. Let your worries drift away. Turn your pain over to God, the mighty love of the universe, the healing force of heaven. Prepare for a miracle. Your pain will dissipate.

HAVE FAITH

Surrender is letting go of resistance and allowing solutions and healing to shower in.

When we focus on the problem, the problem becomes larger; when we focus on solutions, solutions become larger. This is the oxymoron of surrender. We are made strong through giving up. We can take hold of our faith and trust the universe will bring solutions and healing into our lives and into the lives of those we love. We needn't worry. We can give up resistance and strife. Surrender is the beginning of a better day. It is our gateway to a miraculous future.

Have faith in the universe

We are all cared for in unique and wondrous ways. Consider again the tiny sparrow and the fragile wild flower, or the calm river that flows exactly where its waters are needed. Everything moves in synchrony. Each molecule is orchestrated in beautiful rhythm and harmony. Have faith in this reality. Have faith in the universe. It will sustain you. You will be protected and cared for as you journey toward your destiny.

The opposite of faith is doubt. How often have you doubted things will work out? Reflect back upon your story. Look at your life as a narrative. Consider some of the challenges you have faced. Play them out in your mind. Most importantly, remember how these situations ended. What happened? How were you cared for? What did you learn as a result of your trials? Stay with these thoughts for a while. Give your narrative time and space. Write on the reflection pages. Discover. We are finding faith.

Hopefully, you discover stories of survival and victory. I am reminded of the old adage, what doesn't kill us makes us stronger. Challenges strengthen our faith. They give the journey and our personality fiber and resilience. We overcome doubt and despondency. When we look back and realize the times we have been cared for, it becomes easier to have faith. We have always been cared for fully and completely, why would it be any different in our future? These questions and reflections build confidence and trust.

Having complete faith in the universe is a source of overwhelming joy. We are brought to a place that is sacred and profound. Worry disappears and peace reigns in the heart, mind, and spirit. We are one with our soul. We are placed in a position of neutrality, where nothing can shake us or challenge our emotional or spiritual wellness. We are free from suffering and despair. We will know that negative feelings are optional. We will no longer be victims of doubt or fear. We can choose freedom!

Trust in a higher power

Another cornerstone of faith is trusting in a higher power. I use the term higher power to be synonymous to a God of your personal understanding. There are as many ideas about who God is as there are people in the world. We each have our own perceptions and interpretations. We have religious teachings, yet we can balance these with personal, spiritual, intimate understandings. You may worship Buddha, Mohammed, Jesus, Mary, Mother Earth, or another deity. Or, you might be uncomfortable with the concept of a higher power in which case we can remember Corey's definition of spirituality that involves feelings of unity in the universe. Now, let's explore some questions. What is your personal relationship with your higher power? What does your spiritual journey look like? Even more importantly, do you trust that your greatest needs will be met? Use the reflection pages to explore your thoughts and feelings.

Faith requires trust. If we say we have faith and do not trust, faith wanes. Some of us live as if we are playing a game of chess. We constantly calculate our next move, trying to hold on to all our pawns, horses, rooks, and bishops; while guarding our king and queen. We go after one check after another, hoping for the eventual checkmate. We dread a stalemate for that means we must start all over again. Faith is being content in the stalemate. It is giving up all our pieces, even our queen, if that is the path life gives us. Faith is knowledge -deep down- that our lives will be good despite the logistics of our game or for that matter, if we feel like we are winning or losing. We can apply the slogan it's not if you win or lose; it's how you play the game.

HAVE FAITH

Trust your higher power, God, or the unity of the universe, whichever fits for you. Enjoy the journey. Surrender your pawns, plays, and moves. Your higher power will not let you down. You will receive energy that is infinite and unfailing. You can rest in love; journey in abundance. Your higher power will see you through any challenge and all trials and tribulations. Your guidance will be healing and complete. We can trust in the power that hung the stars and filled the oceans. Trust in the source that cares for the entire universe in perfect harmony. We are cared for beyond belief. We are loved unconditionally, wholly, and faithfully. We can trust in faith.

Have faith in yourself

Faith in yourself: your own strengths, talents, and abilities might be the most challenging kind of faith of all. Remember lesson fourteen when we explored the value of believing in our inner qualities. We learned how important it is to build self-confidence and gain courage and strength. We discussed the value of self-expression and how this helps us show the world who we are. We can all develop faith in ourselves. It is a process that leads to joy. Faith in our inner strengths and abilities makes the journey more successful and enjoyable. It helps us reach our destiny.

It is now time to actuate our faith in ourselves. We can make a decision to trust and believe in who we are and what we stand for. We have completed many exercises to prepare us for this great event. So here we go.

Either stand or sit up tall. Raise your hands above your head as if you are reaching for the sky. Open your fingers. Get ready to catch all of the energy that will pour down upon you. Recite the following mantra. "I have faith in myself. I believe in who I am. I am ready to face the world and do all that I can." (Or, recite your own mantra, anything that offers you hope and encouragement).

Repeat this until it chimes in your heart. Feel the energy of faith pour upon you spirit. Experience the strength of who you are. Be empowered. Get ready to shine!

YOU ARE WORTH IT

Have faith in the journey

We can also have faith in the journey. We know deep down that our journey will be beautiful as we walk in the light of who we are. Each one of us has a wonderful journey that is uniquely and incredibly designed for us to experience and share with others. Our journeys weave in and through each other, creating the mighty tapestry of love that makes the world such a lovely and miraculous place. We can have faith in the many steps that form our path. We can put one foot in front of the other with kindness, compassion, strength, and love. We will be guided to a bright and meaningful future. We can trust in the process.

The journey is ours to savor and enjoy. One last time, it is the journey not the destination. It is good to have plans, dreams, and goals; but we can enjoy each step along the way. We can have faith that we are moving in a direction that will be rewarding and successful. Have faith in the journey. Have faith in today. Have faith in the moment. God and the universe are guiding us with care and protection. Trust the process. It is our gift.

Believe in the power of love

We can have faith in the power of love. Love is the greatest gift we can discover along the journey. It is what the journey is all about. It is why we are here. Our whole life changes when we discover the treasure of love. We enjoy each moment. We can bask in the joy and peace of happiness.

If you find it too difficult to practice any of the other suggestions in this lesson, simply begin with believing in the power of love. Love is the gateway to faith. It paves the way to believe in the universe, a higher power, the journey, ourselves, even others. Love heals all doubt, worry, fear, and discouragement. It is our life source. It brings freedom and peace.

The power of love transcends the universe. It transforms our hearts. Love uplifts, encourages, changes, and heals. We live in complete joy when we walk in love's path. You do not have to wait any longer. You can embrace love now and believe in its power. You can live in its ecstatic light and energy. You deserve the best. It is time to let love rapture your heart! Do not hesitate. It's alright. Feel it. Breathe it. Become it. Love is here. It is wherever you are. Believe…

Believe in miracles

We are always and forever surrounded by miracles, big and small. The journey is filled with blessings, tiny miracles waiting to unfold in our lives. Have you ever waited and hoped for something to happen, and just when you gave up, there it was? Or has something wonderful happened in your life surprisingly and unexpected? Have you or someone you love experienced the mighty hand of healing? We can believe in the constant presence and grace of miracles. They are continuously surrounding us, even though we do not always see them. Miracles are worked out beyond our knowledge. This is the beauty of the unknown.

Believe in miracles. They are available to each and every one of us. We deserve them. We have earned them. Many of us have spent our lifetimes working to make a difference. We have helped our spouses, children, employers, coworkers, friends, community, and worthy organizations. We are passionate and ambitious women. We follow a purpose. Miracles are life's gifts back to us. We can learn to receive as we have given. We can accept the gifts of the journey. We can embrace the joy they bring.

Have Hope

Faith leads to hope. Have hope for the future. Expect good things will happen. Hope carries us through hard times. It ushers in the rays of sunshine, shining joy on all our tomorrows. Hope creates goodness and prosperity in our future. It is the law of attraction. This law claims that our thoughts create our future. Thoughts are powerful. We can change our world with our thoughts. We can change our lives with our thoughts. We can believe our futures will be bright and watch as the brilliant colors of happiness unfold. Have hope. It will lead you to success.

YOU ARE WORTH IT

Hope is the handmaiden of freedom and peace. It is our passageway to comfort and serenity. Just when you think all hope is gone, think again. It never goes away. It is always with us, beckoning us to try again, give it another shot, or be patient and trust a little while longer. Hope will bring about a new day. It is already changing the world. It wants to change our hearts. We can let it in. We can carry it like a torch. It lights our way even when we feel trapped in darkness and despair. We no longer have to give up. We are assured we will reach our destiny when we keep the faith. We can hold on. We are almost there.

Have hope. Believe in the law of attraction, the great reality of the universe, positive thoughts have the power to create a happy and successful future. Have faith in where you are going. Know that God and the universe have the very best in store for you. Continue putting one foot in front of the other. Walk the paths of a happy destiny. You are worth it all. You are worth a journey that is joyful and fulfilling.

Rest in the care of the universe

Faith encourages us to rest in the care of the universe. When we have faith, we know all is well. We can let go and rest. We are centered in the connection of our mind, body, and soul. We can surrender to what is, what has been, and whatever will be. We can practice mindfulness and acceptance and release all worry, fear, stress, regret, doubt, and resentment. We know we are cared for. We know we are forgiven. We know we are surrounded by grace and mercy. We feel abundance pouring down and embracing our spirits. We can settle in the beauty of the moment knowing we are unconditionally loved and held. Take the hand of faith and rest in the care and compassion of the universe. You will discover happiness and joy overflowing.

We are nearing the end of our journey of discovering self-love, and yet the end is simply the beginning of so much more! I hope you are beginning to feel the gifts of love, peace, abundance, and joy. We can redefine our lives based on our newfound love. We are reaching toward new beginnings. We are reaching toward the stars. We deserve the very best. After all, we are discovering we are worth it.

Corey, Gerald & Marianne (2010) *I Never Knew I had a Choice, explorations in personal growth*, Brooks/Cole Cengage Learning: Belmont, CA.

Germer, Christopher K. (2009) *The Mindful Path to Self-Compassion, Freeing yourself from destructive thoughts and emotions.* The Guilford Press: New York, NY

YOU ARE WORTH IT

Reflections

HAVE FAITH

YOU ARE WORTH IT

HAVE FAITH

YOU ARE WORTH IT

27

Redefine your Life

Hopefully this book has inspired you to continue your journey of self-discovery. We have completed numerous creative techniques; practiced mindfulness based cognitive exercises, completed inventories, narrative suggestions, meditations, reflections, and experimented with guided imagery. We have engaged in the challenge of personal and spiritual growth work. Pat yourself on the back. None of these lessons have been easy. They are meant to challenge and empower you. They are created to guide you toward self-love.

You can now redefine your life based on what you have learned. There is little use in learning without application. We are now equipped to define a life that is built around the fact that we are worth it. We can arrange our lives around the empowering reality that we are worth everything. It is our new narrative. It is a mega boundary from which all other boundaries can flow. We have redefined our self-concept, embracing our awareness of self-worth; and we can now build our lives around our newfound strength. It is our new reality. We are encouraged. We are inspired. We are ready.

Define your journey the way you want to

We begin by defining our journey the way we want to. Place all expectations aside for a moment. Ignore pressure from others. Surrender approval seeking. It is time to live in a way that is best for you. Choose what is most important to you and go from there. It is your life, your journey. It does not belong to anyone else; not your spouse, life partner, boyfriend, girlfriend, friends, or even family members. We can love them dearly and still take care of our own needs and desires. Your happiness and joy are solely yours. You are responsible for your wellbeing. It is *your* gift.

Now picture what you want your life to look like. Visualize. We will utilize guided imagery to create a new life for ourselves in our mind's eye. What does your new life look like? What are you doing? Who is around you? What are you saying? How are you feeling? Close your eyes for a moment and give yourself fully to this purposeful meditation. Let your mind wander and dream of anything and everything. Imagine and drift into a life you have always longed for. Let it be exactly what you want. Do not hold anything back.

Give yourself time for your visualization to become vivid and real. Let it form completely. Fill in the details where you can. Picture your profession. What are your hobbies? How are you relaxing and enjoying your life, your friends, and your loved ones? Where are you living? What does your house or apartment look like? Who are your friends and neighbors? Are you involved in any organizations or activities? Are you pursuing any passions?

Explore and discover as long as it takes for your vision to become clear. Try this activity over a weekend or any time you have a moment to yourself. Do not rush this exercise. Give yourself as long as you need to visualize a future you desire with confidence and clarity. You may find aspects of your ideal future are similar to parts of your life right now. Wonderful! Continue these things. Savor them. They are working for you. You may also discover things that will be new. You may not know how you can make them happen. Do not let this discourage you. The universe will bring you the desires of your heart when you trust and live in love and compassion. Do not give up before you even begin.

REDEFINE YOUR LIFE

Leave the status quo behind

Now that we have pictured our new journey and imagined what we would like in our new life, let's look at some ideas that can help us make our vision a reality. One of the first things we can do is break free of the restrictions of conformity. We have discussed the status quo. When conformity becomes restricting, it is time to differentiate ourselves from the norm. We can leave the status quo behind. Surrender your need for approval. Quit worrying about whether or not you fit in. You will be liberated and feel spectacular when you move away from conformity and venture out in your new life.

Be creative. Think outside of the box. You can follow a destiny that is uniquely and beautifully designed just for you. You do not need understanding, support, or affirmation from anyone but you. It is nice to have encouragement and openly consider feedback, but we can make our final decisions based on what *we* feel is best for us. We no longer have to seek the approval of others.

We can step off the Ferris wheel of "conditions of worth". Carl Rogers, the father of humanistic psychology, used this expression. It involves deriving our level of satisfaction from how others see us. Other people put certain conditions on our worthiness and value; and we try to live up to their expectations. I add the metaphor of the Ferris wheel because many of us feel great when people approve of us and then feel down when we are not meeting the expectations of others. It is like going up and down on a Ferris wheel depending on whether others view us positively or negatively. Instead, we can give ourselves unconditional affirmation and approval. We can move into our new life with inner confidence and ease. It's alright. We deserve the best.

Choose what is important

As you are redefining your life, choose what is important. Charter a new course toward what is most meaningful to you. Do you value family, friends, travel, your profession, a mission dear to your heart, or other passion? Make each and every thing that is important to you part of your future. A meaningful life is a satisfying life. Meaning is intricately connected to joy.

Think back to your visualization for a moment. What are the important things you remember? Who was in the picture? What was the setting? Recall what you were doing. Meaning and value often surface from the subconscious to the conscious when we relax the mind and imagine. What did you discover? These are all clues to what you want for your future. There are no limitations to the imagination. You can create anything you want for yourself. Then believe and it will happen.

Chart your course toward the future

As we draw near to our new beginning, let's look at a few more sailing analogies to bring our journey of self-love full circle. Reflect back to the beginning of this book and my description of learning how to sail the Caribbean gale winds. The Mayan teacher drew illustrative instructions in the white sand to teach me how to turn the sailboat against the strong winds so that I wouldn't get blown out to sea. He later drew a circle to show me it was time to increase the portion of attention I gave myself. I realize today that the strategies for becoming a good sailor can be linked with the basic principles for living my best journey. Allow me to explain.

Redefining our lives is like sailing out on a new course. As we set our course for the future, we can keep in mind we will have to tack through the wind here and there. In sailing, tacking involves maneuvering the boat in various angles (slicing through the wind with the sail strategically pointed in specific directions in order to catch the wind to move in the direction you want to go). Tacking is a way the sailor utilizes the wind so that he or she will not be blown off course. Angling through the breeze keeps the boat on target while making headway toward the ultimate destination. We will encounter challenge as we move forward in our new life. We can intentionally and effectively maneuver through the changing winds of our future, situations and trials that come our way. We can shift and adjust successfully through changing circumstances while moving toward our desired destination.

It is also good to have a few different turns in mind in case you

REDEFINE YOUR LIFE

encounter a gale wind. It is especially hard to turn a boat against a Caribbean gale wind, but necessary so you do not get swept out to sea. I had to practice various turns many times, and yet it prepared me to sail against the most intense winds. Having strategies in place to overcome life's biggest challenges and turn around when necessary is very important as we travel into our future. We will encounter our share of gale winds along the way.

And it might become inevitable at some point in the future that you will have to set out on a new course. Winds and seasons shift and change. The laws of nature are unpredictable. You may have found a pattern of sailing that is bringing you close to your destination and then all of a sudden, the wind changes direction or even dies down entirely. Or, you may find it difficult to get anywhere with the pattern you have chosen. These are common challenges for the sailor. Sometimes the best strategy is to set out on a new course and establish an alternative pattern of action. This is also true in life. We can relate.

But perhaps the most important strategy to know is relax when you can just sail- letting the wind carry you in the general direction you want to go. This is the most enjoyable part of sailing. Sometimes the wind blows you so quickly that the sailboat makes a humming sound. We can let the journey carry us. We can let our higher power guide our journey and allow the universe to care for us along the way. It takes a lot of faith and little effort. We will see great beauty and experience unexplainable peace and joy when we are relaxing in the natural winds of life. We are equipped to navigate and make adjustments if they become necessary. In the meantime, enjoy the ride!

Don't limit yourself

Another suggestion for redefining your life is to not limit yourself. Our perceptions create our reality. What we perceive and how we perceive it becomes our future. In this process, we magnify the aspects of our lives that we focus on. We become more assured and capable when we focus on our strengths and abilities. We limit ourselves when we focus on our weaknesses and limitations. When we look for the positive in situations and people- even ourselves- we become more positive. When we analyze critically and judge ourselves harshly, our worlds darken. Focus on your capabilities, not your limitations. Grow your strengths. Believe in the brilliance of your future.

As you redefine your life, don't limit yourself. Let your new life be all that you want it to be. Follow your dreams. Reach for the stars. Follow your heart. Turn your visualization into a new reality. Go after that career. Pursue your passion. Work in the light of your destiny. You can achieve great things as long as you keep the faith.

Experience all life has to offer

Experiencing all life has to offer leads to fulfillment and joy. We are born to search and discover. It is how we mature and grow. We develop experientially. Sure, there are discontinuous stages of human development that are less fluent and more systematic, yet our experience continuously shapes who we become along the way. When we experience all that we can in life, we become all that we can be. We reach a higher state of maturation than is possible when we limit the discovery process. Experience leads us to our full potential.

Experience all life has to offer. Don't sell yourself short. Feel everything, taste everything, and see everything there is to see. Be present to your experience. Don't miss out. Life offers so many gifts. The journey is filled with abundant opportunities and blessings. Enjoy each and every one of them. And never forget… you are worth it!

You can make your life beautiful

As you redefine your life, keep in mind you can make it beautiful. You are the artist. Your journey is the masterpiece. Think of yourself as your own work of art. Reflect upon the beauty within you for a moment. We all harbor a vision of our most perfect selves somewhere within us, a dream of what we can become. (Lerner, 1985) We can pursue our vision by embracing our beauty and making it a reality in our life. We can paint our lives with the vibrant and rich colors of all our hopes and dreams. We can work toward making them a reality, like an artist labors forward to create a painting, sculpture, or tapestry.

Lerner goes on to say… like the artist painting a picture, occasionally we can step back from the canvas and consider what colors need to be added to make our lives even more beautiful. We can take time to reflect on our growth and progress. We can truly redefine our lives so that they become more brilliant works of art. We can paint portraits of our best selves. We are uncovering the persons we wish to become. And in the process, we can hold before us the vision of what we are becoming. We can continue to focus on the beauty that is unfolding within us day by day. (Lerner, 1985)

You can make your life as beautiful as you dare to imagine. The days of restriction and despondency are behind. Bring out a full pallet of colors. Gaze confidently and hopefully at the canvas and prepare your mind, body, and spirit to begin. We have the tools we need. We have explored health, wealth, and wellness; and we are encountering joy. Start painting your new life when you are ready, keeping in mind your portrait is an ongoing process. You can spend the rest of your life creating more and more beauty and joy. Your journey *is* the masterpiece.

Discover and experience your destiny

We can redefine our lives in a way that helps us discover and experience our destiny. Joy is found in the heart of our destiny. Our destiny is all that we hope for. It *is* what we dream. Perhaps you saw a glimpse of it earlier while visualizing your future. We are meant to discover our path. We are born to realize contentment and joy. It does not have to be on a grand scale. Many find destiny in the simple and small. We all have a destiny. We each have a life purpose. We can begin on the journey of discovery by loving ourselves.

A helpful strategy to move toward your destiny is to live in the open plane of possibility. (Siegel, 2010) This is a mind sight of neutrality, acceptance, and openness. It is living beyond judgment and preconceived notions, bias or reaction. It is a style of living that embraces pure acceptance, loving kindness, and openness to all possibilities. Destiny lies in the open plane of possibility. It is nestled in a field of dreams. Open mindedness and sure footedness will lead you to discover and experience your destiny. Just put one foot in front of the other. Your new life will bring you there!

Appreciate each step along the way

Consider one last suggestion. As you move into your new life, do not forget to appreciate each step along the way. You have so much in store for you. This is only the beginning. You will encounter ups and downs, highs and lows, but like any good ride; your journey will be thrilling and exciting. We have come a long way from where we once were. We are liberated and empowered, hopeful and joyous. We can appreciate our progress and our journey. It has not been easy, but it will be rewarding. We are entering a new day.

Appreciation is the key to peace and happiness. Our lives are enriched when we appreciate ourselves, the universe, others, even fellow travelers we encounter. Appreciation is the gateway to joy. It lights up the darkest situations and helps us through the greatest challenges. It is the loving hand that sculpts our journey into a masterpiece. Appreciate each step along the way. We realize our best lives by living in gratitude.

Our journey together is now complete. We have reached the end of this guide to self-love. But like life and the many issues of personal and spiritual growth, love is a process. You can spend the rest of your life working toward discovering its beauty and grace. Use this book often. Keep it as a resource. Loan it to a friend. The ending of all journeys are the beginnings of new adventures. Embrace your new life. Follow your heart. Live out your vision. It's never too late.

Most importantly, keep believing you are worth it. Don't give up. You might become discouraged, frustrated, and insecure. You will encounter obstacles and challenges. This is the story of life. Thankfully, we do not have to let these challenges become us. We possess a new narrative that is hopeful, integrated, and whole. We are worthy, beautiful, intelligent, talented, kind, compassionate, and resourceful. Did I mention creative? We have what it takes to survive. We can move

REDEFINE YOUR LIFE

beyond survival now. We can move into a world of happiness, peace, and joy.

Let's end with a final visualization. Picture yourself standing on the edge of a brightly colored sea. Feel the soft warm sand between your toes. Visualize a dark orange ball of sun drop behind a hazy evening sky etched in illuminant tangerine and brushed lavender color. Pastel waves lap back and forth against a small boat sitting beside you along the seashore. The boat sits empty and abandoned, and yet the image is peaceful and secure. It points toward a new tomorrow.

You hesitate and contemplate. It is so comfortable along the seashore, but the beauty of the open sea is even more spectacular. After watching pastel colors float unto the shore one by one, you enter the boat. You consider setting sail into the sunset… You prepare to shove off… Then, you do it. You push the boat away from the shoreline, grab the rope, and drop the rudder.

As you move away from the shore, the wind begins to take your sail and sweeps the boat out to sea. You begin sailing along an unfamiliar course, directly into the beautiful sunset. It creates a golden trail of shimmering waves for you to follow. Your course is uncharted, and yet you know deep down it will be beautiful. You are surrounded by freedom and release, serenity and peace. You know you will be alright. The journey will carry you. The universe is caring for you. You have found unconditional love. You can rest and rejoice.

References:

Siegel, Daniel (2010) *The Mindful Therapist, A Clinician's Guide to Mindsight and Neural Integration* W.W. Norton & Company: New York, NY

Lerner, Rokelle (1985) *Daily Affirmations* for Adult Children of Alcoholics, Health Communications Inc.: Deerfield Beach, Fl.

REDEFINE YOUR LIFE

Reflections

YOU ARE WORTH IT

REDEFINE YOUR LIFE

YOU ARE WORTH IT

REDEFINE YOUR LIFE

Amy Lynn's Wellness and Empowerment Services

Amy has a Master's Degree in Psychology and Clinical Mental Health. She holds licensures in Mental Health and Wellness, Professional Counseling, and is a Nationally Certified Counselor. She has empowered hundreds of women through her private practice- Amy Lynn Psychotherapy and Wellness Services. She has authored several books on various subjects of personal discovery and spiritual growth. She has dedicated her life to helping others through her many works.

Amy conducts empowerment groups, workshops, and inspiring talks nationwide. Visit her at ALDPsychotherapy.com to learn more about her services or to schedule an event. She presents encouraging and uplifting material in conjunction with conferences, seminars, retreats, and other engagements. She tailors her material to fit your audience's needs.

Other books by Amy Lynn:

Hidden Castle, a Message of Hope and Recovery

Seeds of the Heart

Bits of Heaven, A Book of Life's Lessons and God's Miracles

When the Petal Falls, a Book of Hope and Healing Abuse

Each Moment a Gift, a Woman's Journey to the Soul

A River of Hope, a Daily Devotional/Meditation Guide

Sacred Peace, a Journey to Inner Freedom